ARCHITECTURAL GRAPHICS

Fifth Edition

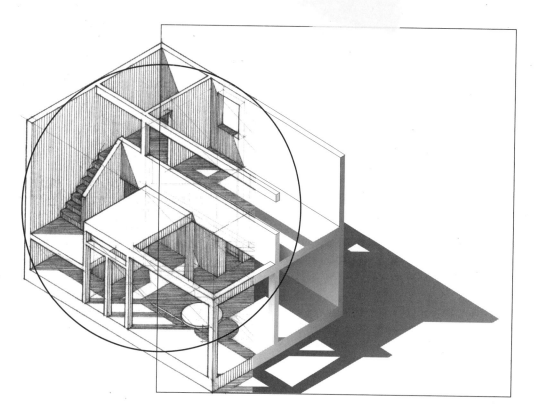

Francis D. K. Ching

JOHN WILEY & SONS, INC.

Copyright © 2009 by John Wiley & Sons, Inc. All rights reserved

Published by John Wiley & Sons, Inc., Hoboken, New Jersey
Published simultaneously in Canada

For general information on our other products and services or for technical support,
please contact our Customer Care Department within the United States at 800-
762-2974, outside the United States at (317) 572-3993 or fax (317) 572-4002.

Wiley also publishes its books in a variety of electronic formats. Some
content that appears in print may not be available in electronic books.

Library of Congress Cataloging-in-Publication Data:

Ching, Frank, 1943-
Architectural graphics / Francis D.K. Ching. -- 5th ed.
    p. cm.
Includes index.
ISBN 978-0-470-39911-8 (pbk.)
1. Architectural drawing. I. Title.
NA2700.C46 2009
720.28'4--dc22
                        2009004203

Printed in the United States of America.

10 9 8 7 6 5 4 3 2

CONTENTS

PREFACE

The first edition of this text introduced students to the range of graphic tools, techniques, and conventions designers use to communicate architectural ideas. The prime objective behind its original formation and subsequent revisions was to provide a clear, concise, and illustrative guide to the creation and use of architectural graphics. While retaining the clarity and visual approach of the earlier editions, this fifth edition of Architectural Graphics incorporates for the first time digital examples alongside the previously hand-drawn illustrations.

Advances in computer technology have significantly altered the process of architectural drawing and design. Current graphics software ranges from 2D drawing programs to 3D surface and solid modelers that aid in the design and representation of buildings, from small houses to large and complex structures. It is therefore important to acknowledge the unique opportunities and challenges digital tools offer in the production of architectural graphics. Whether a drawing is executed by hand or developed with the aid of a computer, however, the standards and judgments governing the effective communication of design ideas in architecture remain the same.

The overall chapter organization remains the same as in the fourth edition. Chapters 1 and 2 introduce the essential tools and techniques of drawing and drafting. While digital tools can augment traditional techniques, the tactile, kinesthetic process of crafting lines on a sheet of paper with a pen or pencil is the most sensible medium for learning the graphic language of drawing.

Chapter 3 introduces the three principal systems of pictorial representation— multiview, paraline, and perspective drawings—and analyzes in a comparative manner the unique viewpoints afforded by each system. Chapters 4 through 6 then focus on the principles and standards governing the conventions and uses of each of the three drawing systems, concepts that apply whether an architectural graphic is created manually or digitally.

The language of architectural graphics relies on the power of a composition of lines to convey the illusion of a three-dimensional construction or spatial environment on a two-dimensional surface, be it a sheet of paper or a computer screen or monitor. Although the line is the quintessential element of all drawing, Chapter 7 demonstrates techniques for creating tonal values and develops strategies for enhancing the pictorial depth of architectural drawings and conveying the illumination of spatial environments. Special thanks go to Nan-ching Tai, who offered his invaluable expertise and assistance in preparing the examples of digital lighting.

PREFACE

Because we design and evaluate architecture in relation to its environment, Chapter 8 extends the role of rendering to establishing context in the drawing of design proposals and indicating the scale and intended use of spaces.

Chapter 9 examines the fundamental principles of graphic communication and illustrate the strategic choices available in the planning and layout of architectural presentations. Incorporated into this discussion is the original chapter on lettering and graphic symbols, which are informative and essential elements to be considered in preparing any presentation.

Drawing with a free hand holding a pen or pencil remains the most direct and intuitive means we have for recording our observations and experiences, thinking through ideas, and diagramming design concepts. Chapter 10 therefore includes additional instruction on freehand sketching and diagramming as well as an expanded section of travel sketches. This terminal position reflects the importance of freehand drawing as a graphic skill and a critical tool for design thinking.

Despite these incremental changes in technology, the fundamental premise of this text endures—drawing has the power to overcome the flatness of a two-dimensional surface and represent three-dimensional ideas in architecture in a clear, legible, and convincing manner. To unlock this power requires the ability both to execute and to read the graphic language of drawing. Drawing is not simply a matter of technique; it is also a cognitive act that involves visual perception, judgment, and reasoning of spatial dimensions and relationships.

1

Drawing Tools and Materials

This chapter introduces the pencils and pens necessary for inscribing lines, the instruments available for guiding the eye and hand while drawing, and the surfaces suitable for receiving the drawn lines. While digital technology continues to further augment and enhance this traditional drawing toolkit, the kinesthetic act of drawing with a hand-held pencil or pen remains the most direct and versatile means of learning the language of architectural graphics.

Pencils are relatively inexpensive, quite versatile, and uniquely responsive to pressure while drawing.

Lead Holders

- Lead holders employ standard 2 mm leads.
- The push-button action of a clutch mechanism allows the exposed length of the lead shaft to be adjusted or withdrawn when the pencil is not in use.
- The lead point, which is capable of a variety of line weights, must be kept well sharpened with a lead pointer.

Mechanical Pencils

- Mechanical pencils utilize 0.3 mm, 0.5 mm, 0.7 mm, and 0.9 mm leads.
- A push-button mechanism advances the lead automatically through a metal sleeve. This sleeve should be long enough to clear the edges of drafting triangles and straightedges.
- The relatively thin leads of mechanical pencils do not require sharpening.
- 0.3 mm pencils yield very fine lines, but the thin leads are susceptible to breaking if applied with too much pressure.
- 0.5 mm pencils are the most practical for general drawing purposes.
- 0.7 mm and 0.9 mm pencils are useful for sketching and writing; avoid using these pencils to produce heavy line weights.

Wood-Encased Pencils

- Wooden drawing pencils are typically used for freehand drawing and sketching. If used for drafting, the wood must be shaved back to expose $3/4"$ of the lead shaft so that it can be sharpened with sandpaper or a lead pointer.

All three styles of pencils are capable of producing quality line drawings. As you try each type out, you will gradually develop a preference for the characteristic feel, weight, and balance of a particular instrument as you draw.

Recommendations for Grades of Graphite Lead

4H

- This dense grade of lead is best suited for accurately marking and laying out light construction lines.
- The thin, light lines are difficult to read and reproduce and should therefore not be used for finish drawings.
- When applied with too much pressure, the dense lead can engrave paper and board surfaces, leaving grooves that are difficult to remove.

2H

- This medium-hard lead is also used for laying out drawings and is the densest grade of lead suitable for finish drawings.
- 2H lines do not erase easily if drawn with a heavy hand.

F and H

- These are general-purpose grades of lead suitable for layouts, finish drawings, and handlettering.

HB

- This relatively soft grade of lead is capable of dense linework and handlettering.
- HB lines erase and print well but tend to smear easily.
- Experience and good technique are required to control the quality of HB linework.

B

- This soft grade of lead is used for very dense linework and handlettering.

Graphite Leads

Grades of graphite lead for drawing on paper surfaces range from 9H (extremely hard) to 6B (extremely soft). Given equal hand pressure, harder leads produce lighter and thinner lines, whereas softer leads produce denser, wider lines.

Nonphoto Blue Leads

Nonphoto blue leads are used for construction lines because their shade of blue tend not to be detected by photocopiers. However, digital scanners can detect the light blue lines, which can be removed by image editing software.

Plastic Leads

Specially formulated plastic polymer leads are available for drawing on drafting film. Grades of plastic lead range from E0, N0, or P0 (soft) to E5, N5, or P5 (hard). The letters E, N, and P are manufacturers' designations; the numbers 0 through 5 refer to degrees of hardness.

The texture and density of a drawing surface affect how hard or soft a pencil lead feels. The more tooth or roughness a surface has, the harder the lead you should use; the more dense a surface is, the softer a lead feels.

Technical Pens

Technical pens are capable of producing precise, consistent ink lines without the application of pressure. As with lead holders and mechanical pencils, technical pens from different manufacturers vary in form and operation. The traditional technical pen utilizes an ink-flow-regulating wire within a tubular point, the size of which determines the width of the ink line.

There are nine point sizes available, from extremely fine (0.13 mm) to very wide (2 mm). A starting pen set should include the four standard line widths— 0.25 mm, 0.35 mm, 0.5 mm and 0.70 mm—specified by the International Organization for Standardization (ISO).

- 0.25 mm line width
- 0.35 mm line width
- 0.50 mm line width
- 0.70 mm line width

- The tubular point should be long enough to clear the thickness of drafting triangles and straightedges.
- Use waterproof, nonclogging, fast-drying black drawing ink.
- Keep points screwed in securely to prevent ink leaking.
- After each use, replace the pen cap firmly to prevent the ink from drying.
- When pens are not in use, store them horizontally.

Since digital tools have reduced the need for manual drafting, a variety of less expensive, low-maintenance technical pens have been developed. Equipped with tubular tips and waterproof, pigment-based ink, these pens are suitable for writing, freehand drawing, as well as drafting with straightedges. They are available in point sizes that range from 0.03 mm to 1.0 mm. Some are refillable and have replaceable nibs.

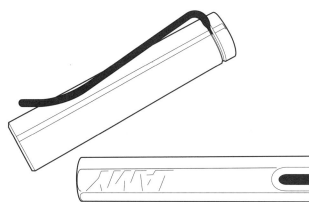

Fountain Pens

Fountain pens typically consist of a reservoir—either a disposable cartridge or an internal piston—containing a water-based ink that is fed to a metal nib by capillary action. While not suitable for drafting, fountain pens are ideal for writing and freehand sketching because they offer ease in drawing fluid, incisive, often expressive lines with little or no pressure.

Fountain pen nibs come in extra-fine, fine, medium and broad sizes; flat tipped nibs are also available for italic and oblique strokes. Some nibs are flexible enough that they respond to individual stroke direction and pressure.

Other Drawing Pens

Gel pens use a thick, opaque ink consisting of pigment suspended in a water-based gel while rollerball pens use a water-based liquid ink. Both offer similar qualities to fountain pens—they are capable of a consistent ink flow and laying down lines with less pressure than that required by regular ballpoint pens.

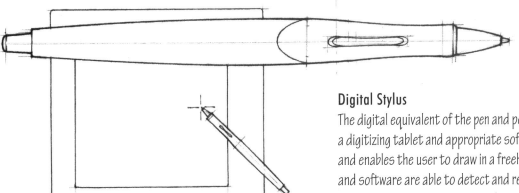

Digital Stylus

The digital equivalent of the pen and pencil is the stylus. Used with a digitizing tablet and appropriate software, it replaces the mouse and enables the user to draw in a freehand manner. Some models and software are able to detect and respond to the amount of hand pressure to mimic more realistically the effects of traditional media.

DRAWING GUIDES

T-Squares

T-squares are straightedges that have a short crosspiece at one end. This head slides along the edge of a drawing board as a guide in establishing and drawing straight parallel lines. T-squares are relatively low in cost and portable but require a straight and true edge against which their heads can slide.

- This end of a T-square is subject to wobbling.

- T-squares are available in 18", 24", 30", 36", 42", and 48" lengths. 42" or 48" lengths are recommended.

- A metal angle secured to the drawing board can provide a true edge.

- Use this length of the straightedge.

- T-squares with clear, acrylic straightedges should not be used for cutting. Metal T-squares are available for this purpose.

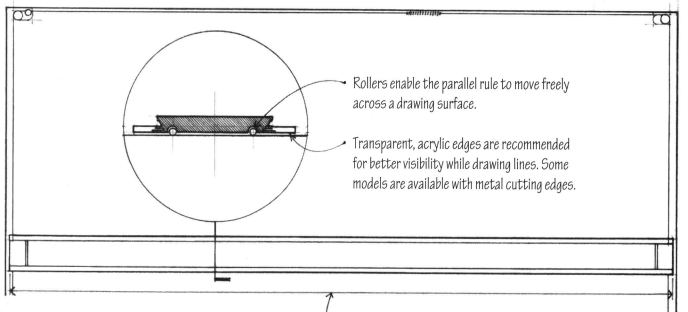

- Rollers enable the parallel rule to move freely across a drawing surface.

- Transparent, acrylic edges are recommended for better visibility while drawing lines. Some models are available with metal cutting edges.

Parallel Rules

Parallel rules are equipped with a system of cables and pulleys that allows their straightedges to move across a drawing board only in a parallel manner. Parallel rules are more expensive and less portable than T-squares but enable one to draft with greater speed and accuracy.

- Parallel rules are available in 30", 36", 42", 48", 54", and 60" lengths. The 42" or 48" length is recommended.

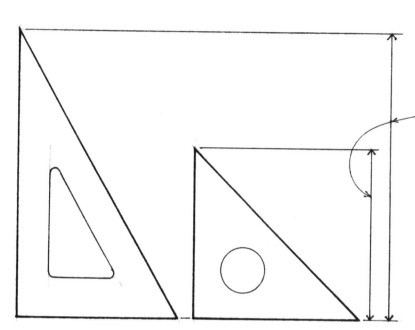

Triangles

Triangles are drafting aids used to guide the drawing of vertical lines and lines at specified angles. They have a right angle and either two 45° angles or one 30° and one 60° angle.

- 4" to 24" lengths are available.
- 8" to 10" lengths are recommended.

- Small triangles are useful for crosshatching small areas and as a guide in handlettering. See page 204.
- Larger triangles are useful in constructing perspectives.

- The 45°–45° and 30°–60° triangles can be used in combination to produce angular increments of 15°. See page 24.

- Triangles are made of clear, scratch-resistant, non-yellowing acrylic to allow a transparent, undistorted view through to the work below. Fluorescent orange acrylic triangles are also available for greater visibility on the drafting surface.
- Machined edges should be polished for precision and to facilitate drawing. Some triangles have raised edges for inking with technical pens.
- Inner edges may be beveled to serve as finger lifts.

- Keep triangles clean by washing with a mild soap and water.
- Triangles should not be used as a straightedge for cutting materials.

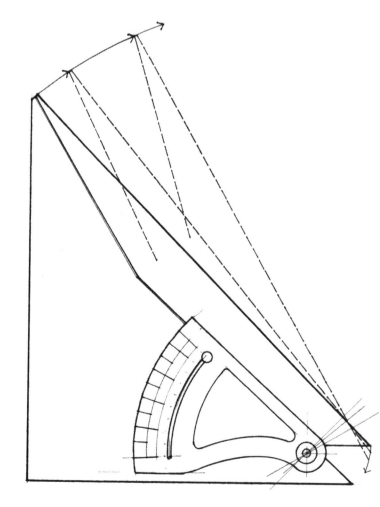

Adjustable Triangles

Adjustable triangles have a movable leg that is held in place with a thumbscrew and a scale for measuring angles. These instruments are useful for drawing such inclined lines as the slope of a stair or the pitch of a roof.

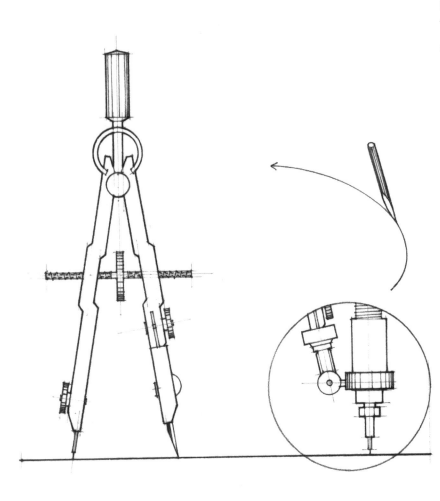

Compasses

The compass is essential for drawing large circles as well as circles of indeterminate radii.

- It is difficult to apply pressure when using a compass. Using too hard a grade of lead can therefore result in too light of a line. A softer grade of lead, sharpened to a chisel point, will usually produce the sharpest line without undue pressure. A chisel point dulls easily, however, and must be sharpened often.

- An attachment allows technical pens to be used with a compass.

- Even larger circles can be drawn by appending an extension arm or using a beam compass.

French Curves

- A variety of French curves are manufactured to guide the drawing of irregular curves.
- Adjustable curves are shaped by hand and held in position to draw a fair curve through a series of points.

Protractors

- Protractors are semicircular instruments for measuring and plotting angles.

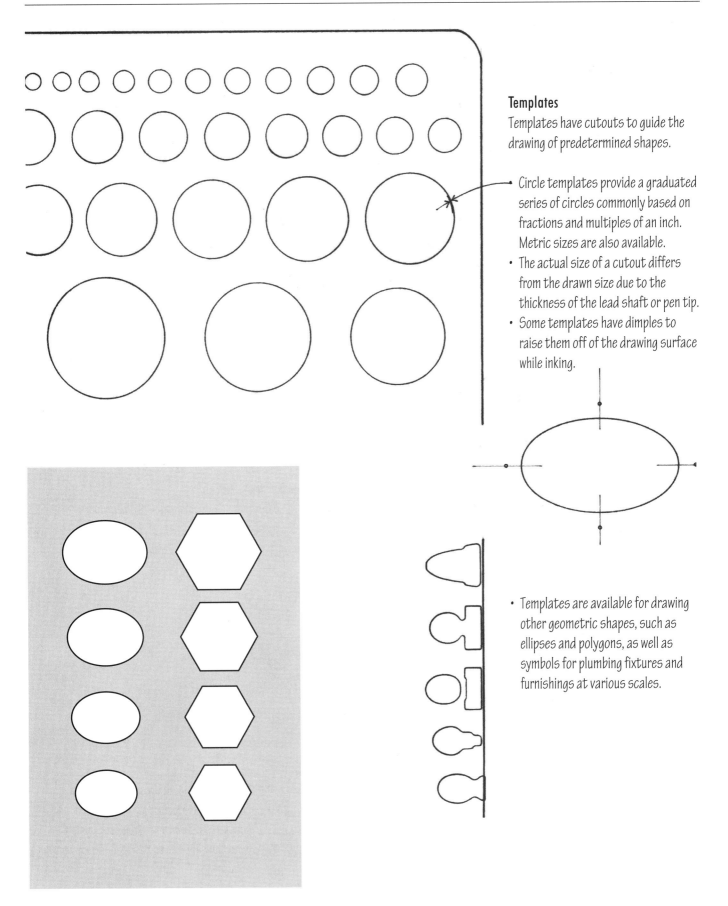

Templates
Templates have cutouts to guide the drawing of predetermined shapes.

- Circle templates provide a graduated series of circles commonly based on fractions and multiples of an inch. Metric sizes are also available.
- The actual size of a cutout differs from the drawn size due to the thickness of the lead shaft or pen tip.
- Some templates have dimples to raise them off of the drawing surface while inking.

- Templates are available for drawing other geometric shapes, such as ellipses and polygons, as well as symbols for plumbing fixtures and furnishings at various scales.

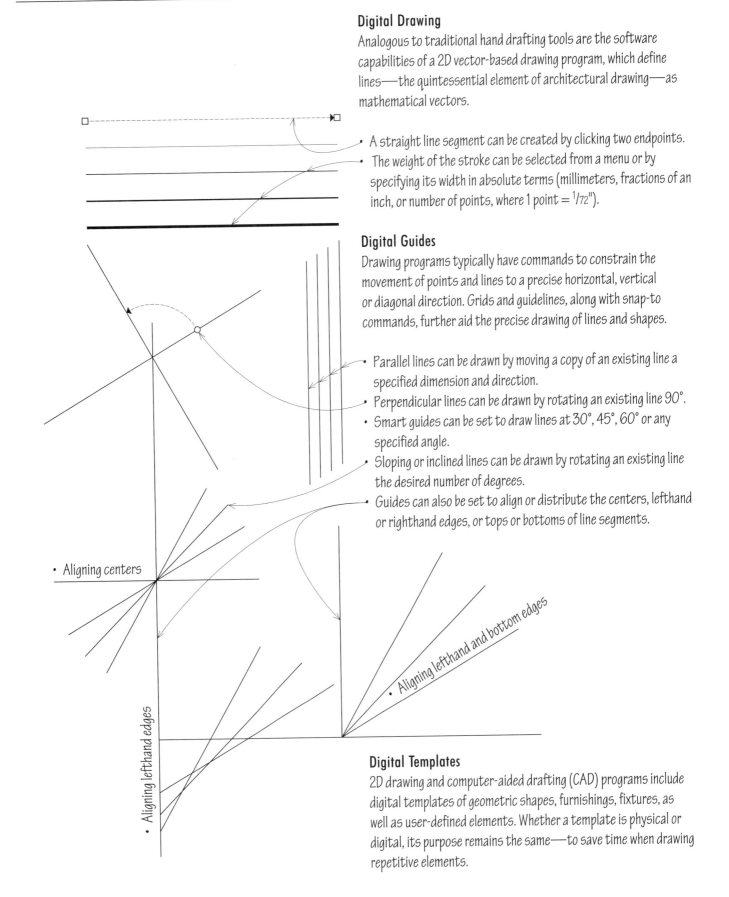

Digital Drawing

Analogous to traditional hand drafting tools are the software capabilities of a 2D vector-based drawing program, which define lines—the quintessential element of architectural drawing—as mathematical vectors.

- A straight line segment can be created by clicking two endpoints.
- The weight of the stroke can be selected from a menu or by specifying its width in absolute terms (millimeters, fractions of an inch, or number of points, where 1 point = $1/72$").

Digital Guides

Drawing programs typically have commands to constrain the movement of points and lines to a precise horizontal, vertical or diagonal direction. Grids and guidelines, along with snap-to commands, further aid the precise drawing of lines and shapes.

- Parallel lines can be drawn by moving a copy of an existing line a specified dimension and direction.
- Perpendicular lines can be drawn by rotating an existing line 90°.
- Smart guides can be set to draw lines at 30°, 45°, 60° or any specified angle.
- Sloping or inclined lines can be drawn by rotating an existing line the desired number of degrees.
- Guides can also be set to align or distribute the centers, lefthand or righthand edges, or tops or bottoms of line segments.

- Aligning centers

- Aligning lefthand and bottom edges

- Aligning lefthand edges

Digital Templates

2D drawing and computer-aided drafting (CAD) programs include digital templates of geometric shapes, furnishings, fixtures, as well as user-defined elements. Whether a template is physical or digital, its purpose remains the same—to save time when drawing repetitive elements.

Erasers

One of the advantages of drawing with a pencil is the ability to easily erase pencil marks. Always use the softest eraser compatible with the medium and the drawing surface. Avoid using abrasive ink erasers.

- Vinyl or PVC plastic erasers are nonabrasive and will not smear or mar the drawing surface.
- Some erasers are saturated with erasing fluid to erase ink lines from paper and drafting films.
- Liquid erasing fluid removes pencil and ink markings from drafting film.

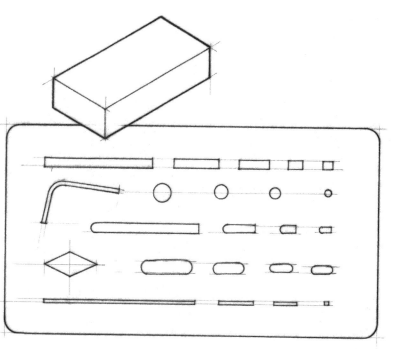

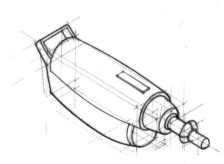

- Electric erasers are very convenient for erasing large areas and ink lines. Compact, battery-operated models are especially handy.

Erasing Shields

Erasing shields have cutouts of various shapes and sizes to confine the area of a drawing to be erased. These thin, stainless-steel shields are especially effective in protecting the drawing surface while using an electric eraser. Ones that have square-cut holes allow the erasure of precise areas of a drawing.

Other Aids

- Drafting brushes help keep the drawing surface clean of erasure fragments and other particles.
- Soft, granular drafting powder is available that provides a temporary protective coating over drawings during drafting, picks up pencil lead dust, and keeps the drawing surface clean. If used too heavily, the powder can cause lines to skip, so use sparingly, if at all.
- Pounce powder may be used to prepare drawing surfaces for inking.

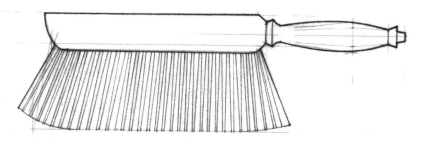

In drawing, "scale" refers to a proportion determining the relation of a representation to the full size of that which is represented. The term also applies to any of various instruments having one or more sets of precisely graduated and numbered spaces for measuring, reading, or transferring dimensions and distances in a drawing.

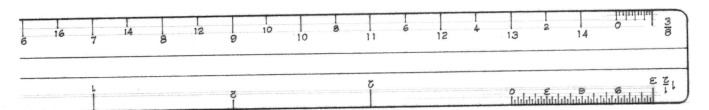

Architect's Scales

An architect's scale has graduations along its edges so that scale drawings can be measured directly in feet and inches.

- Triangular scales have 6 sides with 11 scales, a full-size scale in $1/16"$ increment, as well as the following architectural scales: $3/32"$, $3/16"$, $1/8"$, $1/4"$, $1/2"$, $3/8"$, $3/4"$, $1"$, $1 1/2"$, and $3" = 1'-0"$.

- Flat-beveled scales have either 2 sides with 4 scales or 4 sides with 8 scales.

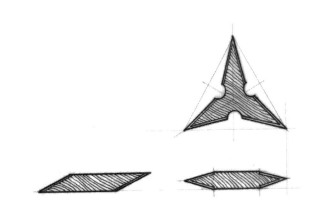

- Both 12" and 6" lengths are available.
- Scales should have precisely calibrated graduations and engraved, wear-resistant markings.
- Scales should never be used as a straightedge for drawing lines.

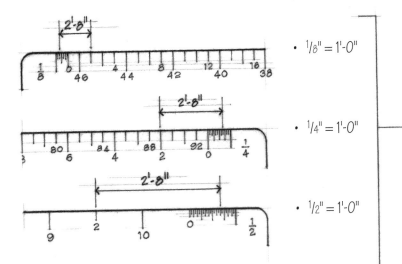

- $1/8" = 1'-0"$

- $1/4" = 1'-0"$

- $1/2" = 1'-0"$

- To read an architect's scale, use the part of scale graduated in whole feet and the division of a foot for increments smaller than a foot.

- The larger the scale of a drawing, the more information it can and should contain.

Engineer's Scales

An engineer's scale has one or more sets of graduated and numbered spaces, each set being divided into 10, 20, 30, 40, 50, or 60 parts to the inch.

- 1" = 10'
- 1" = 100'
- 1" = 1000'

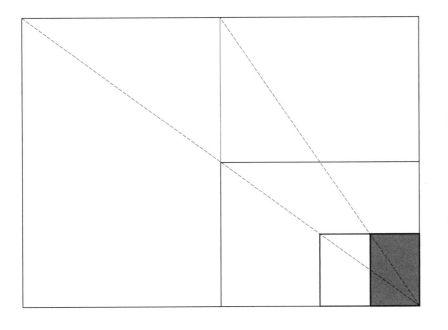

Metric Scales

Metric scales consist of one or more sets of graduated and numbered spaces, each set establishing a proportion of one millimeter to a specified number of millimeters.

- Common metric scales include the following: 1:5, 1:50, 1:500, 1:10, 1:100, 1:1000, 1:20, and 1:200

Digital Scale

In traditional drawing, we think in real-world units and use scale to reduce the drawing to a manageable size. In digital drawing, we actually input information in real-world units, but we should be careful to distinguish between the size of the image viewed on a monitor, which can be reduced and enlarged independent of its real-world size, and the scale of the output from a printer or plotter.

The transparency of tracing papers and films makes them effective for overlay work, allowing the selective drawing or tracing on one sheet and the ability to see through to an underlying drawing.

Tracing Papers

Tracing papers are characterized by transparency, whiteness, and tooth or surface grain. Fine-tooth papers are generally better for inking, whereas medium-tooth papers are more suitable for pencil work.

Sketch-Grade Tracing Paper

- Inexpensive, lightweight tissue is available in white, cream, and yellow or buff colors in rolls 12", 18", 24", 30", and 36" wide.
- Lightweight trace is used for freehand sketching, overlays, and studies.
- Use only soft leads or markers; hard leads can tear the thin paper easily.

Vellum

- Vellum is available in rolls, pads, and individual sheets in 16, 20, and 24 lb. weights.
- Mediumweight 16 lb. vellum is used for general layouts and preliminary drawings.
- 16 or 20 lb. vellum with 100% rag content is a stable, translucent, and erasable paper used for finished drawings.
- Vellum is available with nonreproducible blue square grids, subdivided into 4 x 4, 5 x 5, 8 x 8, or 10 x 10 parts to the inch.
- CAD and 3D-modeling programs have the ability to organize sets of information in different layers. While these levels or categories can be thought of and used as the digital equivalent of tracing paper, they offer more possibilities for manipulating and editing the information they contain than do the physical layers of tracing paper. And once entered and stored, digital information is easier to copy, transfer, and share than traditional drawings.

Drafting Film

Drafting film is a clear polyester film that is durable, dimensionally stable, and translucent enough for clear reproductions and overlay work.

- Drafting film is 3 to 4 mil thick and available in rolls or cut sheets.
- One or both sides may have a nonglare, matte finish suitable for pencil or ink.
- Use only with compatible leads, inks, and erasers.
- Ink lines are removable with erasing fluid or a vinyl eraser saturated with erasing fluid.

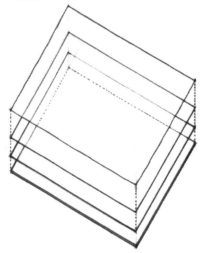

- Drafting tape or dots are required to fix a sheet of vellum or film to the drawing board. Do not use normal masking tape, which can tear the paper surface upon removal.

Illustration Boards

Illustration boards have a paper facing laminated to a cardboard backing.

- Illustration boards are available in single ($1/16$" thick) and double ($3/32$" thick) thicknesses.
- 100% rag paper facings are recommended for finish presentations.
- Coldpress boards have a degree of texture for pencil work; hotpress boards have relatively smooth surfaces more suitable for inking.
- Some brands of illustration boards have white facing papers bonded to a middle core of white stock. Cut edges are therefore consistently white in color, making them useful for constructing architectural models.
- The opacity of illustration boards requires that drawings be laid out directly on the board surface.

The following may be used to cover drawing boards:

- Vinyl covers provide a smooth, even drawing surface; tack holes and cuts heal themselves.
- Cellulose acetate film laminated to a tough paper base provides a smooth, nonglare surface.
- A dense, white illustration board provides an inexpensive drawing surface.

2
Architectural Drafting

Drafting—drawing with the aid of straightedges, triangles, templates, compasses, and scales—is the traditional means of creating architectural graphics and representation, and it remains relevant in an increasingly digital world. Drawing a line with a pen or pencil incorporates a kinesthetic sense of direction and length, and is a tactile act that feeds back into the mind in a way that reinforces the structure of the resulting graphic image. This chapter describes techniques and pointers for drafting lines, constructing geometric figures and shapes, and performing such operations as subdividing a given length into a number of equal parts. Understanding these procedures will result in more efficient and systematic representation of architectural and engineering structures; many are often useful in freehand sketching as well. Interspersed are digital equivalents of hand-drafting techniques to illustrate the principles that underlie all drawing, whether done by hand or on the computer.

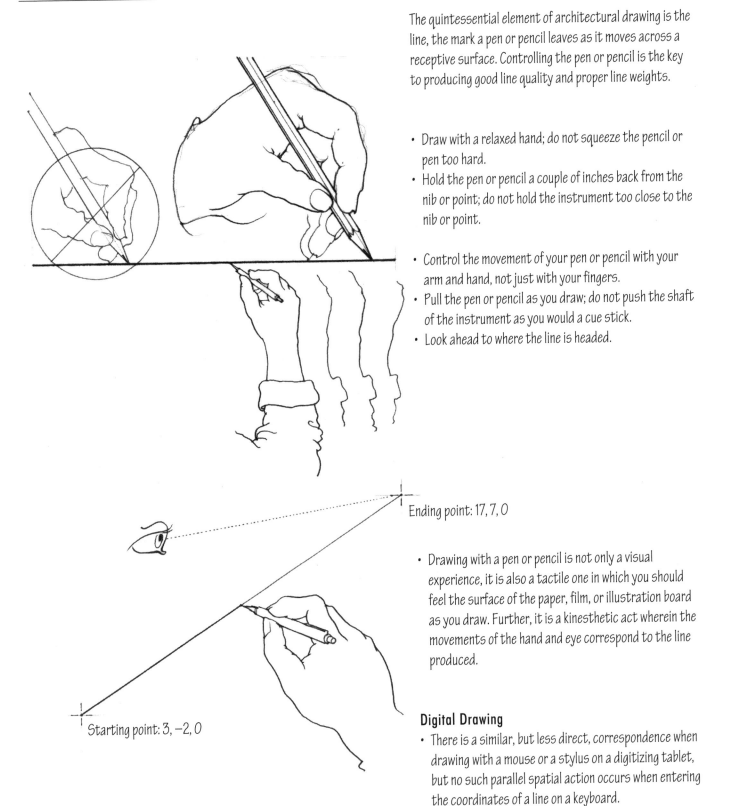

The quintessential element of architectural drawing is the line, the mark a pen or pencil leaves as it moves across a receptive surface. Controlling the pen or pencil is the key to producing good line quality and proper line weights.

• Draw with a relaxed hand; do not squeeze the pencil or pen too hard.
• Hold the pen or pencil a couple of inches back from the nib or point; do not hold the instrument too close to the nib or point.

• Control the movement of your pen or pencil with your arm and hand, not just with your fingers.
• Pull the pen or pencil as you draw; do not push the shaft of the instrument as you would a cue stick.
• Look ahead to where the line is headed.

Ending point: 17, 7, 0

• Drawing with a pen or pencil is not only a visual experience, it is also a tactile one in which you should feel the surface of the paper, film, or illustration board as you draw. Further, it is a kinesthetic act wherein the movements of the hand and eye correspond to the line produced.

Starting point: 3, −2, 0

Digital Drawing
• There is a similar, but less direct, correspondence when drawing with a mouse or a stylus on a digitizing tablet, but no such parallel spatial action occurs when entering the coordinates of a line on a keyboard.

All lines serve a purpose in drawing. It is essential that, as you draw, you understand what each line represents, whether it be an edge of a plane, a change in material, or simply a construction guideline.

The following types of lines, whether drawn by hand or on a computer, are typically used to make architectural graphics easier to read and interpret:

- Solid lines delineate the form of objects, such as the edge of a plane or the intersection of two planes. The relative weight of a solid line varies according to its role in conveying depth.

- Dashed lines, consisting of short, closely spaced strokes, indicate elements hidden or removed from our view.

- Centerlines, consisting of thin, relatively long segments separated by single dashes or dots, represent the axis of a symmetrical object or composition.
- Grid lines are a rectangular or radial system of light solid lines or centerlines for locating and regulating the elements of a plan.

- Property lines, consisting of relatively long segments separated by two dashes or dots, indicate the legally defined and recorded boundaries of a parcel of land.

- Break lines, consisting of relatively long segments joined by short zigzag strokes, are used to cut off a portion of a drawing.

- Utility lines consist of relatively long segments separated by a letter indicating the type of utility.

In theory, all lines should be uniformly dense for ease of readability and reproduction. Line weight is therefore primarily a matter of width or thickness. While inked lines are uniformly black and vary only in width, pencil lines can vary in both width and tonal value, depending on the hardness of the lead used, the tooth and density of the surface, and the speed and pressure with which you draw. Strive to make all pencil lines uniformly dense and vary their width to achieve differing line weights.

Heavy

- Heavy solid lines are used to delineate the profiles of plan and section cuts (see pages 48 and 65) as well as spatial edges (see page 93).
- Use H, F, HB, or B leads; pressing too hard to draw a bold line indicates that you are using too hard of a lead.
- Use a lead holder or draw a series of closely spaced lines with a 0.3 mm or 0.5 mm mechanical pencil; avoid using a 0.7 mm or 0.9 mm pencil for drawing heavy line weights.

Medium

- Medium-weight solid lines indicate the edges and intersections of planes.
- Use H, F, or HB leads.

Light

- Lightweight solid lines suggest a change in material, color, or texture, without a change in the form of an object.
- Use 2H, H, or F leads.

Very Light

- Very light solid lines are used to lay out drawings, establish organizing grids, and indicate surface textures.
- Use 4H, 2H, H, or F leads.

- The visible range and contrast of line weights should be in proportion to the size and scale of a drawing.

Digital Line Weights

- A distinct advantage to drawing or drafting by hand is that the results are immediately discernible to the eye. When using drawing or CAD software, one may select a line weight from a menu or by specifying a stroke width in absolute units (millimeters, fractions of an inch, or number of points, where 1 point = $^1/72$"). In either case, what one views on a monitor may not match the output from a printer or plotter. One should therefore always run a test print or plot to ascertain whether or not the resulting range and contrasts in the line weights of a drawing are appropriate. Note, however, that if changes in line weight are necessary, it is often much easier to make them in a digital drawing than in a hand drawing.

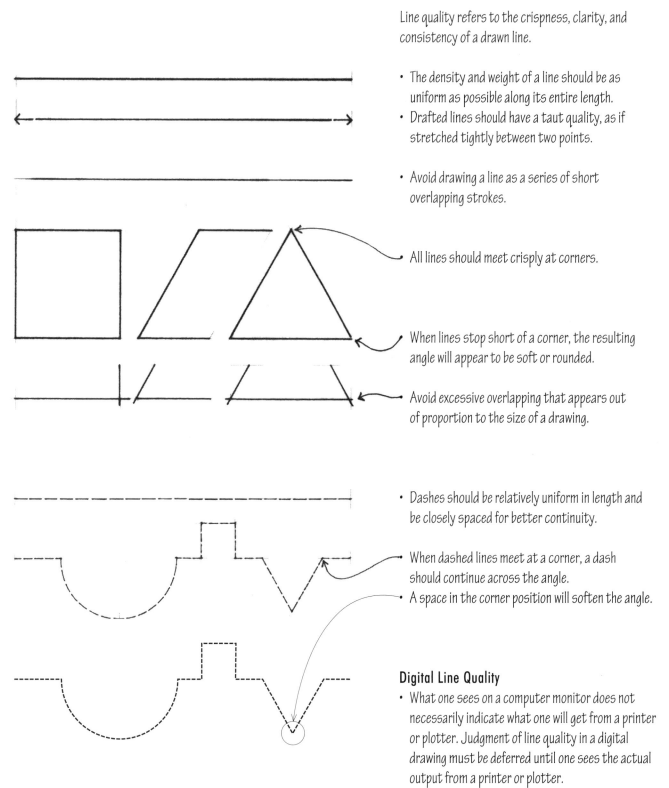

Line quality refers to the crispness, clarity, and consistency of a drawn line.

- The density and weight of a line should be as uniform as possible along its entire length.
- Drafted lines should have a taut quality, as if stretched tightly between two points.

- Avoid drawing a line as a series of short overlapping strokes.

- All lines should meet crisply at corners.

- When lines stop short of a corner, the resulting angle will appear to be soft or rounded.

- Avoid excessive overlapping that appears out of proportion to the size of a drawing.

- Dashes should be relatively uniform in length and be closely spaced for better continuity.

- When dashed lines meet at a corner, a dash should continue across the angle.
- A space in the corner position will soften the angle.

Digital Line Quality
- What one sees on a computer monitor does not necessarily indicate what one will get from a printer or plotter. Judgment of line quality in a digital drawing must be deferred until one sees the actual output from a printer or plotter.
- The lines produced by vector drawing programs are based on mathematical formulas and usually print or plot better than those of raster images.

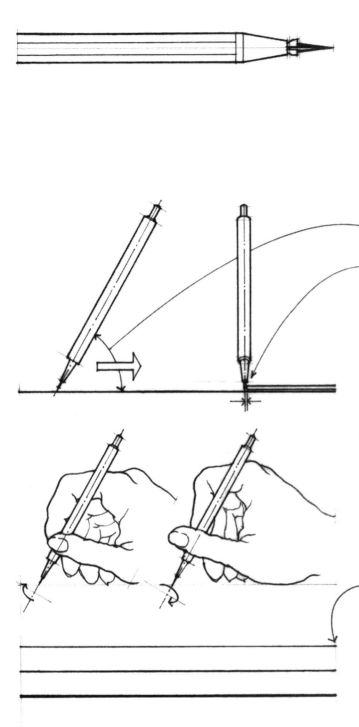

- The point of the lead in a lead holder should have a taper about $^3/_8''$ long; if the taper is too short or too rounded, the point will dull quickly.
- There are a variety of mechanical sharpeners available. If you use a sandpaper pad to sharpen leads, slant the lead at a low angle to achieve the correct taper.
- 0.3 mm or 0.5 mm leads for mechanical pencils do not require sharpening.

- Position your body to draw over the upper straightedge of a T-square, parallel rule, or triangle, never the lower edge.
- Hold the pencil at a 45° to 60° angle; hold technical pens at a slightly steeper angle.
- Pull the pen or pencil along the straightedge in a plane perpendicular to the drawing surface, leaving a very slight gap between the straightedge and the nib of the pen or the point of the pencil. Do not push the pen or pencil as if it were a cue stick.
- Do not draw into the corner where the straightedge meets the drawing surface. Doing so dirties the equipment and causes blotting of ink lines.

- Draw with a steady pace—not too fast, not too slowly—and with even pressure. This will help prevent a line from feathering or fading out along its length.

- To help a pencil point wear evenly and keep it fairly sharp, rotate the shaft of the lead holder or mechanical pencil between your thumb and forefinger slowly as you draw the entire length of a line.

- A line should start and end in a positive manner. Applying slight additional pressure at the beginning and ending of a stroke will help accomplish this.
- Strive for single-stroke lines. Achieving the desired line weight, however, may require drawing a series of closely spaced lines.

- Try to keep drawings clean by washing hands and equipment often, and by lifting and moving tools rather than dragging or sliding them across the drawing surface.
- Protect the drawing surface by keeping areas of it covered with lightweight tracing paper and exposing only the area in which you are working. The transparency of the tracing paper helps maintain a visual connection to the context of the drawing.

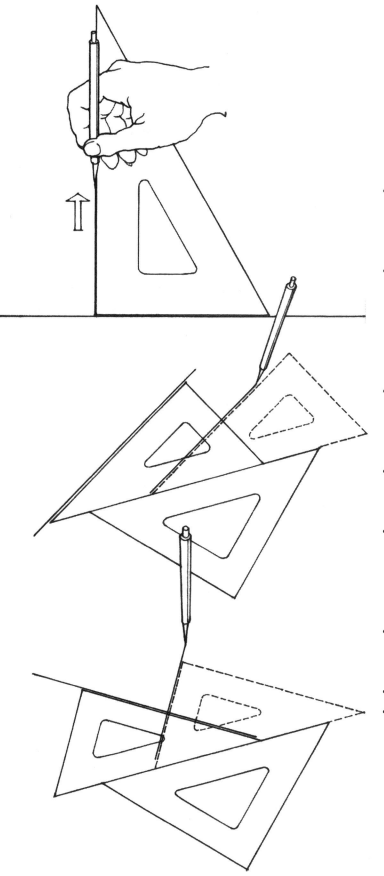

- When drawing vertical lines perpendicular to the edge of a T-square or parallel rule, use a drafting triangle and turn your body so that you can draw them in a manner similar to the way you draw horizontal lines.
- Avoid simply drawing the vertical lines by sitting still and sliding the pen or pencil up or down the edge of the triangle.

- Drawing a series of parallel lines using two triangles is useful when the series is at some angle other than the standard 30°, 45°, 60°, or 90° angle of drafting triangles.
- Position the hypotenuse of one triangle against the hypotenuse of the other and align one side of the upper triangle with the given line.
- Hold the bottom triangle firmly while you slide the other triangle to the desired positions.

- To draw a perpendicular to a given line, first position the hypotenuse of one triangle against the hypotenuse of the other.
- Align one side of the upper triangle with the given line.
- Hold the bottom triangle firmly while you slide the upper triangle until the perpendicular side is in the proper position.

Subdivisions

In principle, it is always advisable to work from the larger part to the smaller. The successive repetition of short lengths or measurements can often result in an accumulation of minute errors. It is therefore advantageous to be able to subdivide an overall length into a number of equal parts. Being able to subdivide any given length in this manner is useful for constructing the risers and runs of a stairway, as well as for establishing the coursing of such construction as a tiled floor or masonry wall.

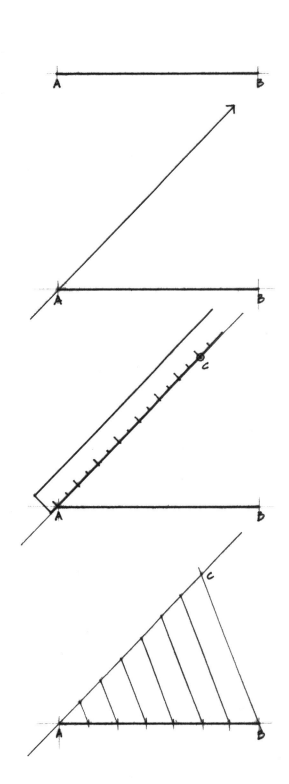

- To subdivide a line segment AB into a number of equal parts, draw a line at a convenient angle between 10° and 45° through the starting point. Using an angle that is too acute would make it difficult to ascertain the exact point of intersection.

- Along this line, use an appropriate scale to mark off the desired number of equal divisions.

- Connect the end points B and C.
- Draw lines parallel to BC to transfer the scaled divisions to line AB.

A distinct advantage of digital drawing programs is they allow us to try out graphic ideas and easily undo them if unworkable. We can lay out and develop work on screen and either print it out or save the file for future editing. Questions of scale and placement can be deferred since these aspects can be adjusted as required during the creation of the final graphic image. In hand drafting, the result of the drawing process is seen immediately but adjustments to scale and placement are difficult to make.

Digital Multiplication

The ability to create, move and place copies of a line or shape is easily accomplished in digital drawing programs.

- We can copy and move any line or shape a specified distance in a given direction, repeating this process as many times as necessary to achieve the desired number of equally spaced copies.

Digital Subdivision

We can subdivide any line segment in a manner similar to the process we use in hand drafting. We can also distribute lines and shapes evenly between the two endpoints of the line segment. Whether subdividing by hand drafting or in a digital drawing program, the process of working from the general to the specific, from the larger whole to the smaller parts, remains the same.

- Given line segment AB, draw a line segment at any angle through point A and copy the line segment as many times as necessary to equal the desired number of subdivisions.

- Move the last line segment to point B.

- Select all of the line segments and distribute them evenly to create the desired number of equal divisions.

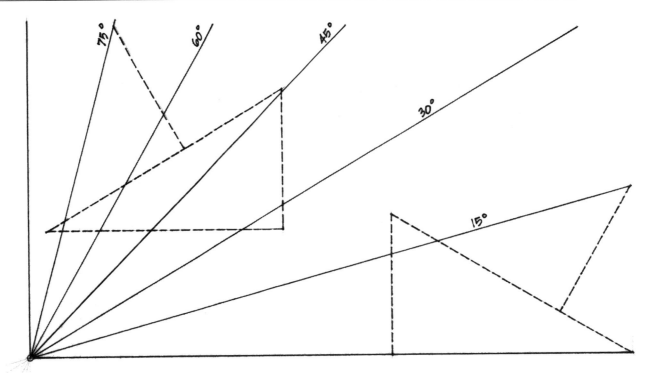

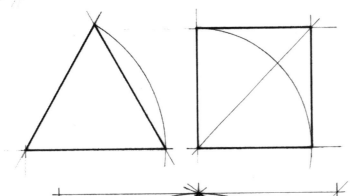

Angles and Shapes

We use the standard drafting triangles to construct 30°, 45°, 60°, and 90° angles. Using both 45°–45° and 30°–60° triangles in combination, we can also easily construct 15° and 75° angles. For other angles, use a protractor or an adjustable triangle.

The diagrams to the left illustrate how to construct three common geometric shapes—an equilateral triangle, a square and a pentagon.

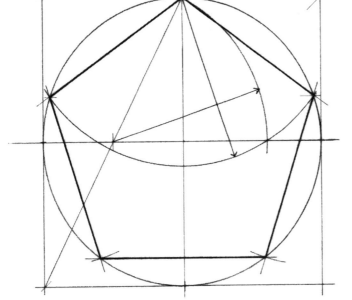

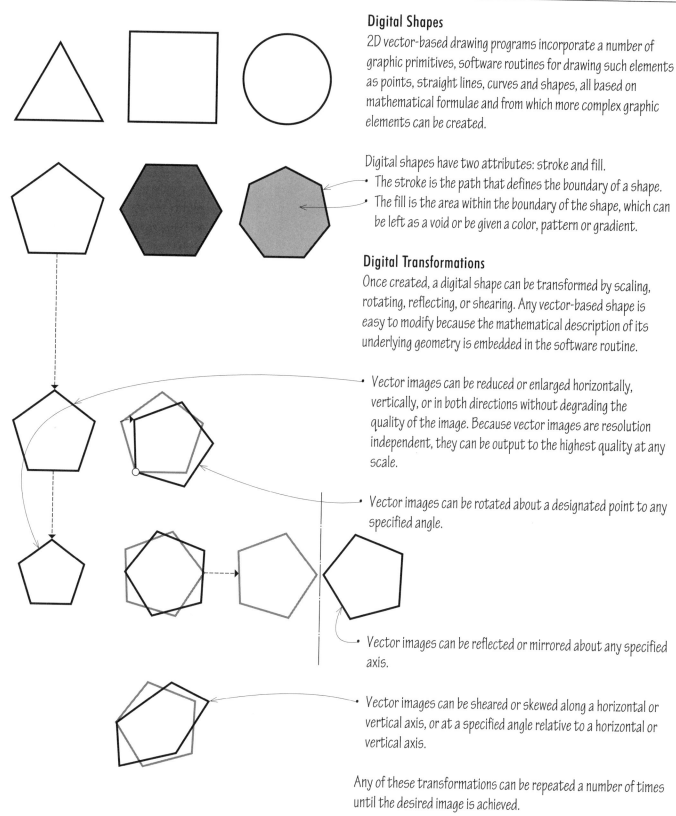

Digital Shapes

2D vector-based drawing programs incorporate a number of graphic primitives, software routines for drawing such elements as points, straight lines, curves and shapes, all based on mathematical formulae and from which more complex graphic elements can be created.

Digital shapes have two attributes: stroke and fill.
* The stroke is the path that defines the boundary of a shape.
* The fill is the area within the boundary of the shape, which can be left as a void or be given a color, pattern or gradient.

Digital Transformations

Once created, a digital shape can be transformed by scaling, rotating, reflecting, or shearing. Any vector-based shape is easy to modify because the mathematical description of its underlying geometry is embedded in the software routine.

* Vector images can be reduced or enlarged horizontally, vertically, or in both directions without degrading the quality of the image. Because vector images are resolution independent, they can be output to the highest quality at any scale.

* Vector images can be rotated about a designated point to any specified angle.

* Vector images can be reflected or mirrored about any specified axis.

* Vector images can be sheared or skewed along a horizontal or vertical axis, or at a specified angle relative to a horizontal or vertical axis.

Any of these transformations can be repeated a number of times until the desired image is achieved.

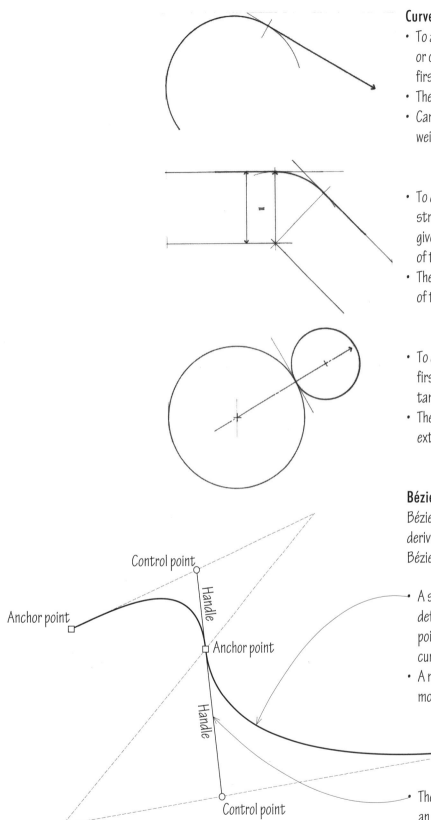

Curved Lines

- To avoid drawing a mismatched tangent to a circle or curved line segment, draw the curvilinear element first.
- Then draw the tangent from the circle or arc.
- Care should be taken to match the pen or pencil line weights of circles and arcs to the rest of the drawing.

- To draw an arc of a given radius tangent to two given straight line segments, first draw lines parallel to the given lines at a distance equal to the desired radius of the arc.
- The intersection of these lines establishes the center of the desired arc.

- To draw two circles that are tangent to each other, first draw a line from the center of one to the desired tangential point on its circumference.
- The center of the second circle must lie along the extension of this line.

Bézier Curves

Bézier curves refers to a class of mathematically derived curves developed by French engineer Pierre Bézier for CAD/CAM operations.

- A simple Bézier curve has two anchor points, which define the endpoints of the curve, and two control points, which lie outside the curve and control the curvature of the path.
- A number of simple Bézier curves can be joined to form more complex curves.

- The colinear relationship between the two handles at an anchor point ensures a smooth curvature wherever the path changes curvature.

Control point

Handle

Anchor point

Anchor point

Handle

Anchor point

Control point

3
Architectural Drawing Systems

The central task of architectural drawing is representing three-dimensional forms, constructions, and spatial environments on a two-dimensional surface. Three distinct types of drawing systems have evolved over time to accomplish this mission: multiview, paraline, and perspective drawings. This chapter describes these three major drawing systems, the principles behind their construction, and their resulting pictorial characteristics. The discussion does not include media that involve motion and animation, made possible by computer technology. Nevertheless, these visual systems of representation constitute a formal graphic language that is governed by a consistent set of principles. Understanding these principles and related conventions is the key to creating and reading architectural drawings.

All three major drawing systems result from the way a three-dimensional subject is projected onto a two-dimensional plane of projection, or more simply, onto the picture plane.

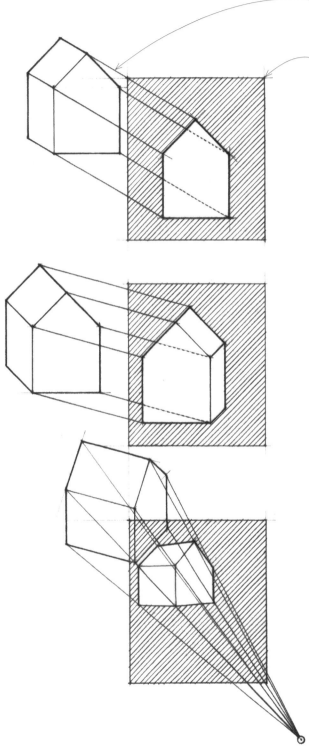

- Projectors transfer points on the subject to the picture plane. These projectors are also called sightlines in perspective projection.
- The drawing surface or sheet of paper is the virtual equivalent of the picture plane.

Three distinct projection systems result from the relationship of the projectors to each other as well as to the picture plane.

Orthographic Projection
- Projectors are parallel to each other and perpendicular to the picture plane.
- Axonometric projection is a special case of orthographic projection.

Oblique Projection
- Projectors are parallel to each other and oblique to the picture plane.

Perspective Projection
- Projectors or sightlines radiate from a central point that represents a single eye of the observer.

Once the information for a three-dimensional construction or environment has been entered into a computer, 3D CAD and modeling software can theoretically present the information in any of these projection systems.

When we study how each projection system represents the same subject, we can see how different pictorial effects result. We categorize these pictorial systems into multiview drawings, paraline drawings, and perspective drawings.

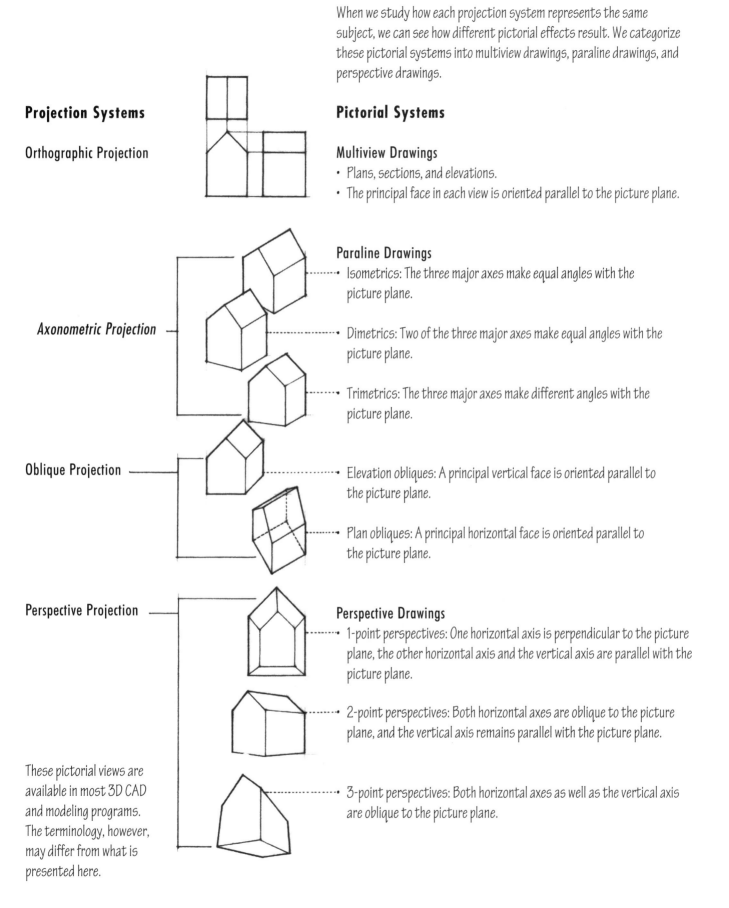

Projection Systems

Orthographic Projection

Axonometric Projection

Oblique Projection

Perspective Projection

These pictorial views are available in most 3D CAD and modeling programs. The terminology, however, may differ from what is presented here.

Pictorial Systems

Multiview Drawings
- Plans, sections, and elevations.
- The principal face in each view is oriented parallel to the picture plane.

Paraline Drawings
- Isometrics: The three major axes make equal angles with the picture plane.

- Dimetrics: Two of the three major axes make equal angles with the picture plane.

- Trimetrics: The three major axes make different angles with the picture plane.

- Elevation obliques: A principal vertical face is oriented parallel to the picture plane.

- Plan obliques: A principal horizontal face is oriented parallel to the picture plane.

Perspective Drawings
- 1-point perspectives: One horizontal axis is perpendicular to the picture plane, the other horizontal axis and the vertical axis are parallel with the picture plane.

- 2-point perspectives: Both horizontal axes are oblique to the picture plane, and the vertical axis remains parallel with the picture plane.

- 3-point perspectives: Both horizontal axes as well as the vertical axis are oblique to the picture plane.

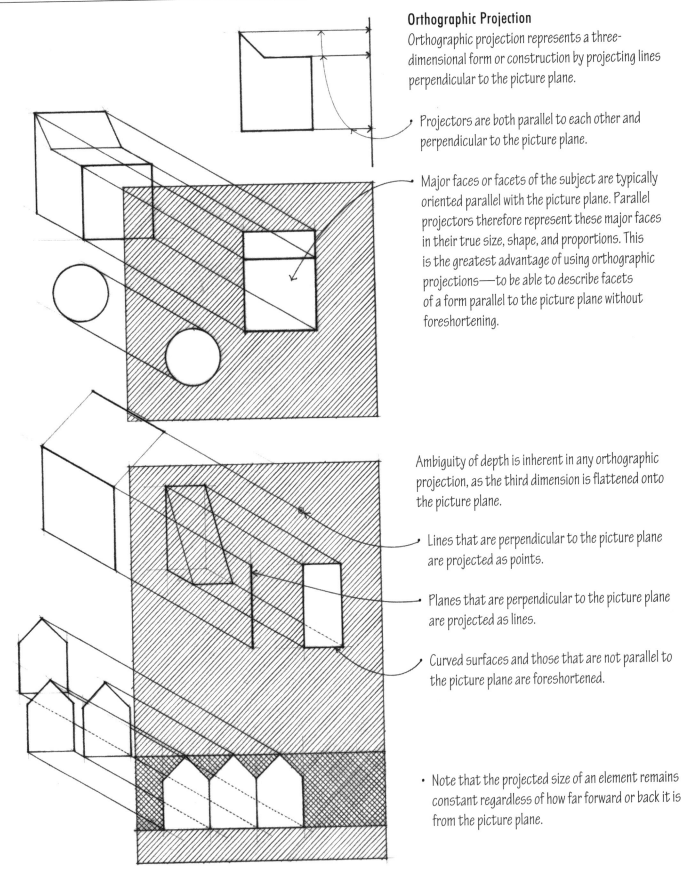

Orthographic Projection

Orthographic projection represents a three-dimensional form or construction by projecting lines perpendicular to the picture plane.

• Projectors are both parallel to each other and perpendicular to the picture plane.

• Major faces or facets of the subject are typically oriented parallel with the picture plane. Parallel projectors therefore represent these major faces in their true size, shape, and proportions. This is the greatest advantage of using orthographic projections—to be able to describe facets of a form parallel to the picture plane without foreshortening.

Ambiguity of depth is inherent in any orthographic projection, as the third dimension is flattened onto the picture plane.

• Lines that are perpendicular to the picture plane are projected as points.

• Planes that are perpendicular to the picture plane are projected as lines.

• Curved surfaces and those that are not parallel to the picture plane are foreshortened.

• Note that the projected size of an element remains constant regardless of how far forward or back it is from the picture plane.

Any single orthographic projection cannot convey facets of a subject that are oblique or perpendicular to the picture plane. Only by looking at related orthographic projections can this information be discerned. For this reason, we use the term "multiview drawings" to describe the series of orthographic projections necessary to fully and accurately describe a three-dimensional subject.

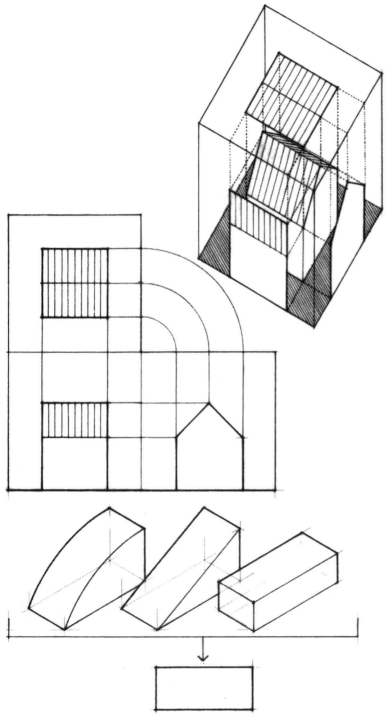

- If we enclose an object within a transparent picture-plane box, we can name the images projected orthographically onto the principal picture planes.
- Top views are orthographic projections cast onto the horizontal picture plane. In architectural drawing, top views are called plans.
- Front and side views are orthographic projections cast onto the vertical picture planes. In architectural drawing, front and side views are called elevations.
- See Chapter 4 for floor plans and sections, which are orthographic projections of cuts made through a building.

- To make it easier to read and interpret how a series of orthographic projections describe a three-dimensional whole, we arrange the views in an orderly and logical fashion.
- The most common layout results when we unfold the transparent picture-plane box into a single plane represented by the drawing surface. The top or plan view revolves upward to a position directly above and vertically aligned with the front or elevation view, while the side view revolves to align horizontally with the front view. The result is a coherent set of related orthographic views.

- Although these three objects have different forms, their top views appear to be identical. Only by looking at related orthographic projections are we able to understand the three-dimensional form of each object. We should therefore study and represent three-dimensional forms and constructions through a series of related orthographic projections.
- The mind must be able to read and assemble a set of multiview drawings to fully understand the nature of the three-dimensional subject.

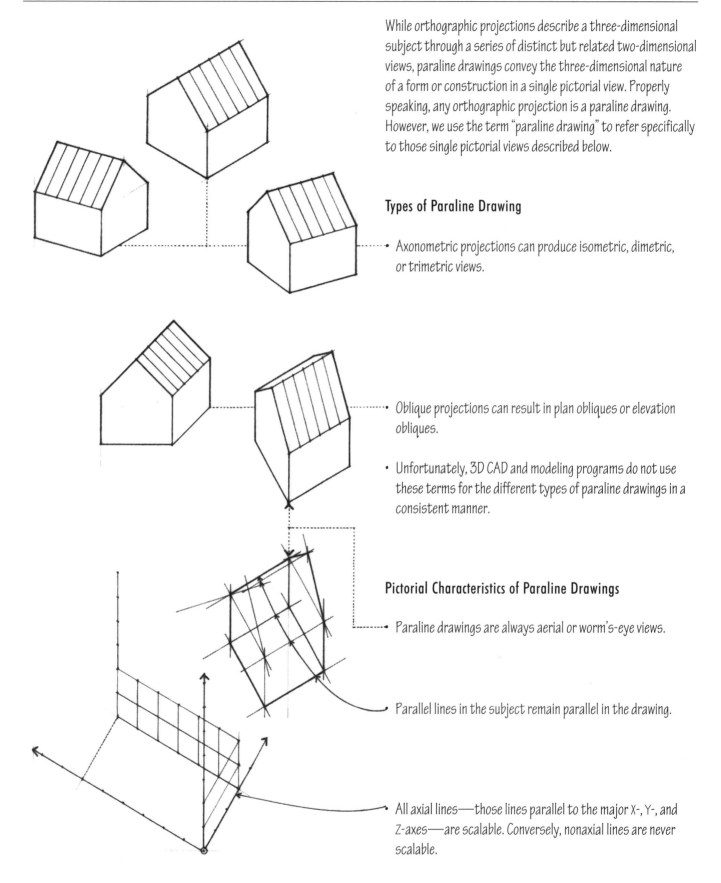

While orthographic projections describe a three-dimensional subject through a series of distinct but related two-dimensional views, paraline drawings convey the three-dimensional nature of a form or construction in a single pictorial view. Properly speaking, any orthographic projection is a paraline drawing. However, we use the term "paraline drawing" to refer specifically to those single pictorial views described below.

Types of Paraline Drawing

- Axonometric projections can produce isometric, dimetric, or trimetric views.

- Oblique projections can result in plan obliques or elevation obliques.

- Unfortunately, 3D CAD and modeling programs do not use these terms for the different types of paraline drawings in a consistent manner.

Pictorial Characteristics of Paraline Drawings

- Paraline drawings are always aerial or worm's-eye views.

- Parallel lines in the subject remain parallel in the drawing.

- All axial lines—those lines parallel to the major X-, Y-, and Z-axes—are scalable. Conversely, nonaxial lines are never scalable.

Axonometric Projection

An axonometric projection is an orthographic projection of a three-dimensional form that is inclined to the picture plane in such a way that its three principal axes are foreshortened. The term "axonometric" is often misused to describe paraline drawings of oblique projections or the entire class of paraline drawings. Strictly speaking, axonometric projection is a form of orthographic projection in which the projectors are parallel to each other and perpendicular to the picture plane. The difference between orthographic multiview drawings and an axonometric single-view drawing is simply the orientation of the object to the picture plane.

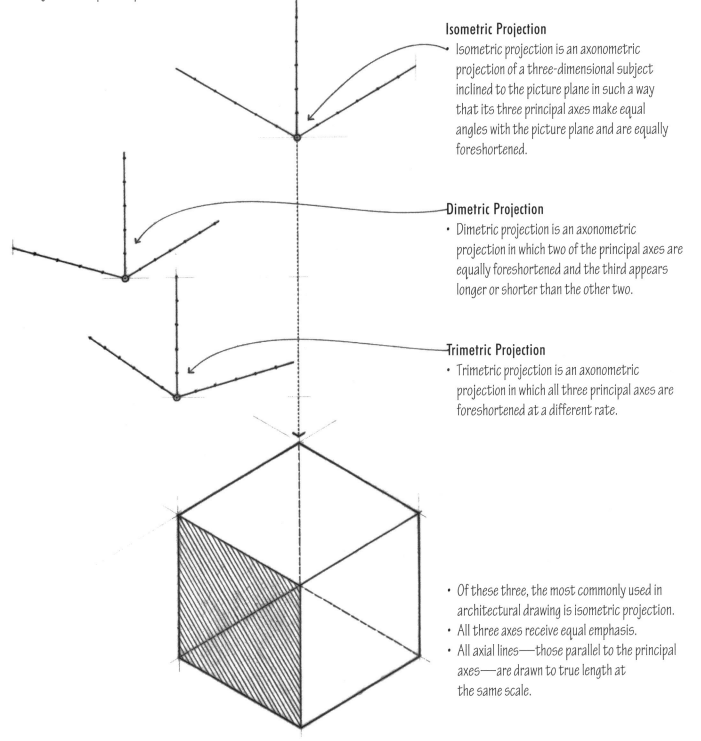

Isometric Projection

- Isometric projection is an axonometric projection of a three-dimensional subject inclined to the picture plane in such a way that its three principal axes make equal angles with the picture plane and are equally foreshortened.

Dimetric Projection

- Dimetric projection is an axonometric projection in which two of the principal axes are equally foreshortened and the third appears longer or shorter than the other two.

Trimetric Projection

- Trimetric projection is an axonometric projection in which all three principal axes are foreshortened at a different rate.

- Of these three, the most commonly used in architectural drawing is isometric projection.
- All three axes receive equal emphasis.
- All axial lines—those parallel to the principal axes—are drawn to true length at the same scale.

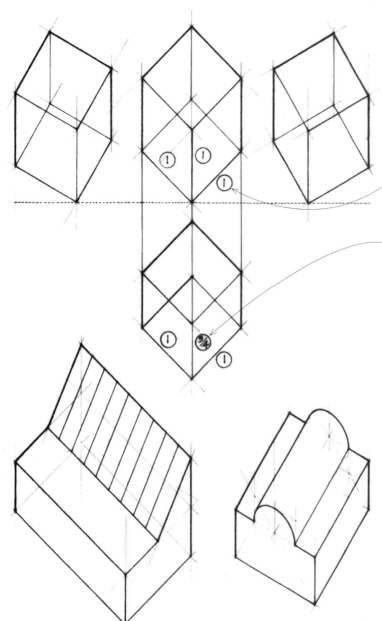

Oblique Projection

Oblique projection represents a three-dimensional form or construction by projecting parallel lines at some convenient angle other than 90° to the picture plane. A principal face or set of planes of the subject is usually oriented parallel to the picture plane and is therefore represented in accurate size, shape, and proportion.

- For convenience, the receding lines perpendicular to the picture plane are typically drawn to the same scale as the lines parallel to the picture plane.
- The receding lines may be foreshortened to $^3/_4$ or $^1/_2$ their true scaled length to offset the appearance of distortion.

In architectural drawing, there are two principal types of oblique drawings: plan obliques and elevation obliques.

Plan Obliques

- Plan obliques orient the horizontal planes of the subject parallel to the picture plane. These horizontal planes are therefore shown in true size and shape, while the two principal sets of vertical planes are foreshortened.
- Plan obliques have a higher angle of view than isometric drawings.
- An advantage in constructing plan obliques is the ability to use floor plans as base drawings.

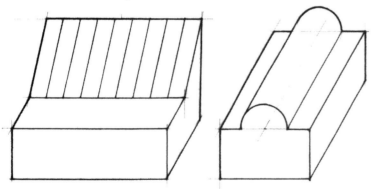

Elevation Obliques

- Elevation obliques orient one principal set of vertical planes of the subject parallel to the picture plane. This set is therefore shown in true size and shape, while the other vertical set and the principal horizontal set of planes are both foreshortened.
- The face selected to be parallel to the picture plane should be the longest, the most complex, or the most significant face of the building or construction.

Perspective Projection

Perspective projection portrays a three-dimensional form or construction by projecting all of its points to a picture plane (PP) by straight lines that converge at a fixed point representing a single eye of the observer.

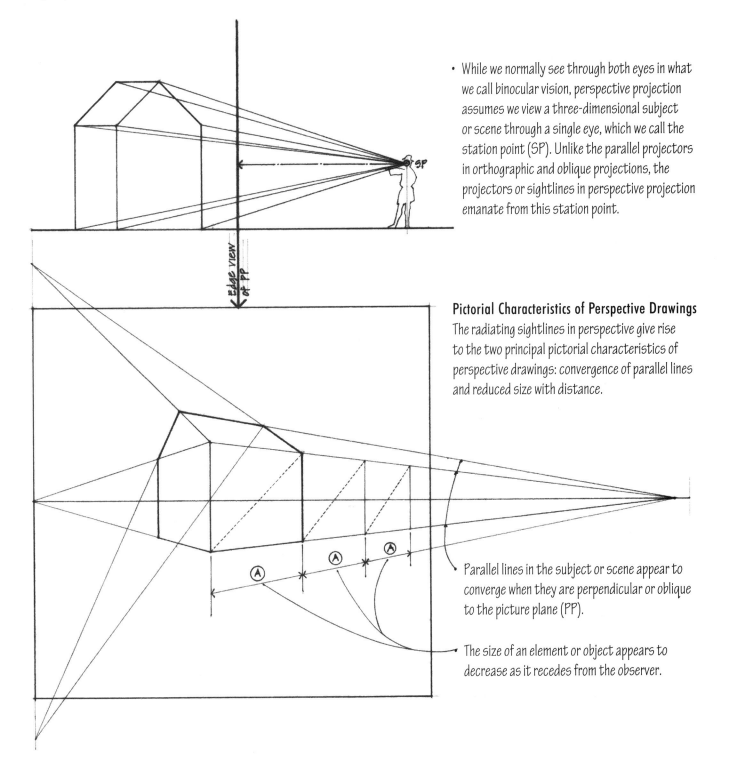

- While we normally see through both eyes in what we call binocular vision, perspective projection assumes we view a three-dimensional subject or scene through a single eye, which we call the station point (SP). Unlike the parallel projectors in orthographic and oblique projections, the projectors or sightlines in perspective projection emanate from this station point.

Pictorial Characteristics of Perspective Drawings

The radiating sightlines in perspective give rise to the two principal pictorial characteristics of perspective drawings: convergence of parallel lines and reduced size with distance.

Parallel lines in the subject or scene appear to converge when they are perpendicular or oblique to the picture plane (PP).

The size of an element or object appears to decrease as it recedes from the observer.

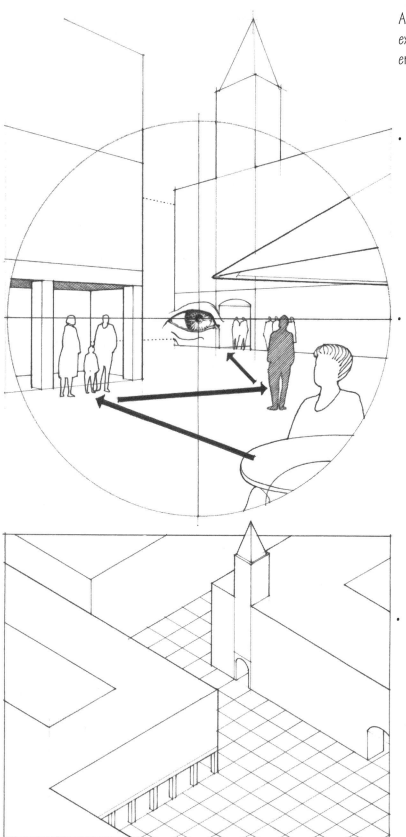

A well-drawn perspective excels in conveying the experience of being in a three-dimensional spatial environment.

- The experiential nature of a perspective drawing relies on our ability to define at least three layers of depth within a scene: a foreground, a middleground, and a background.

- Perspective drawings assume there is an observer located at a specific point in space and looking in a particular direction.

- Multiview and paraline drawings, on the other hand, do not make reference to the point of view of an observer. We can view the drawings from various angles and be comfortable in reading the objective information. Our eyes can roam over the expanse of a plan or paraline drawing and be able to correctly interpret the graphic information.

- We can use a series of perspectives—what we call serial vision—to convey the experience not only of being in a place but also of moving through a sequence of spaces.

- 3D modeling programs often have the ability to create a sequential series of perspective views and animate a walk-through or fly-through of a building or spatial environment. There is an ongoing question regarding how to use these capabilities to simulate more effectively the way we experience space.

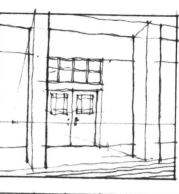

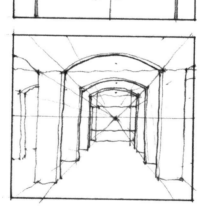

- There is little advantage in drawing a perspective of a small-scale object, such as a chair or structural detail, unless it exists in a spatial environment. At these scales, the degree of convergence of parallel lines is so slight that a paraline view is usually a better and more efficient choice.

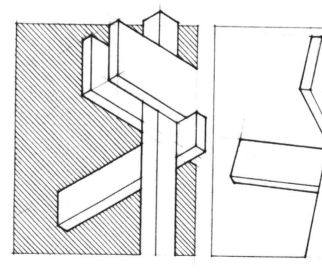

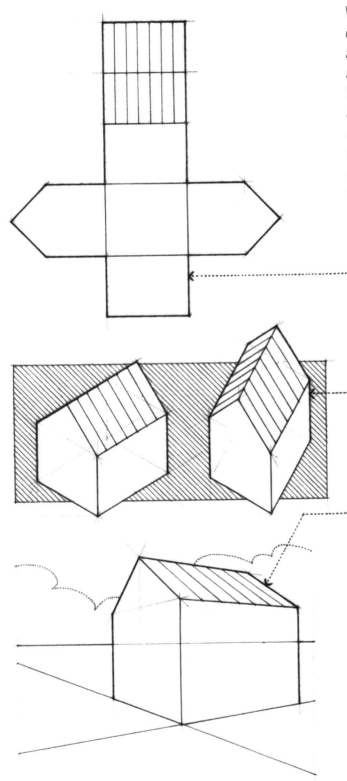

We use architectural drawings to initiate, explore, develop, and communicate design ideas. No one drawing can ever reveal everything about its subject. Each pictorial system of representation provides an alternative way of thinking about and representing what we see before us or envision in the mind's eye. The choice of a particular drawing system influences how we view the resulting graphic image, establishes which design issues are made visible for evaluation and scrutiny, and directs how we are inclined to think about the subject of the drawing. In selecting one drawing system over another, therefore, we make conscious as well as unconscious choices about what to reveal as well as what to conceal.

Point of View

- Multiview drawings represent a three-dimensional subject through a series of distinct, but related, two-dimensional views.
- These are abstract views that the viewer must assemble in the mind to construct an objective reality.

- Paraline drawings describe the three-dimensional nature of the same subject in a single view.
- These views combine the scalability of multiview drawings and the easy-to-understand, pictorial nature of perspectives.

- Perspectives are experiential views that convey a sense of being present in a spatial environment.
- Perspectives depict an optical reality rather than the objective reality of multiview and paraline drawings.
- It is a paradox that multiview drawings are relatively easy to develop but often difficult to interpret, while perspective drawings are challenging to construct but usually easy to understand.

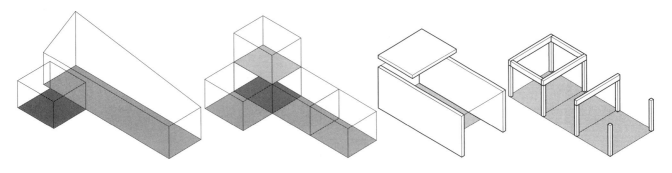

Trying out different spatial and formal possibilities

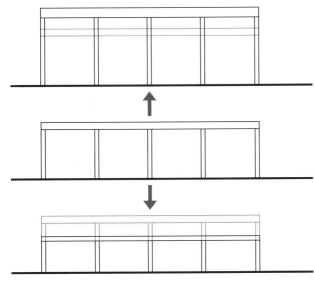

Trying out different proportional relationships

Digital Views

A distinct advantage of digital drawing over traditional drawing is the ability to experiment with design modifications, study alternative points of view, or try out different drawing techniques. These advantages arise from the ability to undo an action or series of operations, or to save one version of a drawing while working on a copy and return to the saved version if necessary.

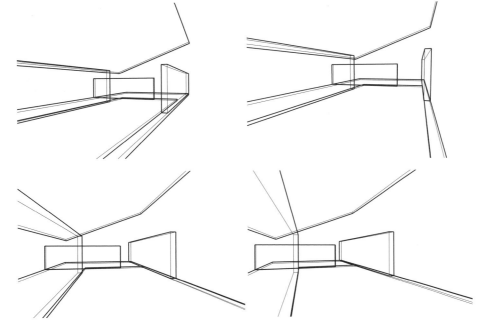

Trying out different points of view

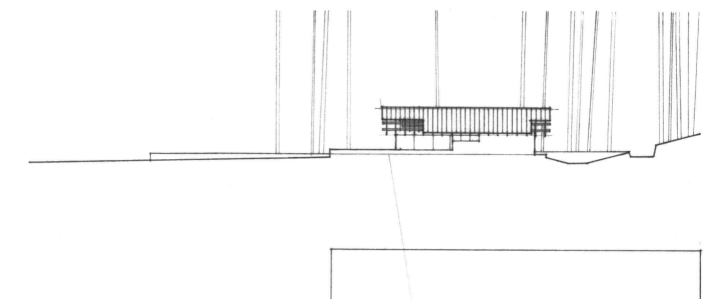

Scale & Detail

Architectural drawings are typically executed at a reduced scale to fit onto a certain size sheet of paper, vellum, or illustration board. Even digital printers and plotters have paper size limitations. The scale of a drawing determines how much detail can be included in the graphic image. Conversely, how much detail is desirable determines how large or small the scale of a drawing should be.

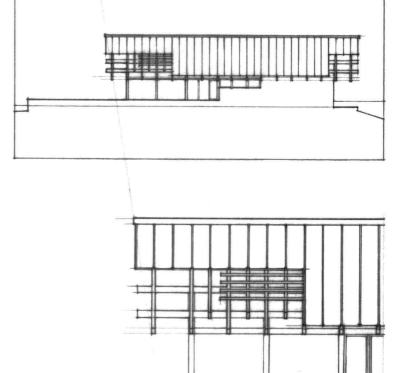

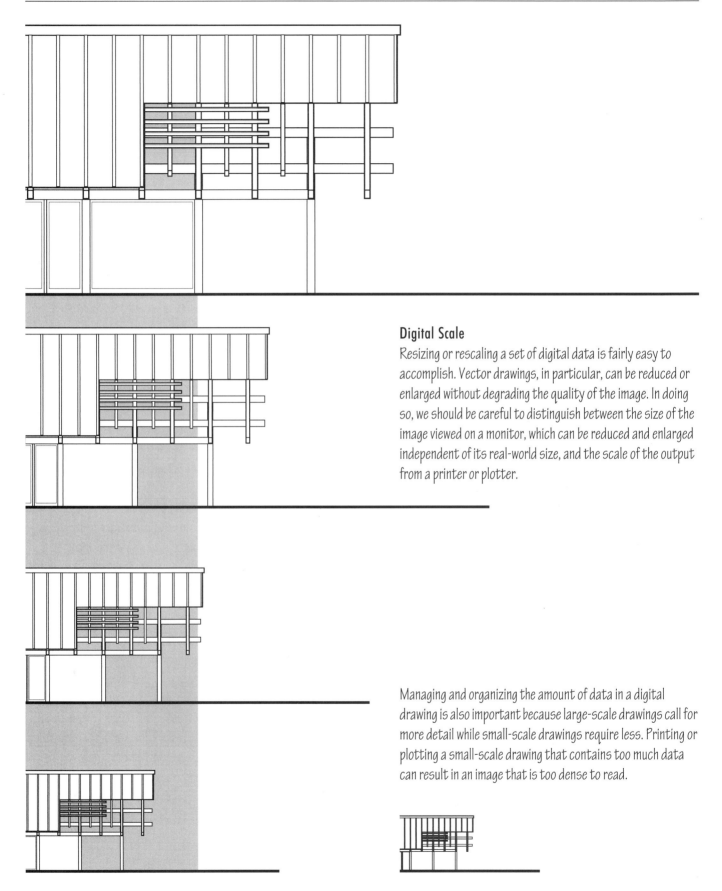

Digital Scale

Resizing or rescaling a set of digital data is fairly easy to accomplish. Vector drawings, in particular, can be reduced or enlarged without degrading the quality of the image. In doing so, we should be careful to distinguish between the size of the image viewed on a monitor, which can be reduced and enlarged independent of its real-world size, and the scale of the output from a printer or plotter.

Managing and organizing the amount of data in a digital drawing is also important because large-scale drawings call for more detail while small-scale drawings require less. Printing or plotting a small-scale drawing that contains too much data can result in an image that is too dense to read.

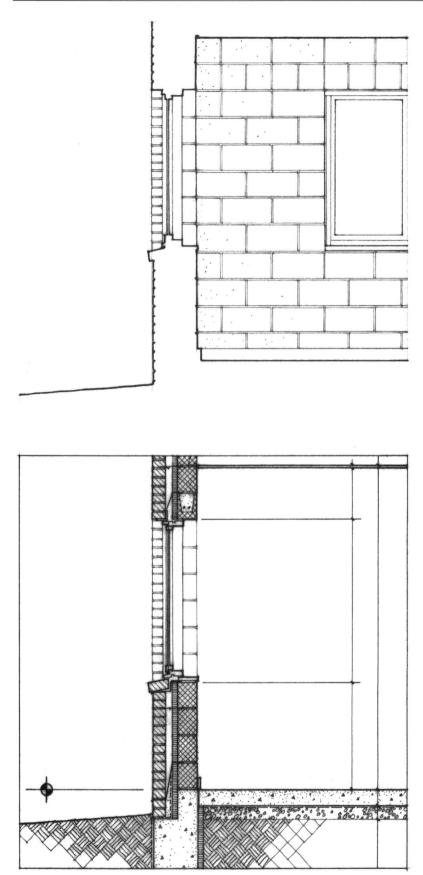

Design & Construction Drawings

In architectural design, we use drawings to convey the experiential qualities of spatial compositions and environments. Design drawings, therefore, focus on illustrating and clarifying the essential solid-void nature of forms and spaces, scale and proportional relationships, and other sensible qualities of space. For these reasons, design drawings convey information primarily through graphic means.

Construction drawings, on the other hand, are intended to instruct the builder or fabricator about the implementation or construction of a design. These contract drawings, which constitute part of a legal document, often rely on abstract conventions and include dimensions, notes, and specifications.

4

Multiview Drawings

Multiview drawings comprise the drawing types we know as plans, elevations, and sections. Each is an orthographic projection of a particular aspect of a three-dimensional object or construction. These orthographic views are abstract in the sense that they do not match optical reality. They are a conceptual form of representation based on what we know about something rather than on the way it might appear to the eye. In architectural design, multiview drawings establish two-dimensional fields on which we are able to study formal and spatial patterns as well as scalar and proportional relationships in a composition. The ability to regulate size, placement, and configuration also makes multiview drawings useful in communicating the graphic information necessary for the description, fabrication, and construction of a design.

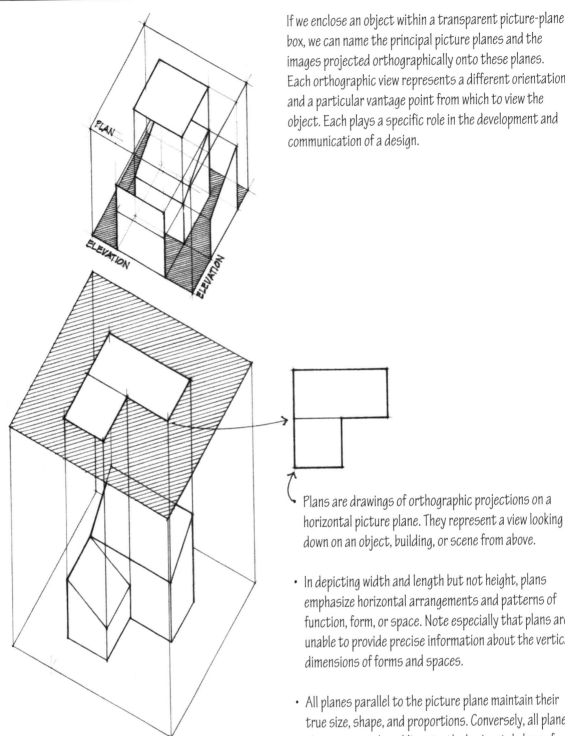

If we enclose an object within a transparent picture-plane box, we can name the principal picture planes and the images projected orthographically onto these planes. Each orthographic view represents a different orientation and a particular vantage point from which to view the object. Each plays a specific role in the development and communication of a design.

Plans are drawings of orthographic projections on a horizontal picture plane. They represent a view looking down on an object, building, or scene from above.

• In depicting width and length but not height, plans emphasize horizontal arrangements and patterns of function, form, or space. Note especially that plans are unable to provide precise information about the vertical dimensions of forms and spaces.

• All planes parallel to the picture plane maintain their true size, shape, and proportions. Conversely, all planes that are curved or oblique to the horizontal plane of projection are foreshortened.

• In architectural drawing, there are distinct types of plan views for depicting various horizontal projections of a building or site: floor plans, reflected ceiling plans, site plans, and roof plans.

A floor plan represents a section of a building as it would appear if cut through by a horizontal plane with the upper portion removed. The floor plan is an orthographic projection of the portion that remains.

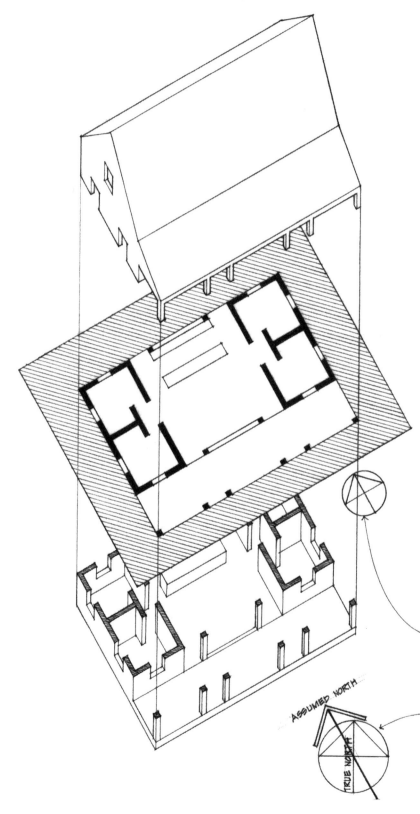

- Floor plans typically show the configuration of walls and columns, the shape and dimensions of spaces, the pattern of window and door openings, and the connections between spaces as well as between inside and outside.
- The plane of the horizontal cut is usually located about 4 feet above the floor, but this height can vary according to the nature of the building design.
- The horizontal section cuts through all walls and columns, as well as through all door and window openings.
- Beyond the plane of the cut, we see the floor, counters, tabletops, and similar horizontal surfaces.

Digital Plans
In 3D modeling programs, "front and back" or "hither and yon" clipping planes, perpendicular to a vertical line of sight, can be employed to create a floor plan from a digital model.

- We use a north arrow to indicate the orientation of a floor plan. The normal convention is to orient floor plans with north facing up or upward on the drawing sheet.
- If a major axis of the building is less than 45° east or west of north, we can use an assumed north to avoid wordy titles, such as "north-northeast elevation," or "south-southwest elevation."

ASSUMED NORTH

TRUE NORTH

Drawing a Floor Plan

This series of drawings illustrates the sequence in which a plan drawing is executed. Although this sequence can vary, depending on the nature of the building design being drawn, always try to proceed from the most continuous, regulating elements to those that are contained or defined by the elements.

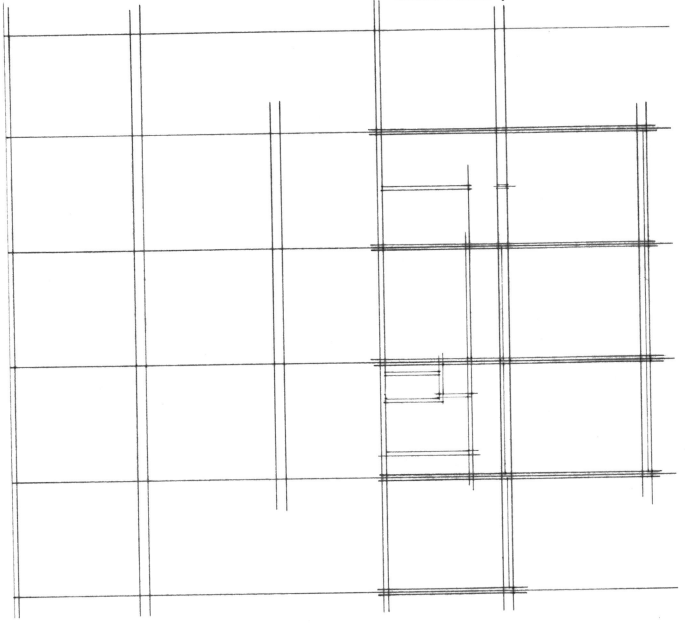

- First, establish the major lines that regulate the position of structural elements and walls.
- A grid of centerlines is a convenient and effective means of indicating a structural or modular system.

- Next, give proper thickness to the major walls and other structural elements such as posts and columns.

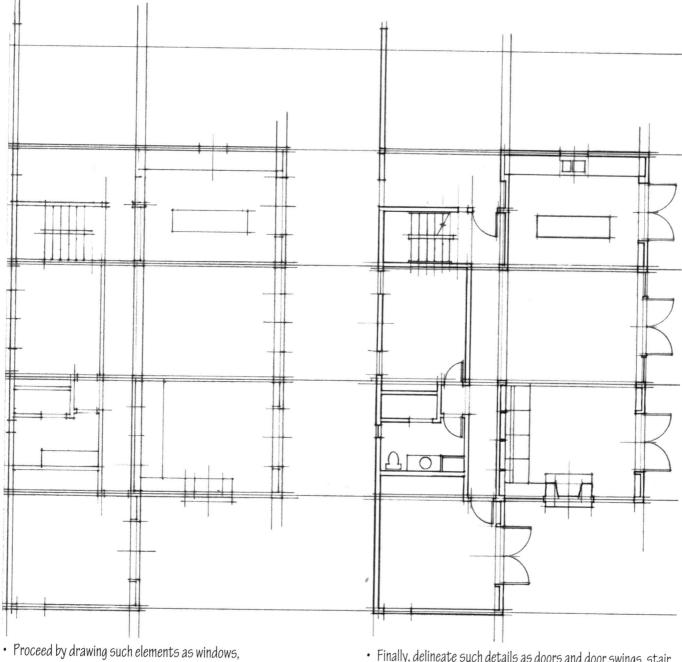

• Proceed by drawing such elements as windows, doorways, and stairways.

• Finally, delineate such details as doors and door swings, stair treads and railings, and built-in furnishings.

Defining the Plan Cut

Critical to the reading of a floor plan is the ability to distinguish between solid matter and spatial void and to discern precisely where mass meets space. It is therefore important to emphasize in a graphic way what is cut in a floor plan, and to differentiate the cut material from what we can see through space below the plane of the cut.

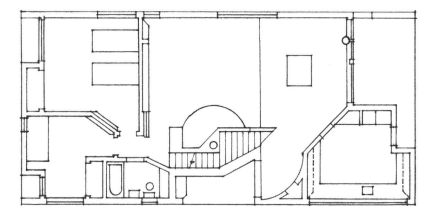

- To the left is the first floor plan of the Vanna Venturi House in Philadelphia, designed by Robert Venturi in 1962. It is drawn with a single line weight.

- To convey depth in a floor plan, we can use a hierarchy of line weights.
- The heaviest line weight profiles the plan shapes of cut elements. As a profile line, this cut line must be continuous; it can never intersect another cut line or terminate at a line of lesser weight.
- Intermediate line weights delineate edges of horizontal surfaces that lie below the plane of the plan cut but above the floor. The farther away a horizontal surface is from the plane of the plan cut, the lighter the line weight.
- The lightest line weights represent surface lines. These lines do not signify any change in form; they simply represent the visual pattern or texture of the floor plane and other horizontal surfaces.

- Drawing scale influences the range of line weights that one can use to convey spatial depth. Small-scale drawings utilize a tighter range of line weights than do large-scale drawings.

Poché and Spatial Depth

We can emphasize the shape of cut elements with a tonal value that contrasts with the spatial field of the floor plan. We refer to this darkening of cut walls, columns, and other solid matter as poché.

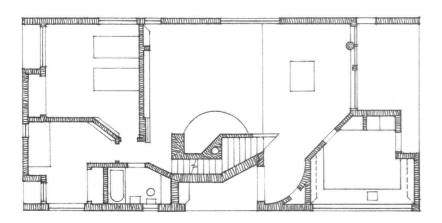

- Poché establishes a figure-ground relationship between solid matter and spatial void.
- It is typical to blacken the cut elements in small-scale plans in order to clarify their figures.

- If only a moderate degree of contrast with the drawing field is desired, use a middle-gray value to emphasize the cut elements. This is especially important in large-scale plans, when large areas of black can carry too much visual weight or create too stark a contrast.

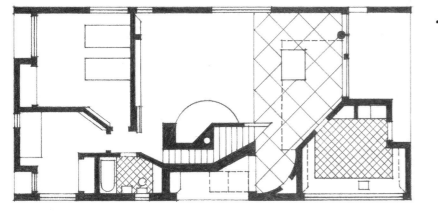

- If such plan elements as flooring patterns and furniture give the field of the drawing a tonal value, a dark gray or black tone may be necessary to produce the desired degree of contrast between solid matter and spatial void.

Digital Floor Plans

When using drawing or CAD software to create floor plans, distinguishing between solid matter and spatial void remains important. As with hand drafting, we should use a range of contrasting line weights to distinguish the profile of the elements that are cut in plan from the elements seen below the plane of the cut.

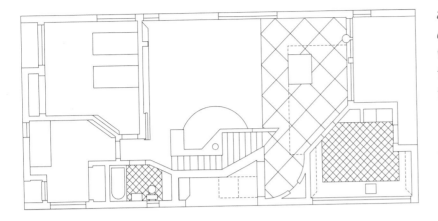

- This floor plan uses the same line weight throughout. At a glance, it is difficult to discern what is cut in plan.

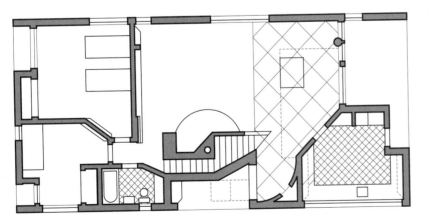

- This floor plan uses the heaviest line weight to profile the plan shapes of cut elements; intermediate line weights to delineate edges of horizontal surfaces that lie below the plane of the plan cut but above the floor; and the lightest line weight to represent surface lines.

- This floor plan emphasizes the shape of cut elements with a tonal value or poché that contrasts with the spatial field of the floor plan.

When using drawing or CAD software to create floor plans, avoid using colors, textures, and patterns to make the drawings more pictorial than they need to be. The primary emphasis should remain on articulating the plan cut and the relative depth of elements below the plane of the cut.

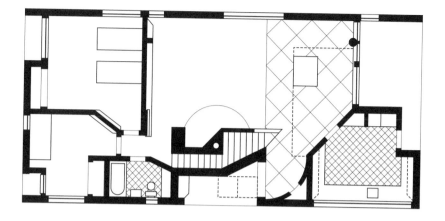

- A dark gray or black tone may be necessary to produce the desired degree of contrast between solid matter and spatial void in a floor plan, especially at small drawing scales.

- An advantage of digital drawing programs is the relative ease with which they can create large areas of tonal value. This can be useful when contrasting a floor plan with its context.

- This last example illustrates how the tonal value scheme can be reversed, with the cut elements being assigned the lightest value and the space being rendered with a range of darker values.

Doors and Windows

We are not able to show the appearance of doors in a plan view. For this information, we must rely on elevations. What a floor plan does show, however, are the location and width of door openings, and to a limited degree, the door jambs and type of door operation—whether a door swings, slides, or folds open.

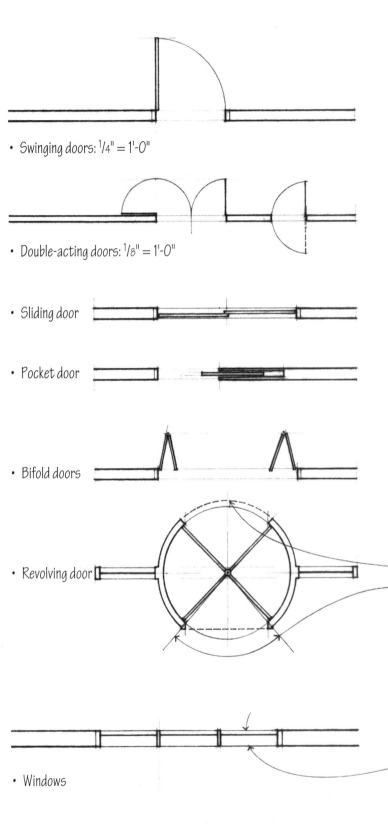

- Swinging doors: $1/4" = 1'-0"$

- Double-acting doors: $1/8" = 1'-0"$

- Sliding door

- Pocket door

- Bifold doors

- Revolving door

Canopy may be straight or curved.
<90°

- Windows

- Draw a swinging door perpendicular to the plane of the wall opening and note the door swing with a quarter circle drawn lightly with a compass or circle template. Be sure that the door width matches that of the door opening.
- Show the thicknesses of doors and door jambs at the scale of $1/4" = 1'-0"$ or larger.

As with doors, we cannot show the appearance of windows in a plan view. A floor plan does disclose the location and width of window openings, and to a limited degree the presence of window jambs and mullions.

- Window sills are not cut through in a floor plan. They should therefore be drawn with a lighter line weight than walls, window mullions, and other cut elements.
- The operation of a window is usually indicated in an elevation drawing.

Stairs

Plan views are able to show the run of a stairway—its horizontal treads and landings—but not the height of the vertical risers.

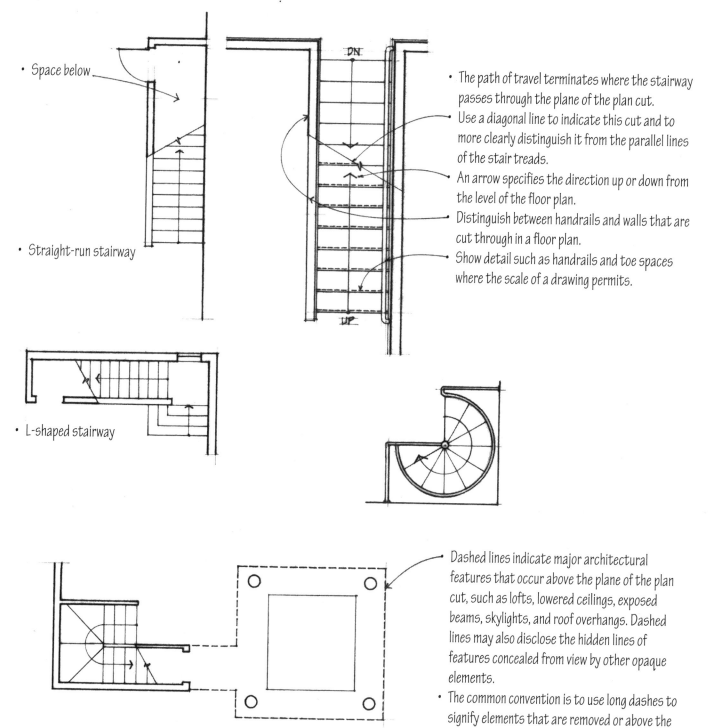

- Space below
- Straight-run stairway
- L-shaped stairway
- Return stair leading to a loft space

- The path of travel terminates where the stairway passes through the plane of the plan cut. Use a diagonal line to indicate this cut and to more clearly distinguish it from the parallel lines of the stair treads.
- An arrow specifies the direction up or down from the level of the floor plan.
- Distinguish between handrails and walls that are cut through in a floor plan.
- Show detail such as handrails and toe spaces where the scale of a drawing permits.

- Dashed lines indicate major architectural features that occur above the plane of the plan cut, such as lofts, lowered ceilings, exposed beams, skylights, and roof overhangs. Dashed lines may also disclose the hidden lines of features concealed from view by other opaque elements.
- The common convention is to use long dashes to signify elements that are removed or above the plane of the plan cut, and shorter dashes or dots for hidden elements below the plan cut.

Scale and Detail

Floor plans are normally drawn at a scale of $1/8" = 1'-0"$ or $1/4" = 1'-0"$. Large buildings and complexes may be drawn at a scale of $1/16" = 1'-0"$ to fit the size of the drawing paper or illustration board.

Digital Scale

In computer graphics, a small-scale drawing that contains too much data can result in an unnecessarily large file as well as a printed or plotted image that is too dense to read.

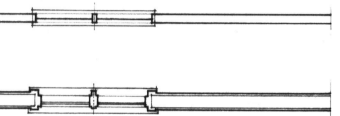

Large-scale plan drawings are useful for the study and presentation of highly detailed spaces, such as kitchens, bathrooms, and stairways. The larger scale enables information about floor finishes, fittings, and trim work to be included.

Conversely, the larger the scale of a floor plan, the more detail we should include. This attention to detail is most critical when drawing the thicknesses of construction materials and assemblies that are cut in a plan view.

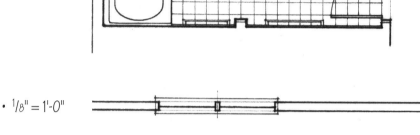

• $^1/_8" = 1'-0"$

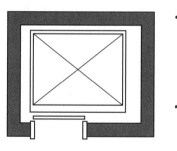

• $^1/_4" = 1'-0"$

• $^3/_8" = 1'-0"$

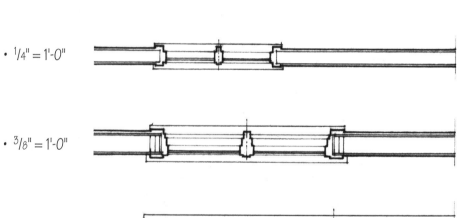

• $^3/_4" = 1'-0"$

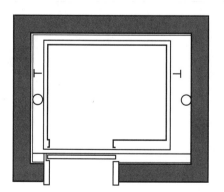

• Pay careful attention to wall and door thicknesses, wall terminations, corner conditions, and stair details. A general knowledge of how buildings are constructed is therefore extremely beneficial when executing large-scale floor plans.

A ceiling plan is a plan of a room as seen from above but having its ceiling surfaces and elements projected downward upon it. For this reason, we usually call this view a reflected ceiling plan.

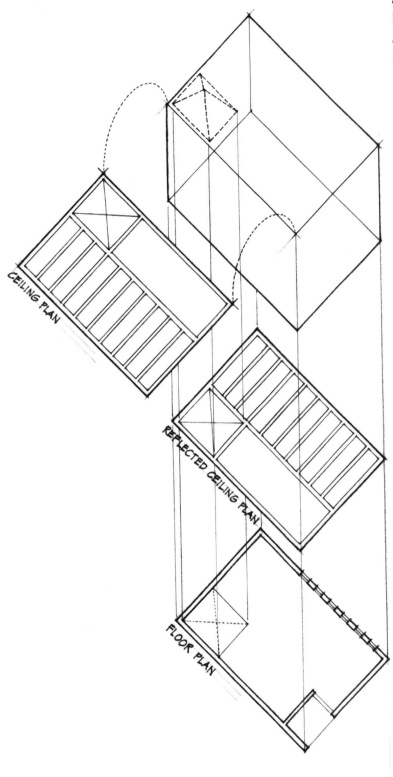

CEILING PLAN

REFLECTED CEILING PLAN

FLOOR PLAN

Reflected Ceiling Plans

• A reflected ceiling plan has the same orientation as the floor plan to which it relates.

• Ceiling plans show such information as the form and material of a ceiling, the location and type of lighting fixtures, exposed structural members or mechanical ductwork, as well as skylights or other openings in the ceiling.

• We typically draw a ceiling plan at the same scale as the floor plan. As with floor plans, it is important to profile all vertical elements that rise to meet the ceiling.

A site plan describes the location and orientation of a building or building complex on a plot of land and in relation to its context. Whether this environment is urban or rural, the site plan should describe the following:

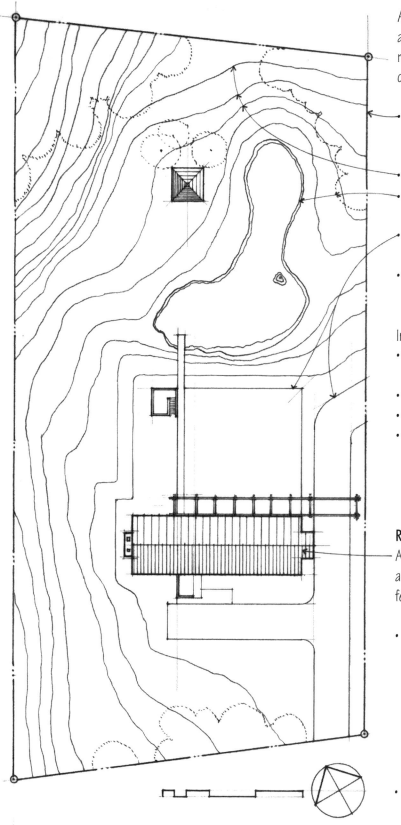

- Legally recorded boundaries of the site, indicated by a broken line consisting of relatively long segments separated by two short dashes or dots
- Physical topography of the terrain with contour lines
- Natural site features, such as trees, landscaping, and watercourses
- Existing or proposed site constructions, such as walks, courts, and roadways
- Architectural structures in the immediate setting that impact the proposed building

In addition, a site plan may include:
- Legal constraints, such as zoning setbacks and rights-of-way
- Existing or proposed site utilities
- Pedestrian and vehicular entry points and paths
- Significant environmental forces and features

Roof Plans

A roof plan is a top view describing the form, massing, and material of a roof or the layout of such rooftop features as skylights, decks, and mechanical housings.

- Roof plans are typically included in the site plan for a proposed building or building complex.

- Graphic scale designates the scale of the site plan and a north arrow indicates the orientation of the site.

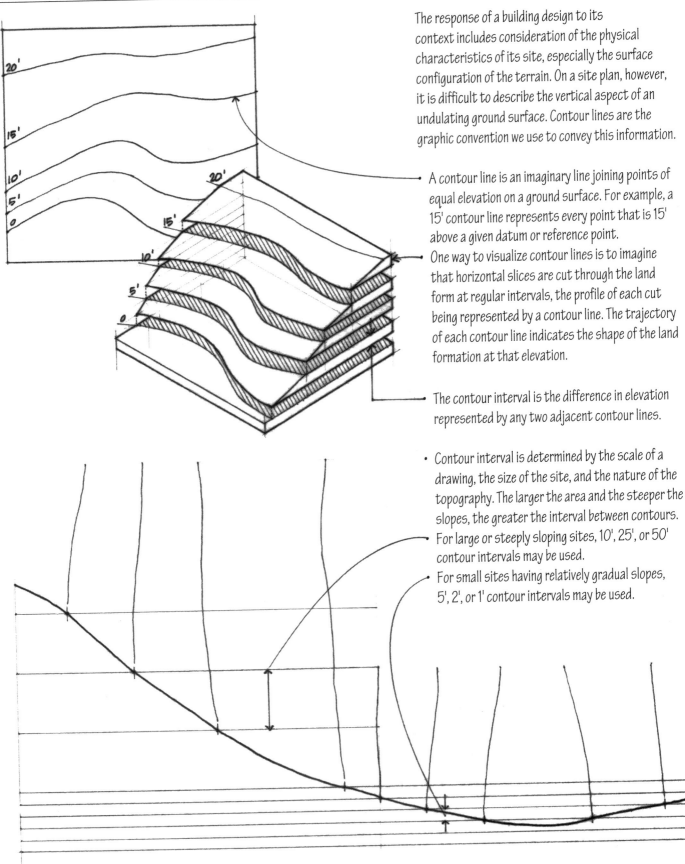

The response of a building design to its context includes consideration of the physical characteristics of its site, especially the surface configuration of the terrain. On a site plan, however, it is difficult to describe the vertical aspect of an undulating ground surface. Contour lines are the graphic convention we use to convey this information.

- A contour line is an imaginary line joining points of equal elevation on a ground surface. For example, a 15' contour line represents every point that is 15' above a given datum or reference point.
- One way to visualize contour lines is to imagine that horizontal slices are cut through the land form at regular intervals, the profile of each cut being represented by a contour line. The trajectory of each contour line indicates the shape of the land formation at that elevation.

- The contour interval is the difference in elevation represented by any two adjacent contour lines.

- Contour interval is determined by the scale of a drawing, the size of the site, and the nature of the topography. The larger the area and the steeper the slopes, the greater the interval between contours.
  - For large or steeply sloping sites, 10', 25', or 50' contour intervals may be used.
  - For small sites having relatively gradual slopes, 5', 2', or 1' contour intervals may be used.

The horizontal distances between contour lines are a function of the slope of the ground surface. We can discern the topographical nature of a site by reading this horizontal spacing.

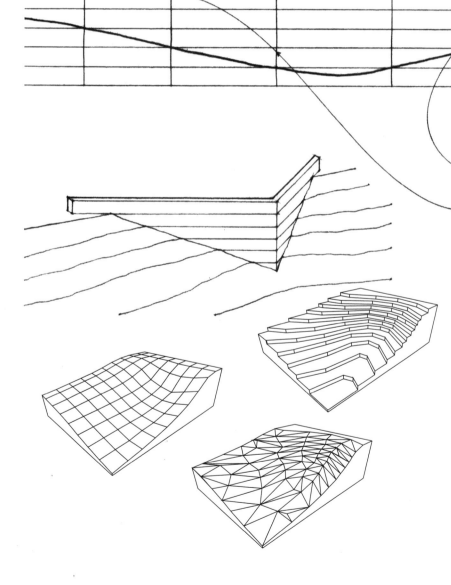

Closely spaced contours indicate a relatively steep rise in elevation.

Equally spaced contours indicate a constant slope.

Widely spaced contours indicate a relatively flat or gently sloping surface.

• Note that contour lines are always continuous and never cross one another. They may coincide in a plan view only when they cut across a vertical surface.

Digital Sites
• 3D CAD and modeling programs have the capability of creating three-dimensional site models. One method produces a stepped model that preserves the visibility of contour lines and intervals. Another creates a warped plane or mesh for shading, consisting of polygonal, usually triangular, faces.

Depending on the size of the site and the available drawing space, site plans may be drawn at an engineering scale of 1" = 20' or 40', or an architectural scale of ¹/₁₆" = 1'-0" or ¹/₃₂" = 1'-0".

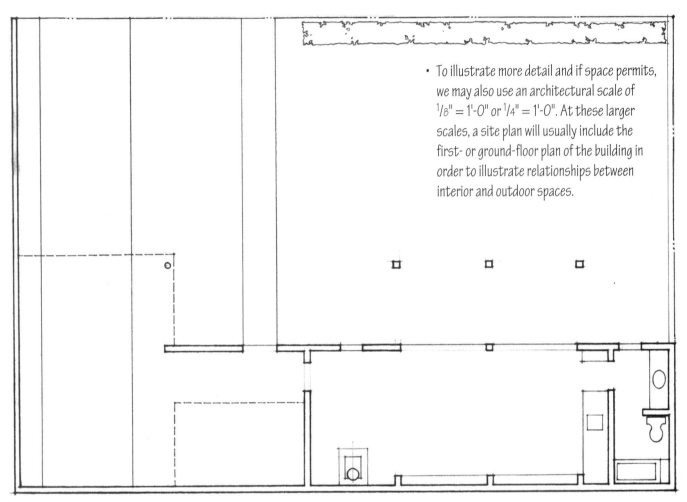

- To illustrate more detail and if space permits, we may also use an architectural scale of ¹/₈" = 1'-0" or ¹/₄" = 1'-0". At these larger scales, a site plan will usually include the first- or ground-floor plan of the building in order to illustrate relationships between interior and outdoor spaces.

- The orientation of a building site is indicated by a north arrow. Whenever possible, north should be oriented up or upward on the drawing sheet or board.
- If a major axis of the building is less than 45° east or west of north, we can use an assumed north to avoid wordy titles for the building elevations, such as "north-northeast elevation," or "south-southwest elevation."
- To make the relationship between a site plan and floor plans clear, they should have the same orientation throughout a presentation.

There are two principal ways to relate a building to its site and context.

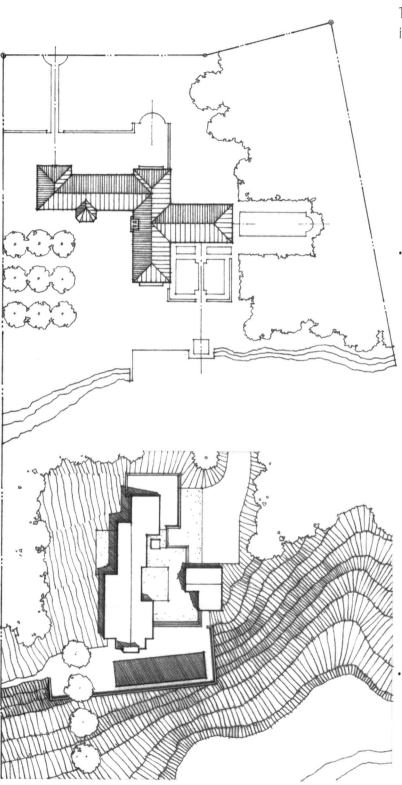

• The first is to draw the building as a darker figure against a lighter background. This approach is especially appropriate when the way in which the roofing material of the building is indicated will establish a tonal value and texture against which the surrounding context must contrast.

• The second approach defines the building as a lighter shape against a darker background. This technique is necessary when rendering shadows cast by the form of the building, or when landscaping elements impart a tonal value to the surrounding context.

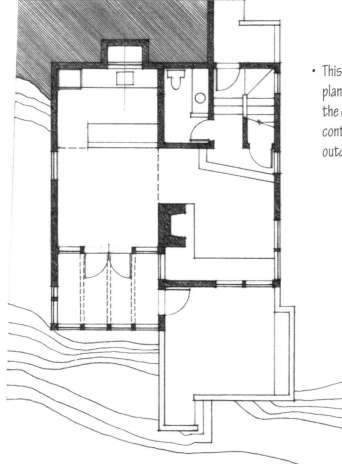

• This drawing combines a floor plan with the site plan. The shape of the floor plan and the poché of the cut plan elements provide a figural quality that contrasts sufficiently with the surrounding field of outdoor space.

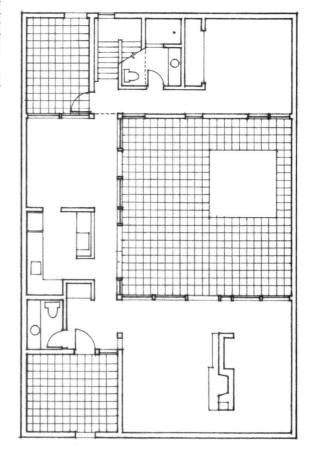

• This drawing illustrates a building whose exterior walls encompass the site; it is therefore a composite floor plan and site plan drawing.

A section is an orthographic projection of an object as it would appear if cut through by an intersecting plane. It opens up the object to reveal its internal material, composition, or assembly. In theory, the plane of the section cut may have any orientation. But in order to distinguish a section drawing from a floor plan—the other type of drawing that involves a slice—we usually assume the plane of the cut for a section is vertical. As with other orthographic projections, all planes parallel to the picture plane maintain their size, shape, and proportions.

We use section drawings to design and communicate the details of a building's construction as well as the assembly of furniture and cabinetry. In architectural graphics, however, the building section is the premier drawing for revealing and studying the relationship between the floors, walls, and roof structure of a building and the dimensions and vertical scale of the spaces defined by these elements.

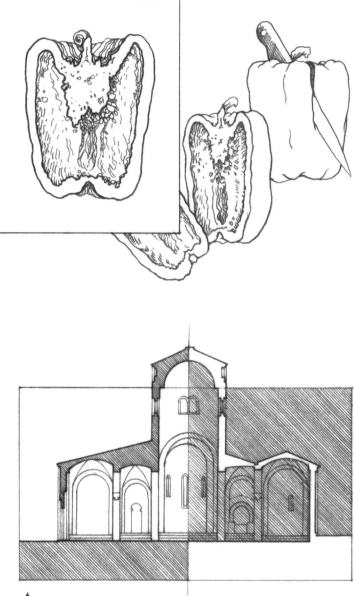

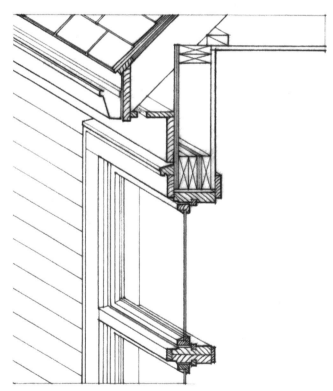

▲
• Design sections emphasize the solid-void relationship between the floors, walls, and roof structure of a building and the vertical dimensions and relationships of the contained spaces.

◀ • Construction sections articulate the structural and material assemblies and details of a building.

A building section represents a vertical section of a building. After a vertical plane slices through the construction, we remove one of the parts. The building section is an orthographic projection of the portion that remains, cast onto a vertical picture plane parallel or coincident with the cutting plane.

• Building sections reveal the shape and vertical scale of interior spaces, the impact of window and door openings on these spaces, and the vertical connections between the internal spaces as well as between inside and outside.

• Beyond the plane of the cut, we see elevations of interior walls, as well as objects and events that occur in front of them but behind the vertical plane of the section cut.

• The conventional symbol for indicating the location of the section cut in a plan drawing is a broken line of long segments separated by short dashes or dots.
• It is not necessary to draw this section line across an entire floor plan, but it should at least overlap the exterior boundaries of the building.
• An arrow at the end of each line points in the direction of view.

Digital Sections
3D-modeling programs utilize "front and back" or "hither and yon" clipping planes to create section drawings.

The Section Cut

Building sections should be cut in a continuous manner, parallel to a major set of walls. Use jogs or offsets in the cutting plane only when absolutely necessary.

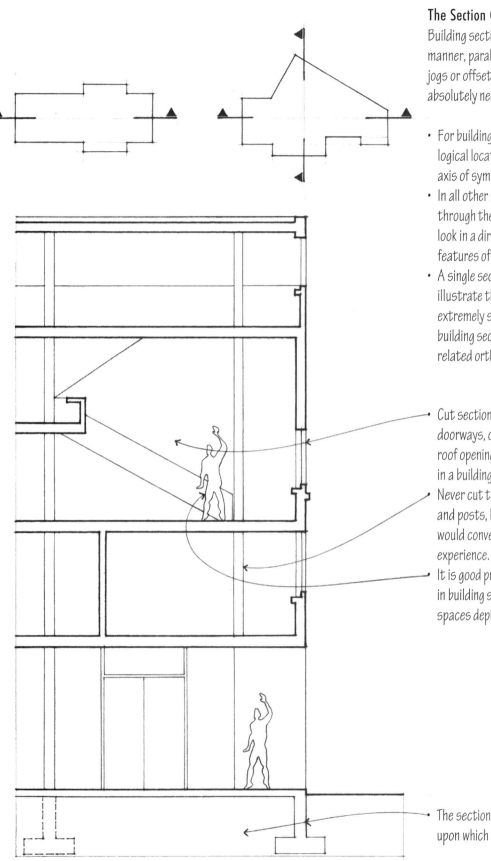

- For buildings having a symmetrical plan, the logical location for a section cut is along the axis of symmetry.
- In all other situations, cut building sections through the most significant spaces and look in a direction that reveals the principal features of the spaces.
- A single section is usually not sufficient to illustrate these qualities unless a building is extremely simple. Remember, too, that the building section is only part of a series of related orthographic views.

Cut sections through window openings, doorways, changes in roof and floor levels, roof openings, and other major spatial events in a building.

Never cut through freestanding columns and posts, lest they read as walls, which would convey an entirely different spatial experience.

It is good practice to include human figures in building sections to convey the scale of the spaces depicted.

The section cut extends to the soil mass upon which a building rests.

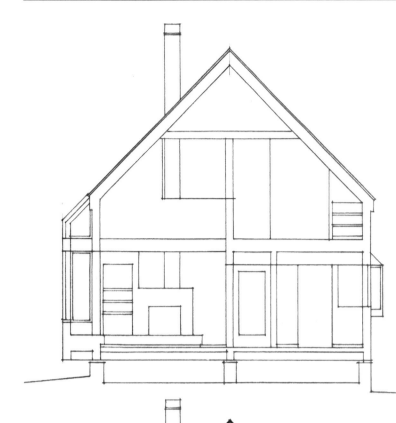

Defining the Section Cut

As with floor plans, it is critical to distinguish between solid matter and spatial void and to discern precisely where mass meets space in a building section. In order to convey a sense of depth and the existence of spatial volumes, we must utilize a hierarchy of line weights or a range of tonal values. The technique we use depends on the scale of the building section, the drawing medium, and the required degree of contrast between solid matter and spatial void.

- This is a building section drawn with a single line weight. It is difficult to discern what is cut and what is seen in elevation beyond the plane of the cut.

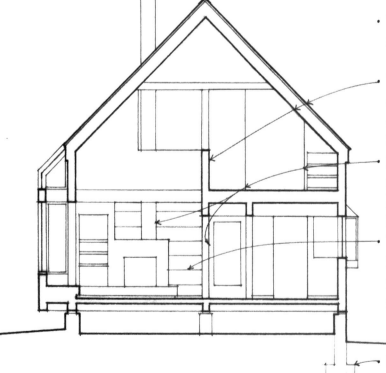

- This drawing uses a hierarchy of line weights to convey a sense of spatial depth.

- The heaviest line weight profiles the shapes of elements cut in the section. Note that these profiles are always continuous; they can never intersect at another cut line or terminate at a line of lesser weight.
- Intermediate line weights delineate those elements that are seen in elevation beyond the section cut. The farther back an element is from the plane of the section cut, the lighter their profile should be.
- The lightest line weights represent surface lines. These lines do not signify any change in form. They simply represent the visual pattern or texture of wall planes and other vertical surfaces parallel to the picture plane.

- In design sections, construction details of foundations and footings below grade need not be indicated. If shown, they are part of the surrounding soil mass and should be drawn lightly.

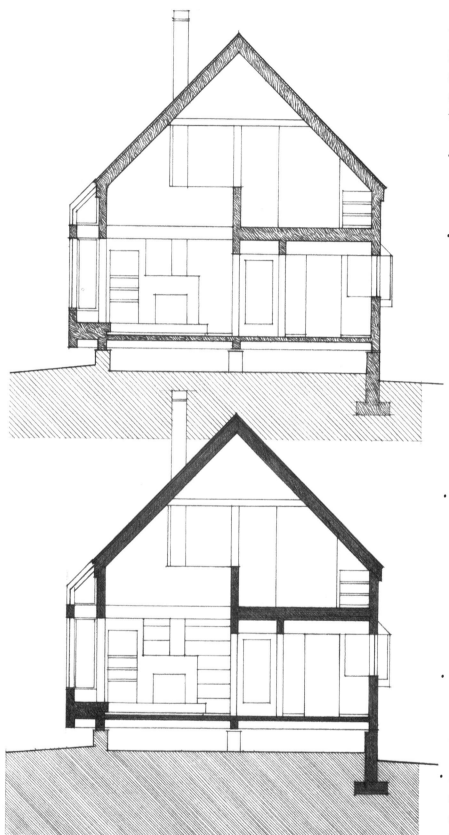

Poché and Spatial Depth

To establish a clear figure-ground relationship between solid matter and spatial void, we can emphasize the shape of cut elements with a tonal value or poché that contrasts with the spatial field of the building section.

- We typically blacken or poché the floor, wall, and roof elements that are cut in small-scale building sections.

- If only a moderate degree of contrast with the drawing field is desired, use a middle-gray value to illuminate the shape of the cut elements. This is especially important in large-scale sections, when large areas of black can carry too much visual weight or create too stark a contrast.

- If vertical elements, such as wall patterns and textures, give the field of the drawing a tonal value, a dark gray or black tone may be necessary to produce the desired degree of contrast between solid matter and spatial void. In this value scheme, use progressively lighter values for elements as they recede into the third dimension.

- Remember that the supporting soil mass is also cut in building and site sections. Any tonal value given to cut elements should therefore continue into this mass.

- If we wish to show a building's foundation system in a section drawing, we should be careful to delineate the below-grade portion as an integral part of the surrounding soil mass.

• This section drawing illustrates how the cut elements can be given a tonal value to heighten their contrast with elements seen in elevation beyond the plane of the cut.

• This drawing shows how the value system can be reversed by toning what is seen in elevation along with the background of the drawing. In this case, the section cut can be left white or be given a fairly light value to contrast with the drawing field.

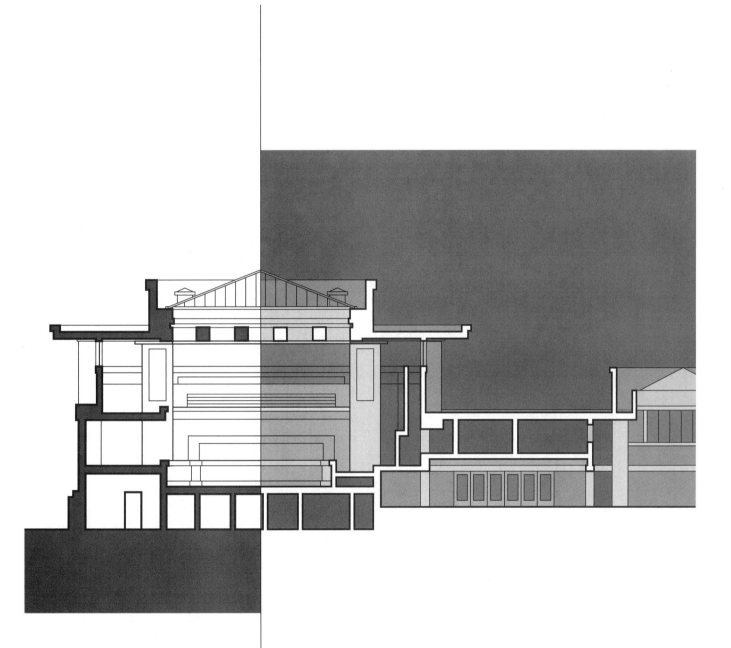

Digital Poché

When using drawing or CAD software to create section drawings, avoid using colors, textures, and patterns to make the drawings more pictorial than they need to be. The primary emphasis should remain on articulating the section cut and the relative depth of elements beyond the plane of the cut.

• These two examples illustrate the use of graphics software to create section drawings. The upper building section uses a vector-based drawing program while the lower drawing uses a raster image to convey the character of a site as well as serve as a contrasting background for the white section cut.

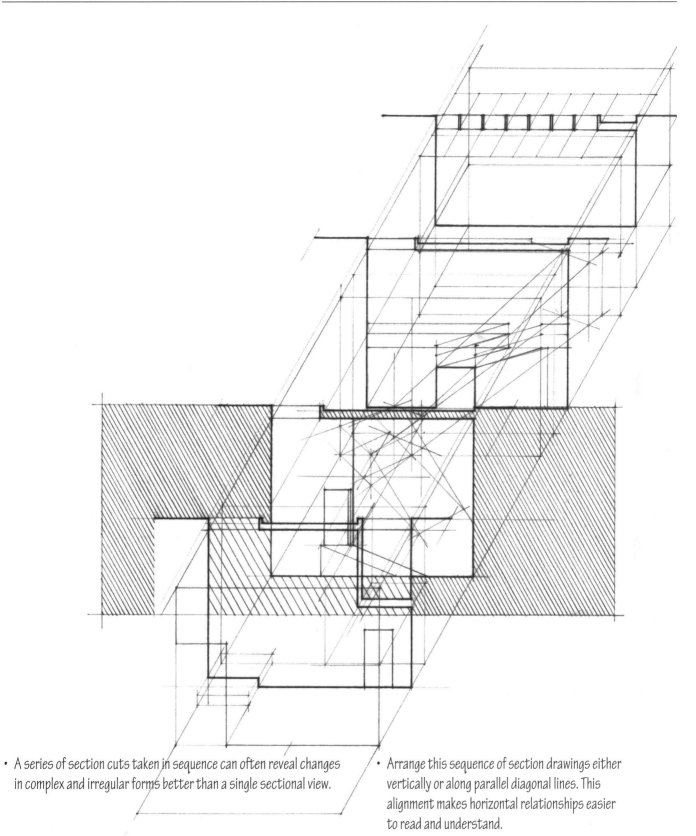

• A series of section cuts taken in sequence can often reveal changes in complex and irregular forms better than a single sectional view.

• Arrange this sequence of section drawings either vertically or along parallel diagonal lines. This alignment makes horizontal relationships easier to read and understand.

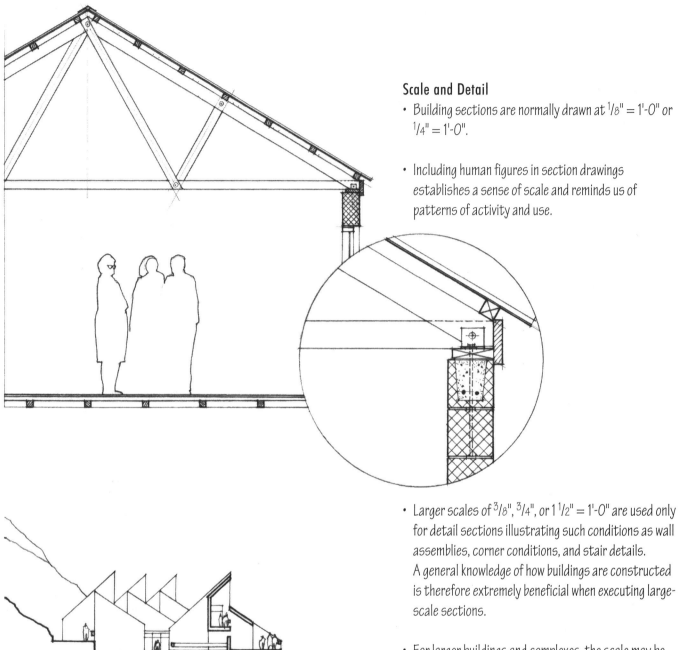

Scale and Detail

- Building sections are normally drawn at $1/8" = 1'-0"$ or $1/4" = 1'-0"$.

- Including human figures in section drawings establishes a sense of scale and reminds us of patterns of activity and use.

- Larger scales of $3/8"$, $3/4"$, or $1\,1/2" = 1'-0"$ are used only for detail sections illustrating such conditions as wall assemblies, corner conditions, and stair details. A general knowledge of how buildings are constructed is therefore extremely beneficial when executing large-scale sections.

- For larger buildings and complexes, the scale may be reduced to $1/16" = 1'-0"$.

Section drawings often extend outward to include the context of a building's site and environment. They are capable of describing the relationship of a proposed structure to the surrounding ground plane and disclosing whether a proposed structure rises from, sits on, floats above, or becomes embedded within the ground mass of the site. In addition, section drawings can effectively illustrate the relationship between the interior spaces of a building and adjoining exterior spaces, as well as the relationships among a number of buildings.

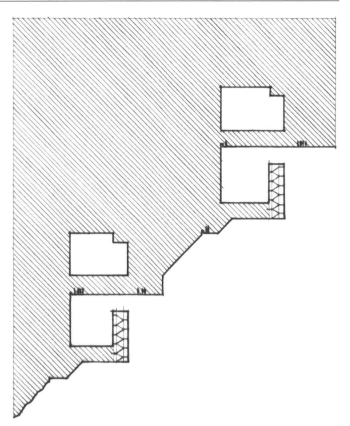

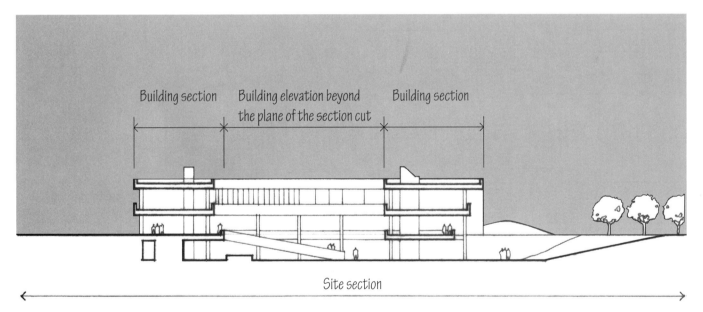

Building section Building elevation beyond the plane of the section cut Building section

Site section

- Whenever possible, but especially in urban settings, building sections should include adjacent structures, either cut through simultaneously in the section or seen in elevation beyond the plane of the cut.

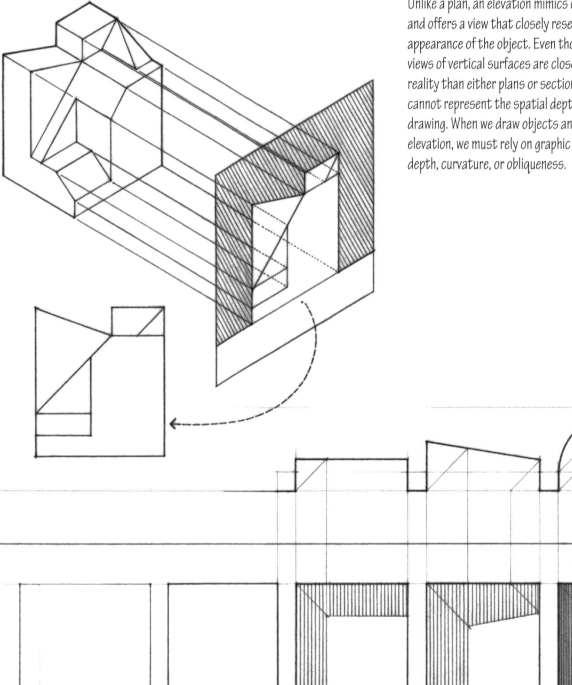

An elevation is an orthographic projection of an object or construction on a vertical picture plane parallel to one of its principal faces.

Unlike a plan, an elevation mimics our upright stance and offers a view that closely resembles the natural appearance of the object. Even though elevation views of vertical surfaces are closer to perceptual reality than either plans or section views, they cannot represent the spatial depth of a perspective drawing. When we draw objects and surfaces in elevation, we must rely on graphic cues to convey depth, curvature, or obliqueness.

A building elevation is the image of a building projected orthographically onto a vertical picture plane. Building elevations convey the external appearance of a building, compressed onto a single plane of projection. They therefore emphasize the exterior vertical faces of a building parallel to the picture plane and define its silhouette in space. They can also illustrate the texture and pattern of cladding materials, as well as the location, type, and dimensions of window and door openings.

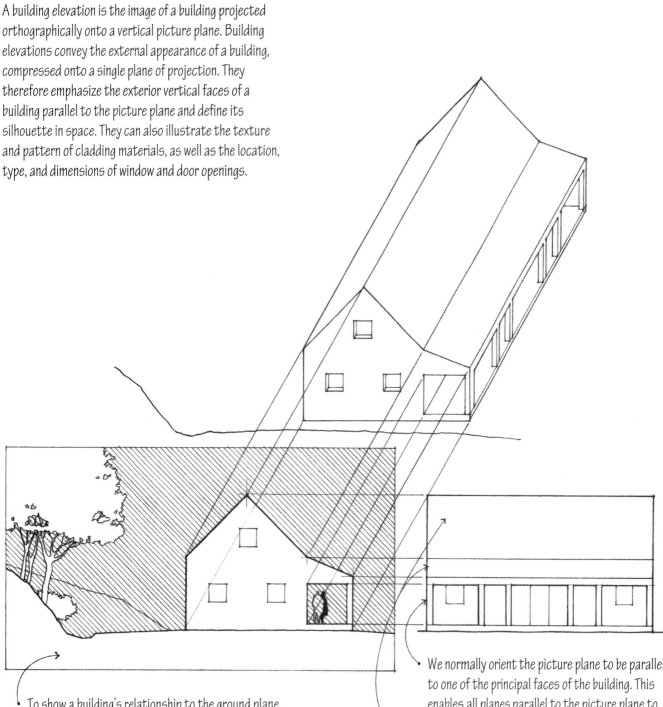

To show a building's relationship to the ground plane, building elevations should include a section cut through the ground mass on which the structure sits. This vertical cut is typically at some distance in front of the building. This distance varies according to what information we wish to display in front of the building and to what degree this context will obscure the form and features of the building.

We normally orient the picture plane to be parallel to one of the principal faces of the building. This enables all planes parallel to the picture plane to retain their true size, shape, and proportions.

Any plane that is curved or oblique to the picture plane will appear foreshortened.

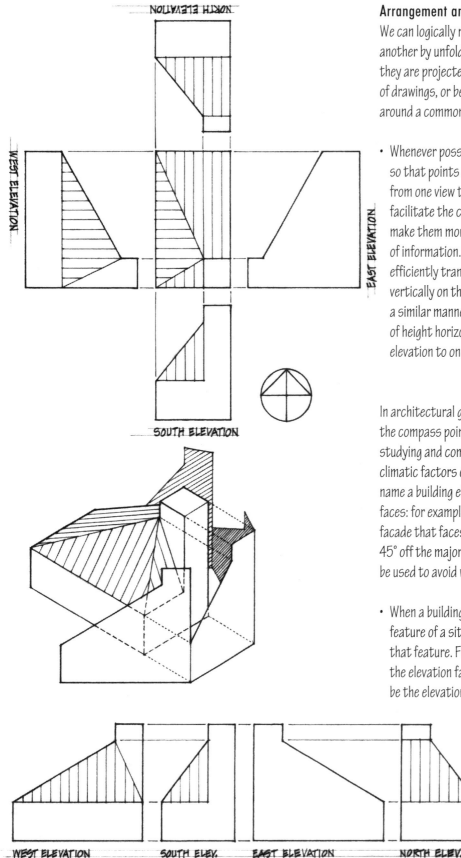

NORTH ELEVATION

WEST ELEVATION

EAST ELEVATION

SOUTH ELEVATION

WEST ELEVATION   SOUTH ELEV.   EAST ELEVATION   NORTH ELEV.

Arrangement and Orientation

We can logically relate a series of building elevations to one another by unfolding the vertical picture planes on which they are projected. They can form a horizontal sequence of drawings, or be related in a single composite drawing around a common plan view.

• Whenever possible, we align related orthographic views so that points and dimensions can be transferred easily from one view to the next. This relationship will not only facilitate the construction of the drawings but will also make them more understandable as a coordinated set of information. For example, once a plan is drawn, we can efficiently transfer the horizontal dimensions of length vertically on the drawing surface to the elevation below. In a similar manner, we can project the vertical dimensions of height horizontally on the drawing surface from one elevation to one or more adjacent elevations.

In architectural graphics, the orientation of a building to the compass points is an important consideration when studying and communicating the effect of sun and other climatic factors on the design. We therefore most often name a building elevation after the direction the elevation faces: for example, a north elevation is the elevation of the facade that faces north. If the face is oriented less than 45° off the major compass points, an assumed north may be used to avoid wordy drawing titles.

• When a building addresses a specific or significant feature of a site, we can name a building elevation after that feature. For example, Main Street Elevation would be the elevation facing Main Street, or Lake Elevation would be the elevation seen from the lake.

Scale and Detail

We usually draw building elevations at the same scale as the accompanying floor plans—$^1/_8$" = 1'-0" or $^1/_4$" = 1'-0". We may use a smaller scale for large buildings and complexes.

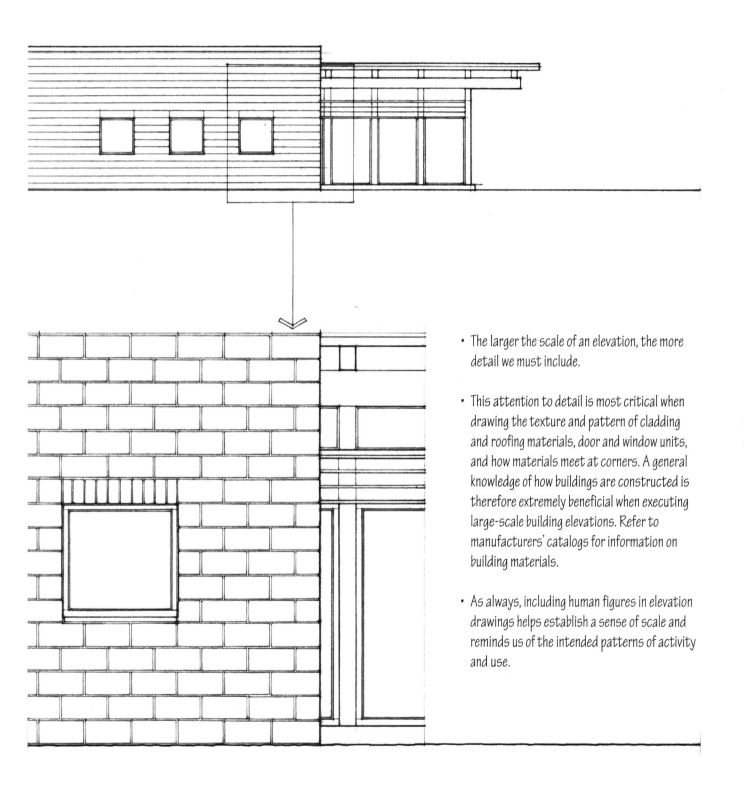

- The larger the scale of an elevation, the more detail we must include.

- This attention to detail is most critical when drawing the texture and pattern of cladding and roofing materials, door and window units, and how materials meet at corners. A general knowledge of how buildings are constructed is therefore extremely beneficial when executing large-scale building elevations. Refer to manufacturers' catalogs for information on building materials.

- As always, including human figures in elevation drawings helps establish a sense of scale and reminds us of the intended patterns of activity and use.

Representing Materials

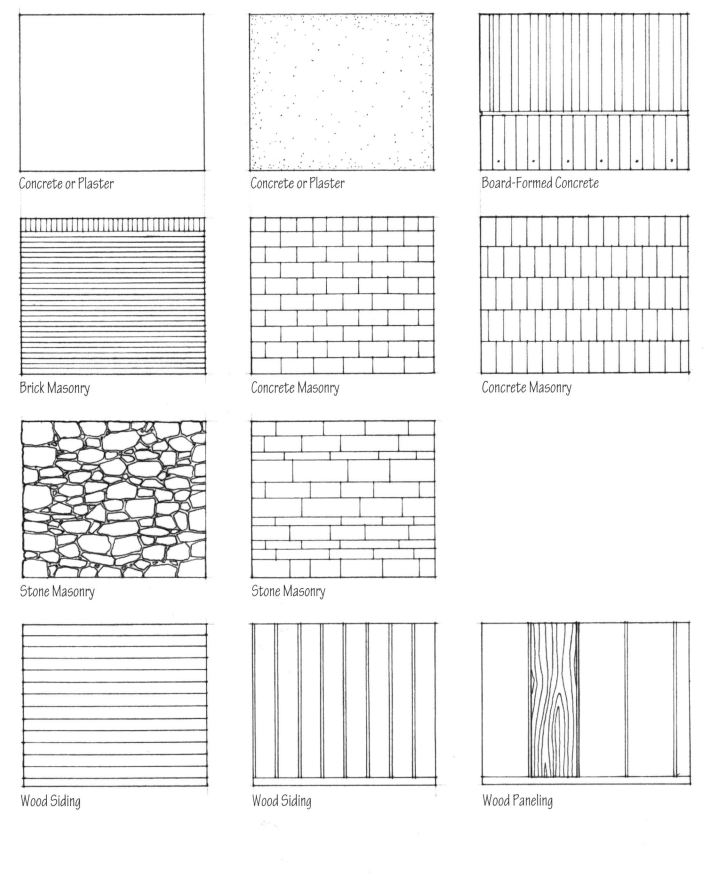

Concrete or Plaster

Concrete or Plaster

Board-Formed Concrete

Brick Masonry

Concrete Masonry

Concrete Masonry

Stone Masonry

Stone Masonry

Wood Siding

Wood Siding

Wood Paneling

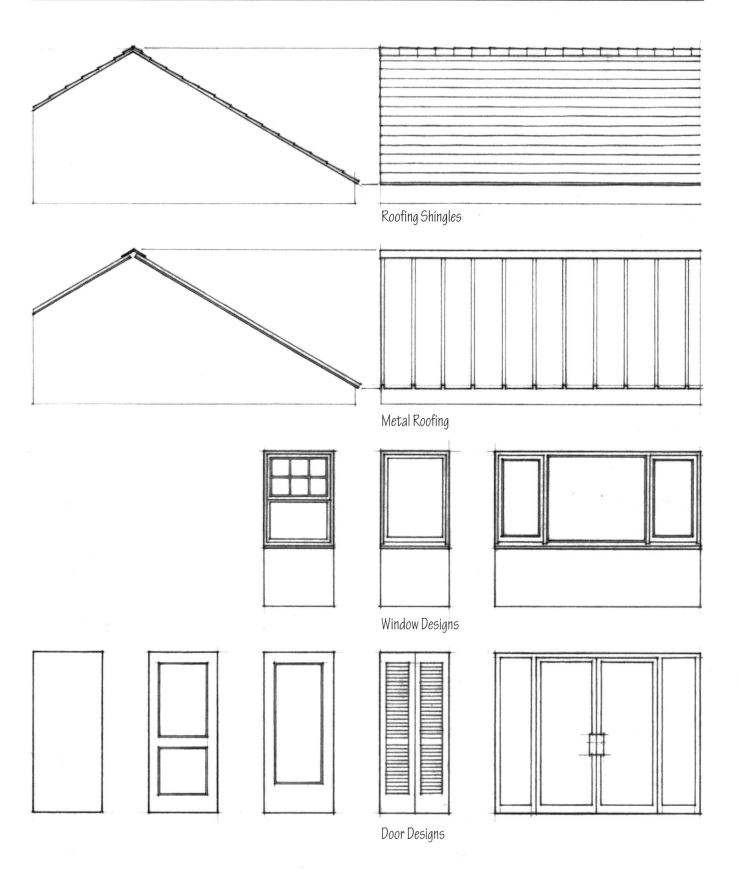

Roofing Shingles

Metal Roofing

Window Designs

Door Designs

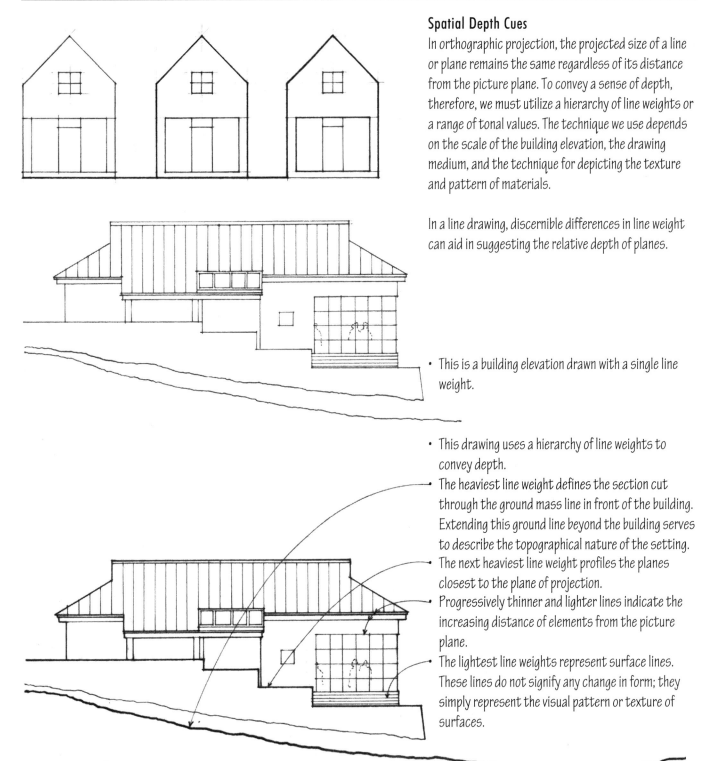

Spatial Depth Cues

In orthographic projection, the projected size of a line or plane remains the same regardless of its distance from the picture plane. To convey a sense of depth, therefore, we must utilize a hierarchy of line weights or a range of tonal values. The technique we use depends on the scale of the building elevation, the drawing medium, and the technique for depicting the texture and pattern of materials.

In a line drawing, discernible differences in line weight can aid in suggesting the relative depth of planes.

• This is a building elevation drawn with a single line weight.

• This drawing uses a hierarchy of line weights to convey depth.
• The heaviest line weight defines the section cut through the ground mass line in front of the building. Extending this ground line beyond the building serves to describe the topographical nature of the setting.
• The next heaviest line weight profiles the planes closest to the plane of projection.
• Progressively thinner and lighter lines indicate the increasing distance of elements from the picture plane.
• The lightest line weights represent surface lines. These lines do not signify any change in form; they simply represent the visual pattern or texture of surfaces.

In an elevation drawing, we try to establish three pictorial zones: the foreground space between the section cut and the façade of the building; the middle-ground that the building itself occupies; and the background of sky, landscape, or structures beyond the building.

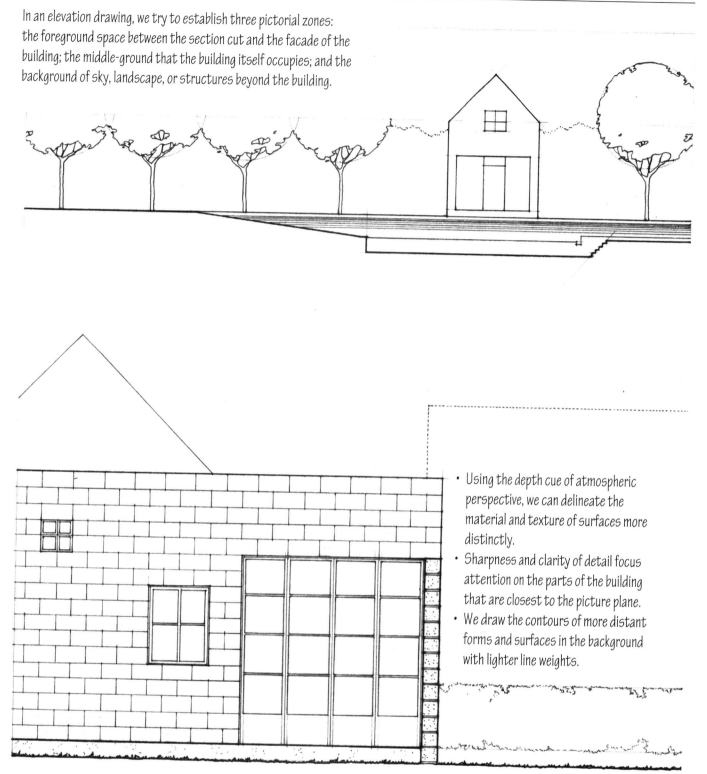

- Using the depth cue of atmospheric perspective, we can delineate the material and texture of surfaces more distinctly.
- Sharpness and clarity of detail focus attention on the parts of the building that are closest to the picture plane.
- We draw the contours of more distant forms and surfaces in the background with lighter line weights.

Spatial Depth Cues

The examples on the previous two pages illustrate the use of varying line weights and detail to convey a sense of spatial depth in the drawing of building elevations. This series of drawings illustrates in a more discrete and abstract way how visual cues can enhance the sense of depth in any orthographic projection.

• Continuity of Outline: We tend to perceive a shape as being in front of another when it has continuity of outline and disrupts the profile of the other shape. Since this visual phenomenon relies on nearer objects overlaying or projecting in front of objects farther away, we often refer to this depth cue simply as overlap.

• By itself, overlap tends to create relatively shallow intervals of space. However, we can achieve a greater sense of intervening space and depth if we combine overlap with other depth cues, such as by varying the line weights of a pure-line drawing. Darker and thicker profile or contour lines tend to advance and appear to be in front of lighter and thinner outlines.

• Atmospheric Perspective: A progressive muting of hues, tonal values, and contrast occurs with increasing distance from the observer. Objects seen up close in the foreground of our visual field typically possess more saturated colors and sharply defined contrasts in value. As they move farther away, their colors become lighter in value and more subdued, and their tonal contrasts more diffuse. In the background, we see mainly shapes of grayed tones and muted hues.

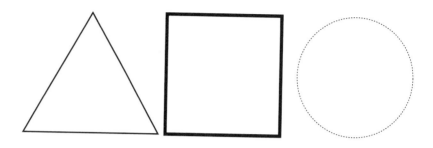

- Perspective of Blur: This depth cue reflects the fact that we normally associate clarity of vision with nearness and blurring of outlines with farness. The graphic equivalent of perspective blur is a diminishing or diffusion of the edges and contours of more distant objects. We can use either a lightly drawn line or a broken or dotted line to delineate these edges of shapes and contours of forms that exist beyond the focus of a drawing.

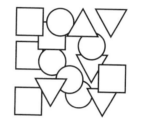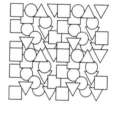

- Texture Perspective: The density of the texture of a surface gradually increases as it recedes into the distance. The graphic technique for depicting the visual phenomenon of texture perspective involves gradually diminishing the size and spacing of the graphic elements used to portray a surface texture or pattern, whether they be dots, lines, or tonal shapes. Proceed from identifying units in the foreground to delineating a textured pattern in the middleground and finally to rendering a tonal value in the background.

- Light and Shade: Any abrupt shift in brightness stimulates the perception of a spatial edge or profile separated from a background surface by some intervening space. This depth cue implies the existence of overlapping shapes and the use of contrasting tonal values in a drawing. See Chapter 7 for more information on the use of tonal values in architectural graphics.

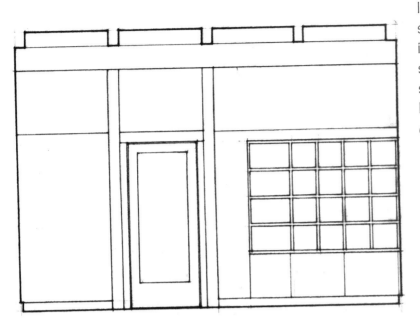

Interior elevations are orthographic projections of significant interior walls of a building. While normally included in the drawing of building sections, they may stand alone to study and present highly detailed spaces, such as kitchens, bathrooms, and stairways. In this case, instead of profiling the section cut, we emphasize instead the boundary line of the interior wall surfaces.

- We normally draw interior elevations at the same scale as the accompanying floor plans—$1/8" = 1'-0"$ or $1/4" = 1'-0"$. To show a greater amount of detail, we may use a scale of $3/8"$ or $1/2" = 1'-0"$.

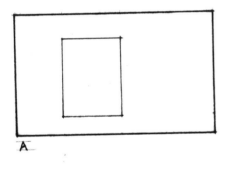

A

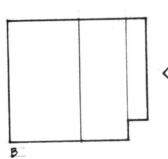

B

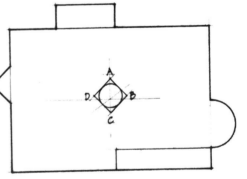

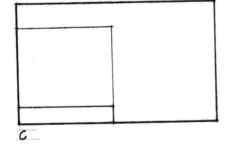

C

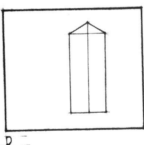

D

- To orient the viewer, we label each interior elevation according to the compass direction toward which we look in viewing the wall.
- An alternative method is to key each interior elevation to a compass on the floor plan of the room.

5

Paraline Drawings

Paraline drawings include a subset of orthographic projections known as axonometric projections—the isometric, dimetric, and trimetric projections—as well as the entire class of oblique projections. Each type offers a slightly different viewpoint and emphasizes different aspects of the drawn subject. As a family, however, they combine the measured precision and scalability of multiview drawings and the pictorial nature of linear perspective. Because of their pictorial quality and relative ease of construction, paraline drawings are appropriate for visualizing an emerging idea in three dimensions early in the design process. They are capable of fusing plan, elevation, and section into a single view and illustrating three-dimensional patterns and compositions of space. Portions of a paraline drawing can be cut away or made transparent to see inside and through things, or expanded to illustrate the spatial relationships between the parts of a whole. At times, they can even serve as a reasonable substitute for a bird's-eye perspective.

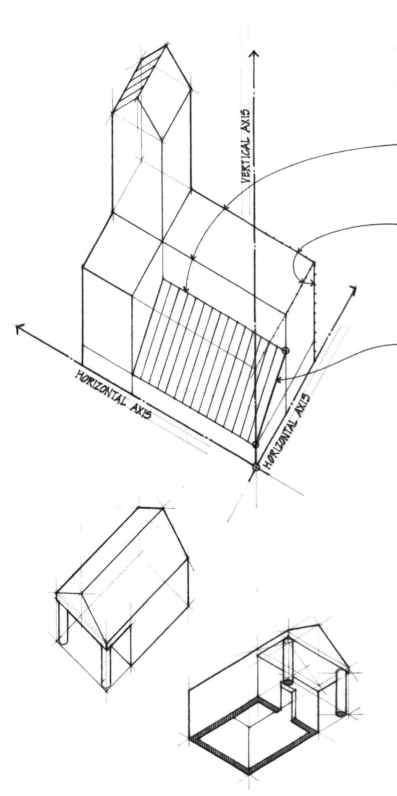

Paraline drawings communicate the three-dimensional nature of an object or spatial relationship in a single image. Hence, they are also called single-view drawings to distinguish them from the multiple and related views of plans, sections, and elevations. They can be distinguished from the other type of single-view drawing, linear perspective, by the following pictorial effects.

• Parallel lines, regardless of their orientation in the subject, remain parallel in the drawn view; they do not converge to vanishing points as in linear perspective.

• Any linear measurement parallel to one of the three major axes—along axial lines—can be made and drawn to a consistent scale. Axial lines naturally form a rectangular grid of coordinates that we can use to find any point in three-dimensional space.

• Nonaxial lines refer to those lines that are not parallel to any of the three principal axes. We cannot measure dimensions along these nonaxial lines, nor can we draw them to scale. To draw nonaxial lines, we must first locate their end points using axial measurements and then connect these points. Once we establish one nonaxial line, however, we can draw any line parallel to that line, since parallel lines in the subject remain parallel in the drawing.

• Paraline drawings present either an aerial view looking down on an object or scene, or a worm's-eye view looking upward. They lack the eye-level view and picturesque quality of linear perspectives. They represent what we know rather than how we see, depicting an objective reality that corresponds more closely to the picture in the mind's eye than to the retinal image of linear perspective.

There are several types of paraline drawings, each named after the method of projection that is used to develop them. Two of the most common in architectural drawing are discussed in this chapter: isometric and oblique drawings.

In both isometric and oblique drawings:
• All parallel lines in the subject remain parallel in the drawing.
• All lines parallel to the principal X-Y-Z- axes can be measured and drawn to scale.

The images that emerge from oblique projections are distinct from isometric views that develop from orthographic projection. The ease with which we can construct an oblique drawing has a powerful appeal. If we orient a principal face of the subject parallel to the picture plane, its shape remains true and we can draw it more easily. Thus, oblique views are especially convenient for representing an object that has a curvilinear, irregular, or complicated face.

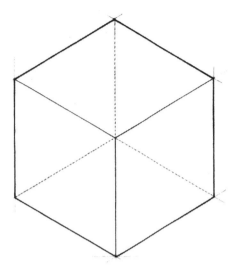

Isometric Drawings
• All three principal sets of planes share equal emphasis.
• The angle of view is slightly lower than that of plan obliques.
• Plans and elevations cannot be used as base drawings.

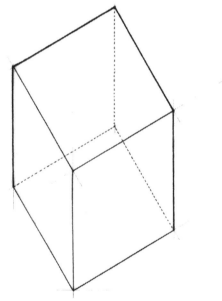

Plan Obliques
• The principal set of horizontal planes oriented parallel to the picture plane is emphasized and can be represented in true size, shape, and proportion.
• Plan views can be utilized as base drawings—a definite advantage when drawing horizontal planes with circular or complex shapes.
• Plan obliques have a higher angle of view than isometric drawings.

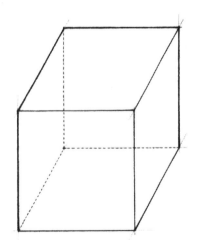

Elevation Obliques
• The principal set of vertical planes oriented parallel to the picture plane is emphasized and can be represented in true size, shape, and proportion. The other vertical set and the principal horizontal set of planes are both foreshortened.
• An elevation can be used as a base drawing. This view should be of the longest, the most significant, or the most complex face of the object or building.

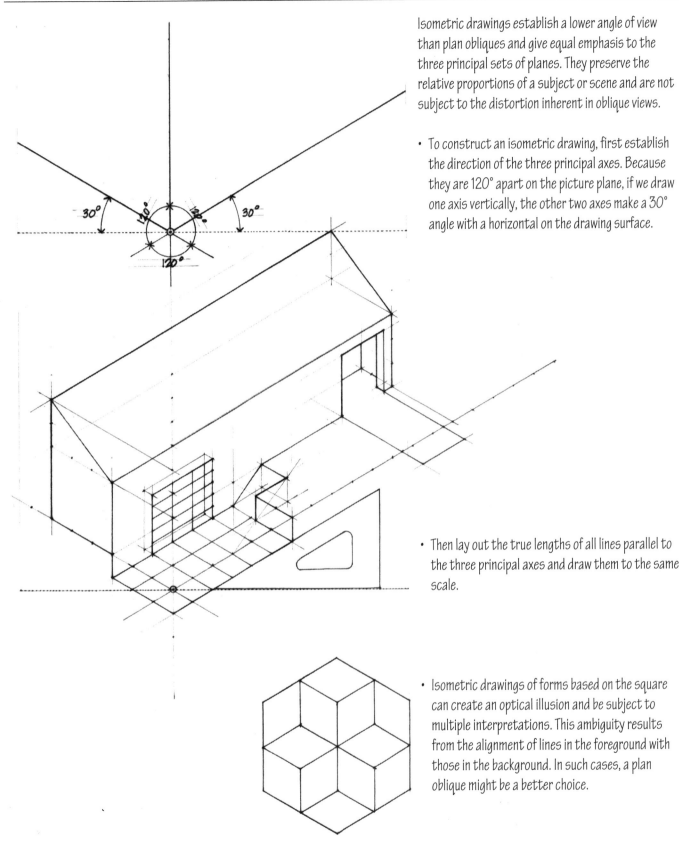

Isometric drawings establish a lower angle of view than plan obliques and give equal emphasis to the three principal sets of planes. They preserve the relative proportions of a subject or scene and are not subject to the distortion inherent in oblique views.

• To construct an isometric drawing, first establish the direction of the three principal axes. Because they are 120° apart on the picture plane, if we draw one axis vertically, the other two axes make a 30° angle with a horizontal on the drawing surface.

• Then lay out the true lengths of all lines parallel to the three principal axes and draw them to the same scale.

• Isometric drawings of forms based on the square can create an optical illusion and be subject to multiple interpretations. This ambiguity results from the alignment of lines in the foreground with those in the background. In such cases, a plan oblique might be a better choice.

Plan obliques present a higher angle of view than isometric drawings and emphasize the set of horizontal planes by revealing their true size, shape, and proportions.

- To construct a plan oblique, begin with a plan drawing and rotate it to the desired angle relative to a horizontal on the drawing sheet or board.
- When drafting a plan oblique, the triangles encourage the use of 45°-45° and 30°-60° angles in establishing the orientation of the principal horizontal planes. Digital graphics programs, however, allow the use of any desired angle.
- Note that we can emphasize one of the sets of vertical planes over the other or show them to be of equal importance by varying this angle.

60°   45°   30°

- In a 45°-45° plan oblique, both principal sets of vertical planes receive equal emphasis.
- In a 30°-60° plan oblique, one principal set of vertical planes receives more emphasis than the other.

- From the rotated plan view, we project the vertical edges and planes of the subject.

- We usually lay out and draw these vertical dimensions to their true lengths.
- To offset the appearance of distortion, we may reduce the vertical dimensions to $1/2$, $2/3$, or $3/4$ of their true lengths.

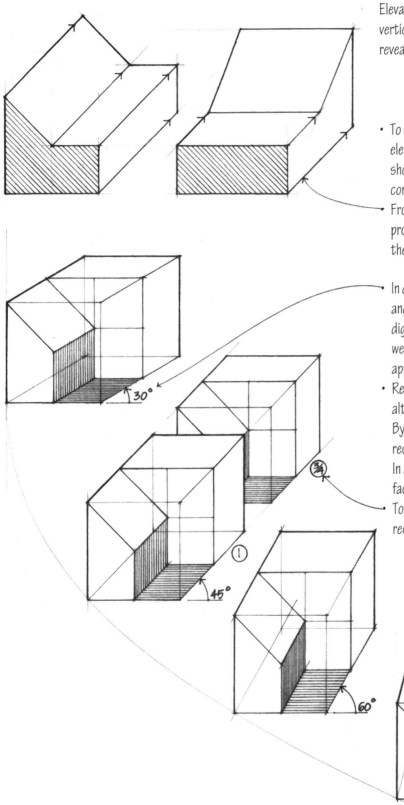

Elevation obliques orient a principal vertical face or set of vertical planes parallel to the picture plane and therefore reveal their true sizes, shapes, and proportions.

- To construct an elevation oblique, we begin with an elevation view of the principal face of the subject. This should be the longest, the most significant, or the most complex face of the subject.
- From significant points in the elevation view, we then project the receding lines back at the desired angle into the depth of the drawing.

- In drafting with triangles, we typically use 45°, 30°, or 60° angles for the receding lines. In sketching or when using digital drawing tools, we need not be as precise, but once we establish an angle for the receding lines, we should apply it consistently.
- Remember that the angle we use for the receding lines alters the apparent size and shape of the receding planes. By varying the angle, the horizontal and vertical sets of receding planes can receive different degrees of emphasis. In all cases, the primary emphasis remains on the vertical faces parallel to the picture plane.
- To offset the appearance of distortion, we may reduce the receding lines to $1/2$, $2/3$, or $3/4$ of their true lengths.

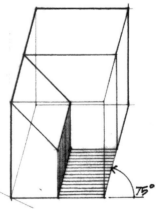

There are three basic approaches to constructing the entire class of paraline drawings. When constructing and presenting a paraline drawing, keep in mind that paraline views are easiest to understand if vertical lines in space are also oriented vertically on the drawing surface.

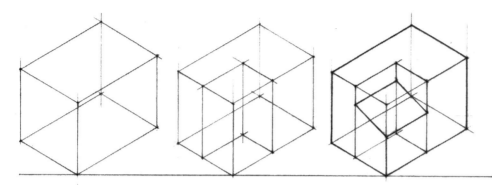

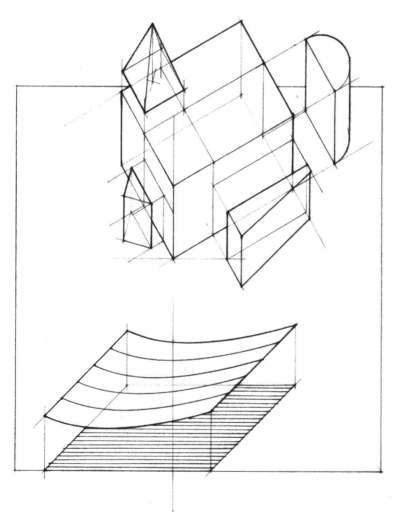

• The first is a subtractive approach appropriate for relatively simple forms. It involves constructing a paraline view of a transparent rectangular box that encompasses the entire volume of the subject, and then working in a subtractive manner to remove material and reveal the form.

• A second approach, appropriate for a composition of discrete forms, reverses the procedure of the subtractive approach. It requires drawing a paraline view of the parent form first, and then adding the subordinate forms.

• The third approach is appropriate for irregularly shaped forms. It begins with a paraline view of a horizontal plane of the subject or the profile of a vertical section cut. We can then extrude the shape vertically or extend it back into the depth of the drawing.

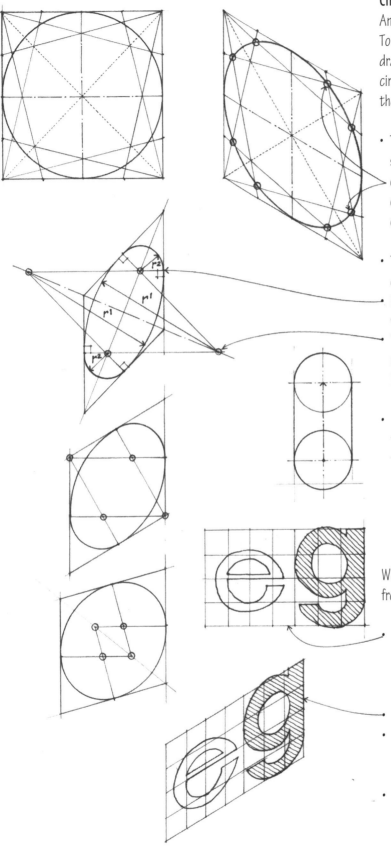

Circles and Freeform Shapes

Any circles oblique to the picture plane appear as ellipses. To draw such a circle in a paraline drawing, we must first draw a paraline view of the square that circumscribes the circle. Then we can use either of two approaches to drawing the circle within the square.

- The first is an approximate method. By dividing the square into quadrants and drawing diagonals from each corner to quarter points along the sides of the square, we can establish eight points along the circumference of the circle.

- The four-center method uses two sets of radii and a compass or circle template.
- From the midpoints of the sides of the square in the paraline view, we extend perpendiculars until they intersect.
- With the four points of intersection as centers and with radii r1 and r2, we describe two sets of arcs in equal pairs between the origin points of the perpendiculars.

- It is often more convenient to draw a plan oblique rather than an isometric of a circular or free-form plan because the plan itself can be used as the base drawing and the horizontal shapes remain true.

We can use a grid to transfer curvilinear or free-form shapes from an orthographic view to the paraline view.

- First, we construct a grid over a plan or elevation view of the shape. This grid may either be uniform or correspond to critical points in the shape. The more complex the shape, the finer the grid divisions should be.
- Then we construct the same grid in the paraline view.
- Next, we locate the points of intersection between the grid and the free-form shape and plot these coordinates in the paraline view.
- Finally, we connect the transferred points in the paraline view.

Spatial Depth Cues

We can enhance the perceived depth of a paraline drawing by utilizing a hierarchy of line weights to distinguish between spatial edges, planar corners, and surface lines.

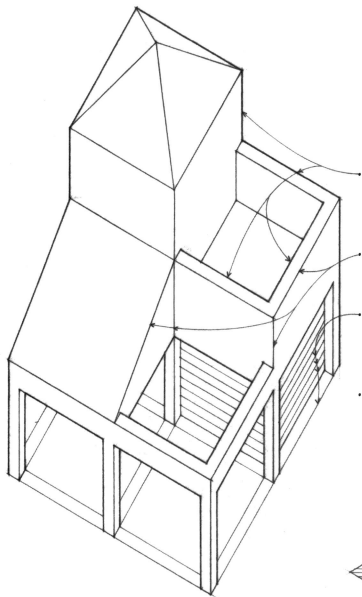

Spatial edges are the boundaries of a form separated from the background by some intervening space.

Planar corners are the intersections of two or more planes that are visible to the eye.

Surface lines are lines that represent an abrupt contrast in color, tonal value, or material; they do not represent a change in form.

- 3D-modeling programs treat lines as the continuous edges of polygons. It may therefore be difficult to define this hierarchy of line weights without first transferring the graphic image to a two-dimensional environment.

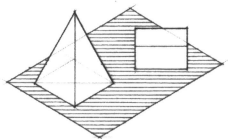

- To separate planes in space, to clarify their different orientations, and especially to distinguish between the horizontal and the vertical, we can use contrasting textures and patterns.

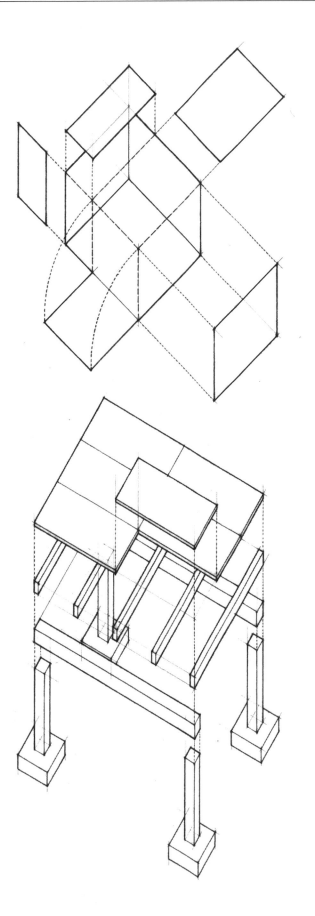

Even though a paraline drawing always presents either an aerial view or a worm's-eye view of a subject, we can construct a paraline view in any of several ways to reveal more than the exterior form and configuration of a design. These techniques allow us to gain visual access to the interior of a spatial composition or the hidden portions of a complex construction. We categorize these techniques into expanded views, cutaway views, phantom views, and sequential views.

Expanded Views

To develop what we call an expanded or exploded view, we merely shift portions of a paraline drawing to new positions in space. The finished drawing appears to be an explosion frozen at a point in time when the relationships between the parts of the whole are most clear.

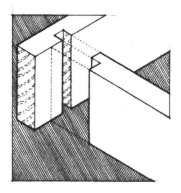

• Expanded views are extremely useful in describing the details, layering, or sequence of a construction assembly. Remember that, as with other drawing types, the larger the scale of a paraline drawing, the more detail you have to show.
• At a larger scale, expanded views can effectively illustrate vertical relationships in multistory buildings as well as horizontal connections across space.

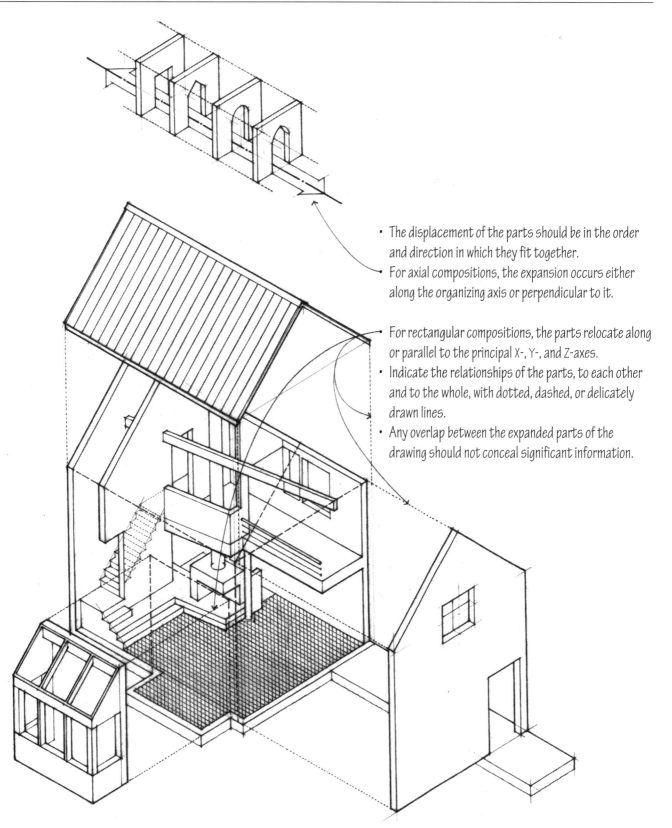

- The displacement of the parts should be in the order and direction in which they fit together.
- For axial compositions, the expansion occurs either along the organizing axis or perpendicular to it.

- For rectangular compositions, the parts relocate along or parallel to the principal X-, Y-, and Z-axes.
- Indicate the relationships of the parts, to each other and to the whole, with dotted, dashed, or delicately drawn lines.
- Any overlap between the expanded parts of the drawing should not conceal significant information.

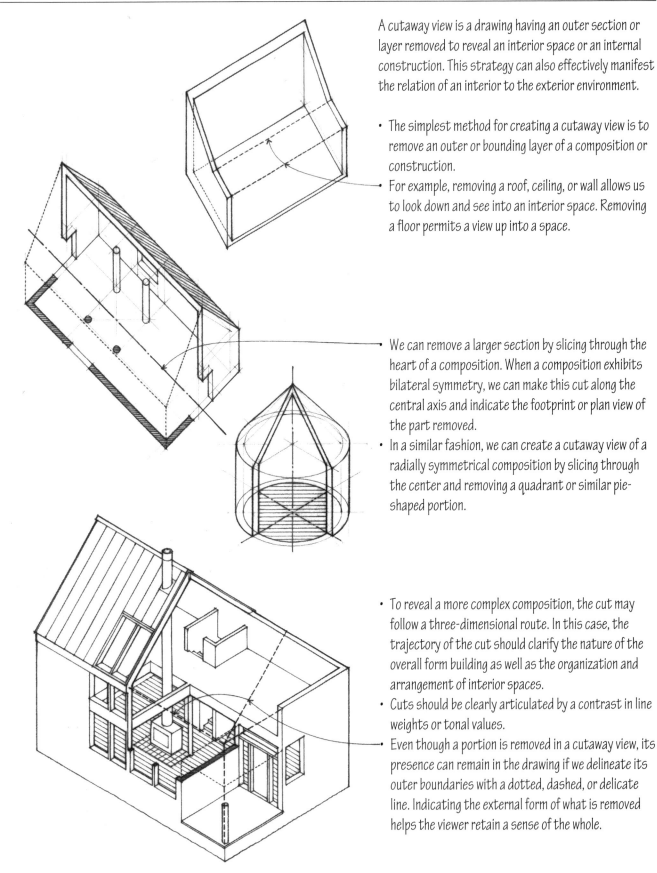

A cutaway view is a drawing having an outer section or layer removed to reveal an interior space or an internal construction. This strategy can also effectively manifest the relation of an interior to the exterior environment.

- The simplest method for creating a cutaway view is to remove an outer or bounding layer of a composition or construction.
- For example, removing a roof, ceiling, or wall allows us to look down and see into an interior space. Removing a floor permits a view up into a space.

- We can remove a larger section by slicing through the heart of a composition. When a composition exhibits bilateral symmetry, we can make this cut along the central axis and indicate the footprint or plan view of the part removed.
- In a similar fashion, we can create a cutaway view of a radially symmetrical composition by slicing through the center and removing a quadrant or similar pie-shaped portion.

- To reveal a more complex composition, the cut may follow a three-dimensional route. In this case, the trajectory of the cut should clarify the nature of the overall form building as well as the organization and arrangement of interior spaces.
- Cuts should be clearly articulated by a contrast in line weights or tonal values.
- Even though a portion is removed in a cutaway view, its presence can remain in the drawing if we delineate its outer boundaries with a dotted, dashed, or delicate line. Indicating the external form of what is removed helps the viewer retain a sense of the whole.

A phantom view is a paraline drawing having one or more parts made transparent to permit the presentation of internal information otherwise hidden from our view. This strategy effectively allows us to unveil an interior space or construction without removing any of its bounding planes or encompassing elements. Thus, we are able to simultaneously see the whole composition and its internal structure and arrangement.

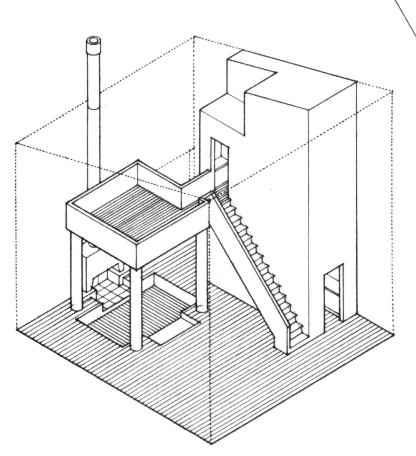

• A phantom line is a broken one consisting of relatively long segments separated by two short dashes or dots.
• In practice, phantom lines may also consist of dashed, dotted, or even delicately drawn lines.
• The graphic description should include the thickness or volume of the parts that are made transparent.

• Condominium Unit No. 5, Sea Ranch, California, 1963–65
Moore, Lyndon, Turnbull, Whitaker

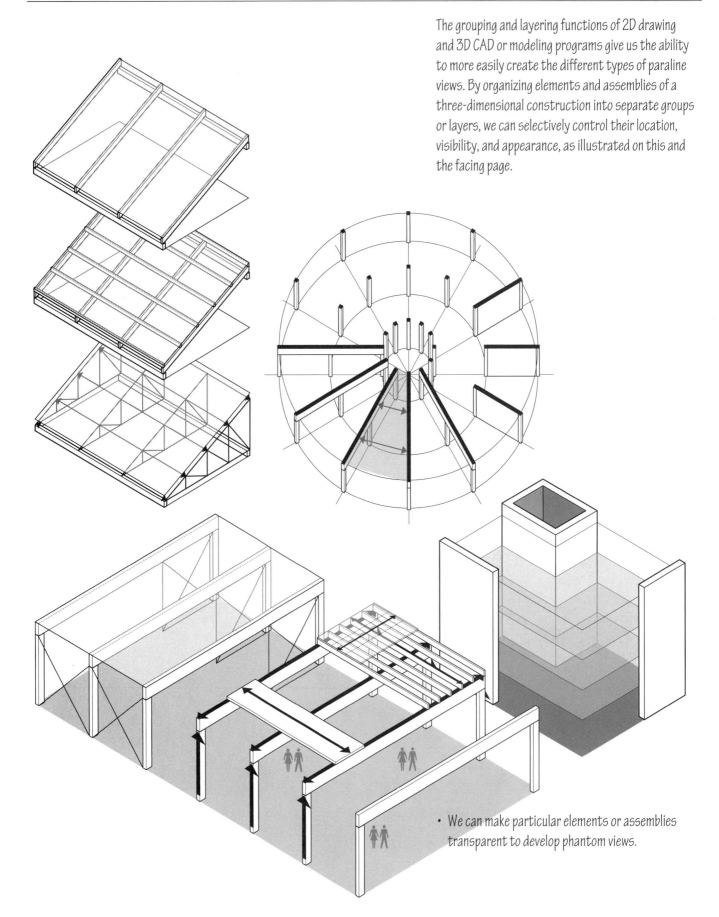

The grouping and layering functions of 2D drawing and 3D CAD or modeling programs give us the ability to more easily create the different types of paraline views. By organizing elements and assemblies of a three-dimensional construction into separate groups or layers, we can selectively control their location, visibility, and appearance, as illustrated on this and the facing page.

• We can make particular elements or assemblies transparent to develop phantom views.

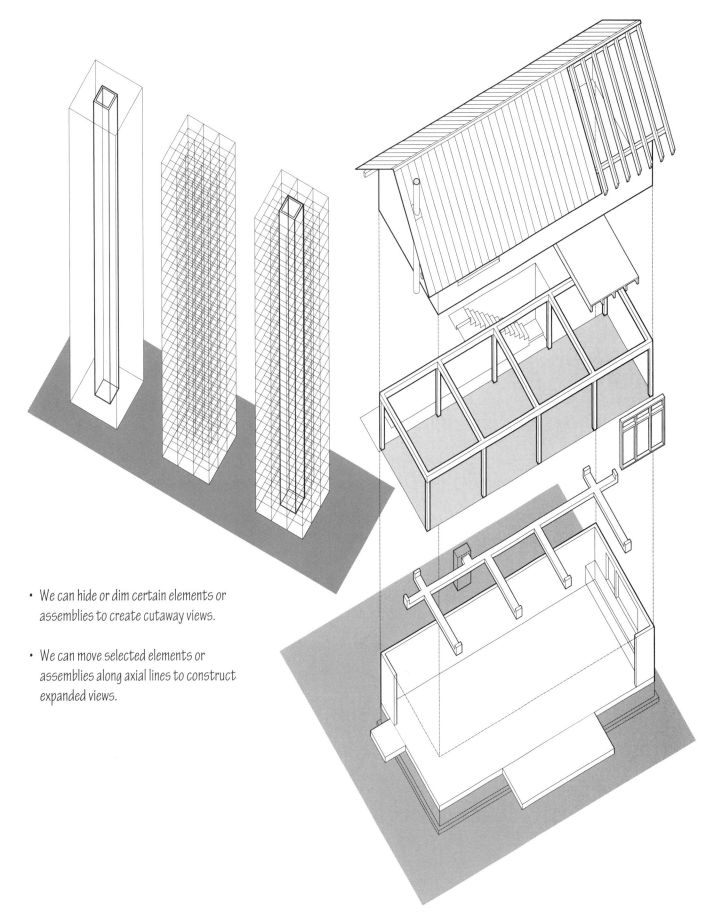

• We can hide or dim certain elements or assemblies to create cutaway views.

• We can move selected elements or assemblies along axial lines to construct expanded views.

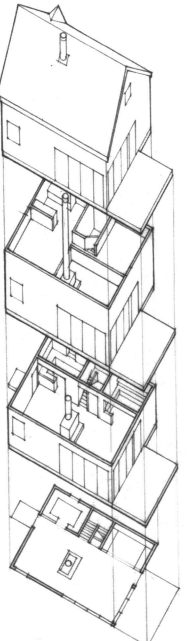

While a paraline is a single-view drawing useful in displaying three-dimensional relationships, a series of paraline views can effectively explain processes and phenomena that occur in time or across space.

• A progression of paraline drawings can explain a sequence of assembly or the stages of a construction, with each view successively building upon the preceding one.

• A similar technique can be used to illustrate the interior organization as well as the overall form of a building utilizing repetitive unit plans. In this case, each floor level successively builds upon the preceding one.

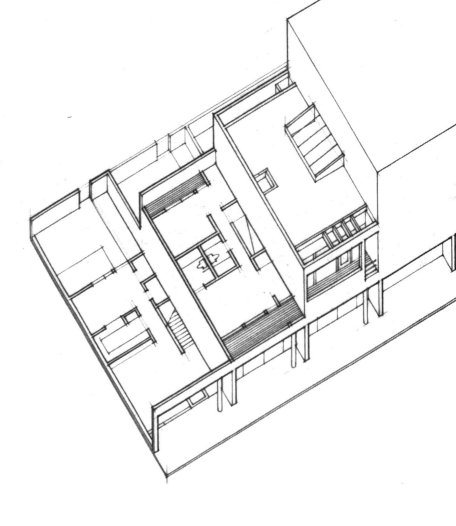

6
Perspective Drawings

"Perspective" properly refers to any of various graphic techniques for depicting volumes and spatial relationships on a flat surface, such as size perspective and atmospheric perspective. The term "perspective," however, most often brings to mind the drawing system of linear perspective. Linear perspective is a technique for describing three-dimensional volumes and spatial relationships on a two-dimensional surface by means of lines that converge as they recede into the depth of a drawing. While multiview and paraline drawings present views of an objective reality, linear perspective offers scenes of an optical reality. It depicts how a construction or environment might appear to the eye of an observer looking in a specific direction from a particular vantage point in space.

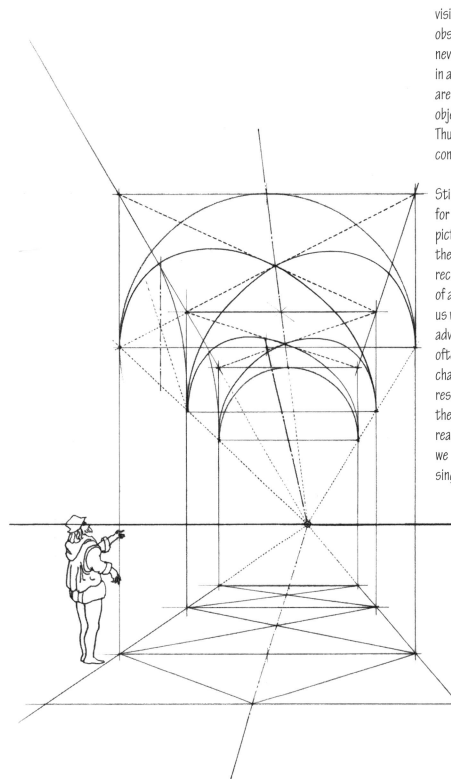

Linear perspective is valid only for monocular vision. A perspective drawing assumes that the observer sees through a single eye. We almost never view anything in this way. Even with the head in a fixed position, we see through both eyes, which are constantly in motion, roving over and around objects and through ever-changing environments. Thus, linear perspective can only approximate the complex way our eyes actually function.

Still, linear perspective provides us with a method for correctly placing three-dimensional objects in pictorial space and illustrating the degree to which their forms appear to diminish in size as they recede into the depth of a drawing. The uniqueness of a linear perspective lies in its ability to provide us with an experiential view of space. This distinct advantage, however, also gives rise to the difficulty often connected with perspective drawing. The challenge in mastering linear perspective is resolving the conflict between our knowledge of the thing itself—how we conceive its objective reality—and the appearance of something—how we perceive its optical reality—as seen through a single eye of the observer.

Perspective projection represents a three-dimensional object by projecting all its points to a picture plane by straight lines converging at a fixed point in space representing a single eye of the observer. This convergence of sightlines differentiates perspective projection from the other two major projection systems—orthographic projection and oblique projection—in which the projectors remain parallel to each other.

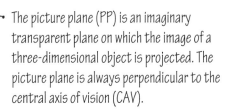

The picture plane (PP) is an imaginary transparent plane on which the image of a three-dimensional object is projected. The picture plane is always perpendicular to the central axis of vision (CAV).

Sightlines are any of the projectors extending from the station point (SP) to various points on what is viewed.

The perspective projection of any point on an object is where the sightline to that point intersects the picture plane.

The central axis of vision (CAV) is the sightline determining the direction in which the observer is assumed to be looking.

The station point (SP) is a fixed point in space representing a single eye of the observer.

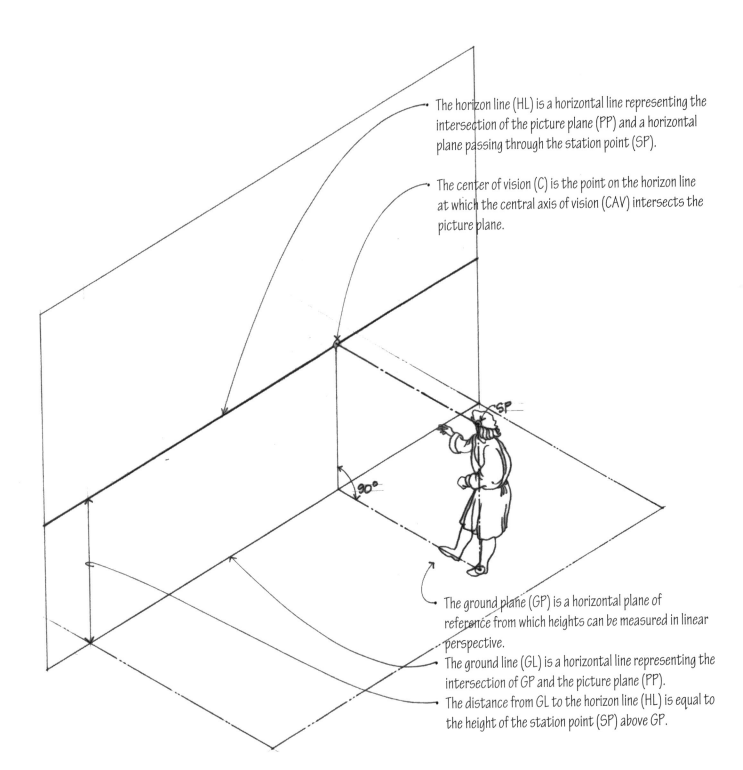

The horizon line (HL) is a horizontal line representing the intersection of the picture plane (PP) and a horizontal plane passing through the station point (SP).

The center of vision (C) is the point on the horizon line at which the central axis of vision (CAV) intersects the picture plane.

The ground plane (GP) is a horizontal plane of reference from which heights can be measured in linear perspective.

The ground line (GL) is a horizontal line representing the intersection of GP and the picture plane (PP).

The distance from GL to the horizon line (HL) is equal to the height of the station point (SP) above GP.

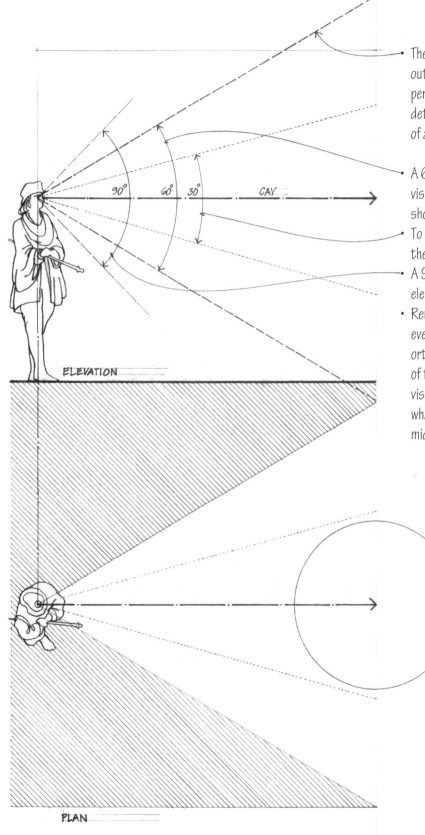

ELEVATION

PLAN

The cone of vision describes the sightlines radiating outward from SP and forming an angle with CAV in linear perspective. The cone of vision serves as a guide in determining what is to be included within the boundaries of a perspective drawing.

A 60° cone of vision is assumed to be the normal field of vision within which the principal aspects of the subject should be placed.

To minimize distortion of circles and circular shapes, they should fall within a 30° cone of vision.

A 90° cone of vision is acceptable for peripheral elements.

Remember that the cone of vision is three-dimensional even though it is seen as a triangular shape in orthographic plans and elevations. Only a small portion of the immediate foreground falls within the cone of vision. As the cone of vision reaches out to gather in what the observer sees, it widens its field, and the middleground and background become more expansive.

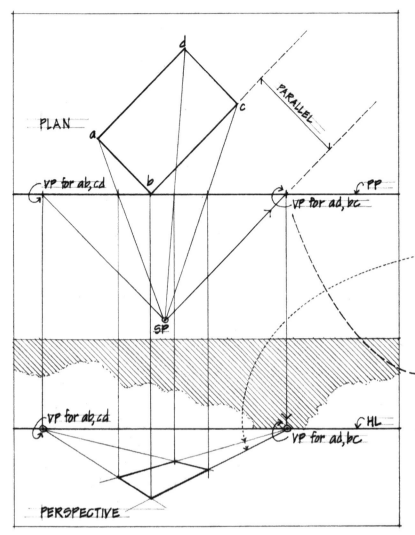

The converging nature of sightlines in linear perspective produces certain pictorial effects. Being familiar with these pictorial effects helps us understand how lines, planes, and volumes should appear in linear perspective and how to place objects correctly in the space of a perspective drawing.

Convergence

Convergence in linear perspective refers to the apparent movement of parallel lines toward a common vanishing point as they recede.

- As two parallel lines recede into the distance, the space between them will appear to diminish. If the lines are extended to infinity, they will appear to meet at a point on the picture plane (PP). This point is the vanishing point (VP) for that particular pair of lines and all other lines parallel to them.
- The vanishing point (VP) for any set of parallel lines is the point where a line drawn from the station point (SP) parallel to the set intersects PP.

The first rule of convergence is that each set of parallel lines has its own vanishing point. A set of parallel lines consists only of those lines that are parallel to one another. If we look at a cube, for example, we can see that its edges comprise three principal sets of parallel lines, one set of vertical lines parallel to the X-axis, and two sets of horizontal lines, perpendicular to each other and parallel to the Y- and Z-axes.

In order to draw a perspective, we must know how many sets of parallel lines exist in what we see or envision and where each set will appear to converge. The following guidelines for the convergence of parallel lines is based solely on the relationship between the observer's central axis of vision (CAV) and the subject.

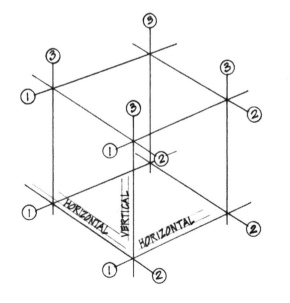

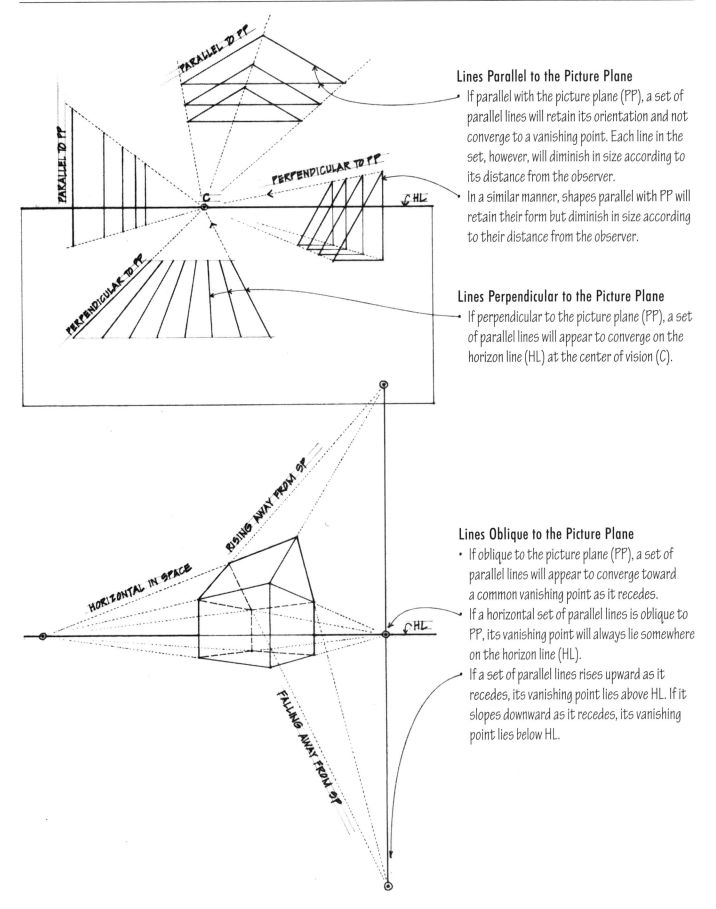

Lines Parallel to the Picture Plane

- If parallel with the picture plane (PP), a set of parallel lines will retain its orientation and not converge to a vanishing point. Each line in the set, however, will diminish in size according to its distance from the observer.
- In a similar manner, shapes parallel with PP will retain their form but diminish in size according to their distance from the observer.

Lines Perpendicular to the Picture Plane

- If perpendicular to the picture plane (PP), a set of parallel lines will appear to converge on the horizon line (HL) at the center of vision (C).

Lines Oblique to the Picture Plane

- If oblique to the picture plane (PP), a set of parallel lines will appear to converge toward a common vanishing point as it recedes.
- If a horizontal set of parallel lines is oblique to PP, its vanishing point will always lie somewhere on the horizon line (HL).
- If a set of parallel lines rises upward as it recedes, its vanishing point lies above HL. If it slopes downward as it recedes, its vanishing point lies below HL.

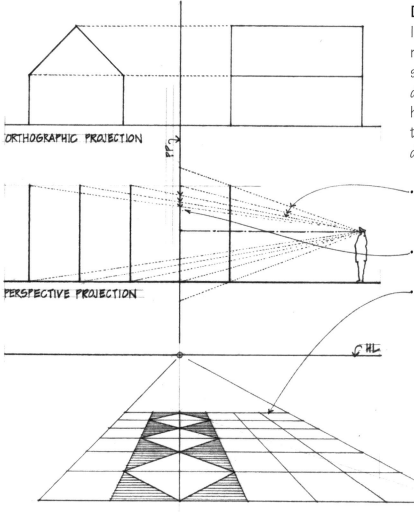

ORTHOGRAPHIC PROJECTION

PERSPECTIVE PROJECTION

Diminution of Size

In orthographic and oblique projection, the projectors remain parallel to each other. Therefore, the projected size of an element remains the same regardless of its distance from the picture plane. In linear perspective, however, the converging projectors or sightlines alter the apparent size of a line or plane according to its distance from the picture plane.

- Converging sightlines reduce the size of distant objects, making them appear smaller than identical objects closer to the picture plane (PP).
- Note also that as an object recedes, sightlines to the object approach the horizon line (HL).
- For example, looking down on a tiled floor pattern, we can see more of the tiles' surfaces in the foreground. As the same-size tiles recede, they appear smaller and flatter as they rise and approach the horizon.

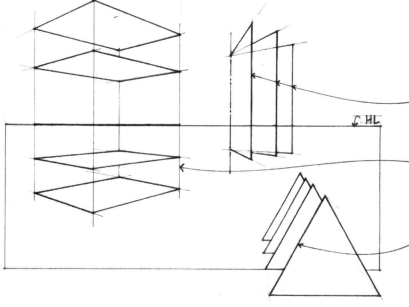

Other Pictorial Effects

Perspective drawings also possess other pictorial characteristics found in multiview and paraline drawing systems.

- Foreshortening refers to the apparent compression in size or length when a facet of an object rotates away from the picture plane (PP).
- In linear perspective, foreshortening also results when a facet of an object perpendicular or oblique to PP moves laterally or vertically with respect to the central axis of vision (CAV).
- In all drawing systems, the overlapping of shapes and forms is an essential visual cue to spatial depth.

The observer's point of view determines the pictorial effect of a perspective drawing. As this viewpoint changes—as the observer moves up or down, to the left or right, forward or back—the extent and emphasis of what the observer sees also changes. In order to achieve the desired view in perspective, we should understand how to adjust the following variables.

Height of the Station Point

The height of the station point (SP) relative to an object determines whether it is seen from above, below, or within its own height.

- For a normal eye-level perspective, SP is at the standing height of a person.
- As SP moves up or down, the horizon line (HL) moves up or down with it.

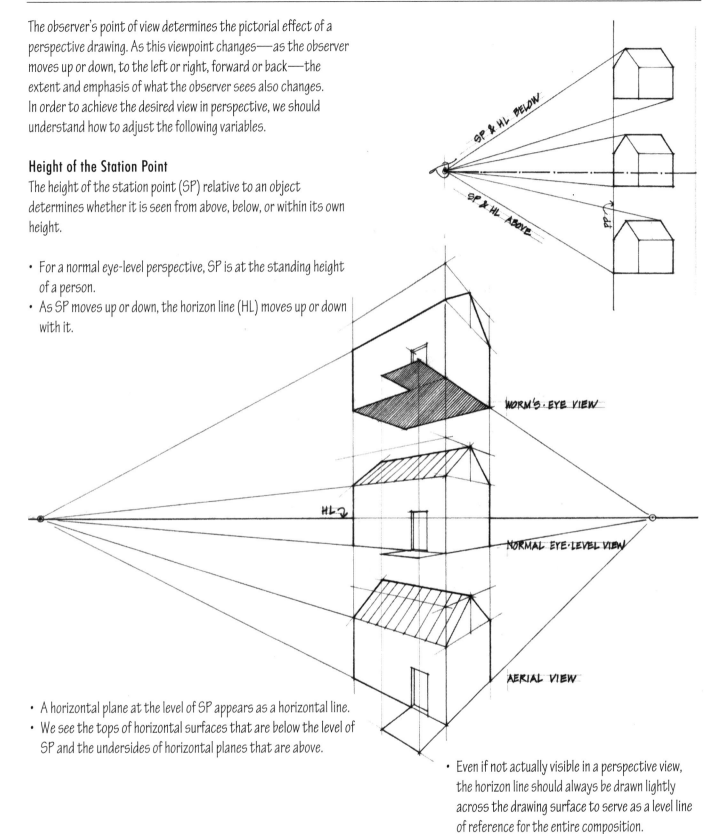

- A horizontal plane at the level of SP appears as a horizontal line.
- We see the tops of horizontal surfaces that are below the level of SP and the undersides of horizontal planes that are above.

- Even if not actually visible in a perspective view, the horizon line should always be drawn lightly across the drawing surface to serve as a level line of reference for the entire composition.

Distance from the Station Point to the Object

The distance from the station point (SP) to an object influences the rate of foreshortening of the object's surfaces that occurs in the perspective drawing.

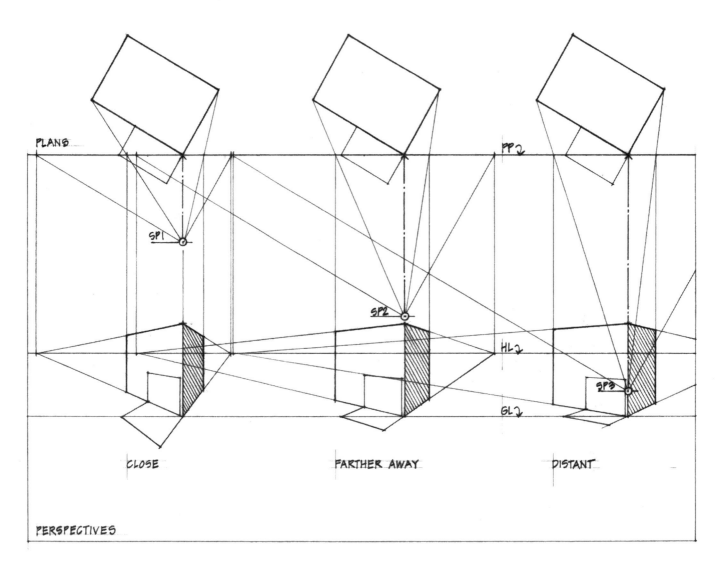

- As the observer's SP moves farther away from the object, the vanishing points for the object move farther apart, horizontal lines flatten out, and perspective depth is compressed.

- As the observer's SP moves forward, the vanishing points for the object move closer together, horizontal angles become more acute, and perspective depth is exaggerated.

- In theory, a perspective drawing presents a true picture of an object only when the eye of the viewer is located at the assumed station point (SP) of the perspective.

Angle of View

The orientation of the central axis of vision (CAV) and the picture plane (PP) relative to an object determines which faces of the object are visible and the degree to which they are foreshortened in perspective.

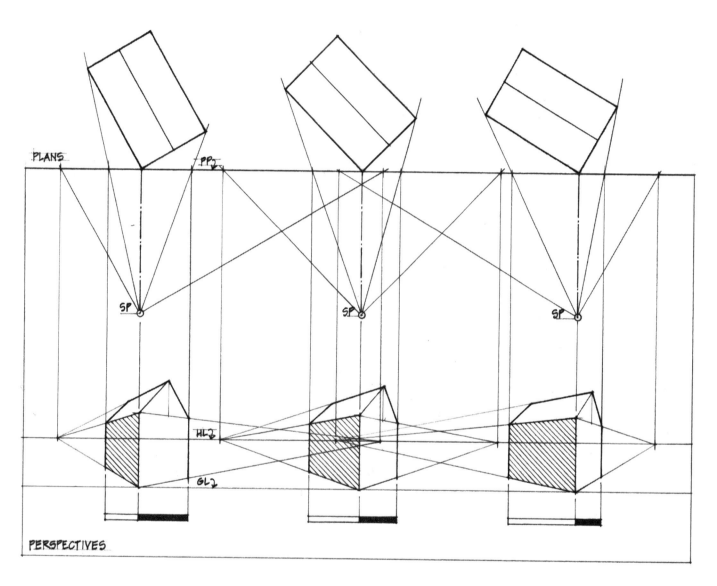

- The more a plane is rotated away from PP, the more it is foreshortened in perspective.

- The more frontal the plane is, the less it is foreshortened.
- When a plane becomes parallel to PP, its true shape is revealed.

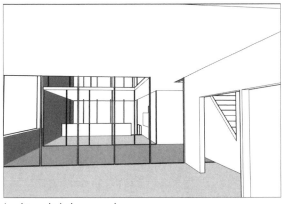

Looking slightly upward

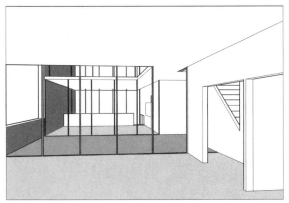

Level line of sight

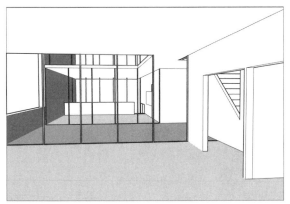

Looking slightly downward

Digital Viewpoints

In constructing a perspective by hand, we must have experience in setting up the station point and the angle of view to predict and achieve a reasonable outcome. A distinct advantage in using 3D CAD and modeling programs is that once the necessary data is entered for a three-dimensional construction, the software allows us to manipulate the perspective variables and fairly quickly produce a number of perspective views for evaluation. 3D CAD and modeling programs, while following the mathematical principles of perspective, can easily create distorted perspective views. Judgment of what a perspective image conveys, whether produced by hand or with the aid of the computer, remains the responsibility of its author.

Illustrated on this and the facing page are examples of computer-generated perspectives, showing how the various perspective variables affect the resulting images. The differences in the perspective views may be subtle but they do affect our perception of the scale of the spaces and our judgment of the spatial relationships the images convey.

- Both one- and two-point perspective assumes a level line of sight, which results in vertical lines remaining vertical. As soon as the observer's line of sight tilts up or down, even a few degrees, the result is technically a three-point perspective.

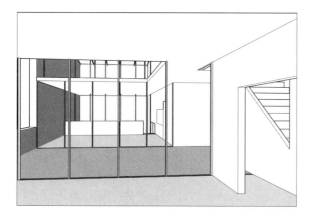

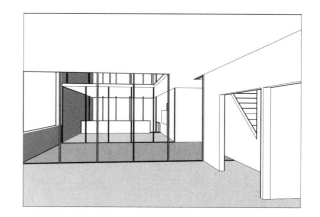

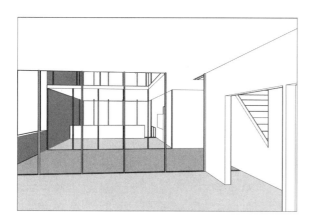

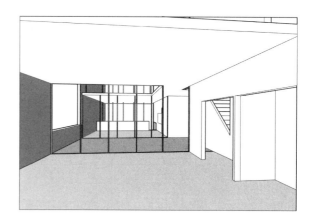

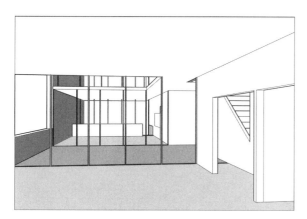

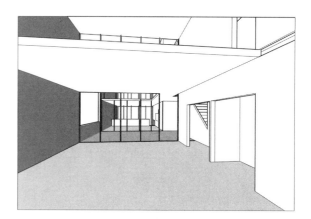

- The desire to see more of a space in a single perspective view often leads to moving the station point of the observer as far back as possible. However, one should always attempt to maintain a reasonable position for the observer within the space being represented.

- Keeping the central portion of a subject or scene within a reasonable cone of vision is critical to avoiding distortion in a perspective view. Widening the angle of view to include more of a space within a perspective can easily lead to distortion of forms and exaggeration of the depth of a space.

Location of the Picture Plane

The location of the picture plane (PP) relative to an object affects only the final size of the perspective image. The closer PP is to the station point (SP), the smaller the perspective image. The farther away PP is, the larger the image. Assuming all other variables remain constant, the perspective images are identical in all respects except size.

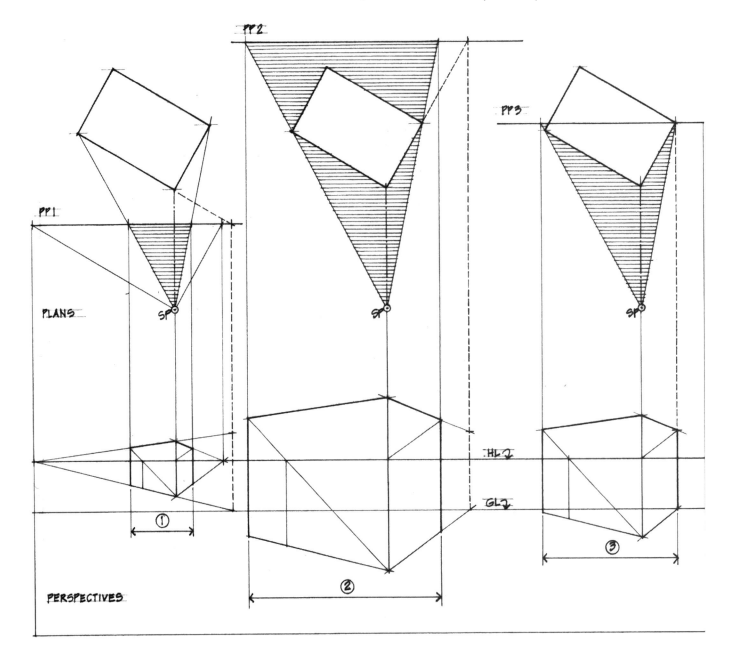

In any rectilinear object, such as a cube, each of the three principal sets of parallel lines has its own vanishing point. Based on these three major sets of lines, there are three types of linear perspective: one-, two-, and three-point perspectives. What distinguishes each type is simply the observer's angle of view relative to the subject. The subject does not change, only our view of it, but the change of view affects how the sets of parallel lines appear to converge in linear perspective.

One-Point Perspective

If we view a cube with our central axis of vision (CAV) perpendicular to one of its faces, all of the cube's vertical lines are parallel with the picture plane (PP) and remain vertical. The horizontal lines that are parallel with PP and perpendicular to CAV also remain horizontal. The lines that are parallel with CAV, however, will appear to converge at the center of vision (C). This is the one point referred to in one-point perspective.

Two-Point Perspective

If we shift our point of view so that we view the same cube obliquely, but keep our central axis of vision (CAV) horizontal, then the cube's vertical lines will remain vertical. The two sets of horizontal lines, however, are now oblique to the picture plane (PP) and will appear to converge, one set to the left and the other to the right. These are the two points referred to in two-point perspective.

Three-Point Perspective

If we lift one corner of the cube off the ground plane (GP), or if we tilt our central axis of vision (CAV) to look down or up at the cube, then all three sets of parallel lines will be oblique to the picture plane (PP) and will appear to converge at three different vanishing points. These are the three points referred to in three-point perspective.

Note that each type of perspective does not imply that there are only one, two, or three vanishing points in a perspective. The actual number of vanishing points will depend on our point of view and how many sets of parallel lines there are in the subject being viewed. For example, if we look at a simple gable-roofed form, we can see that there are potentially five vanishing points, since we have one set of vertical lines, two sets of horizontal lines, and two sets of inclined lines.

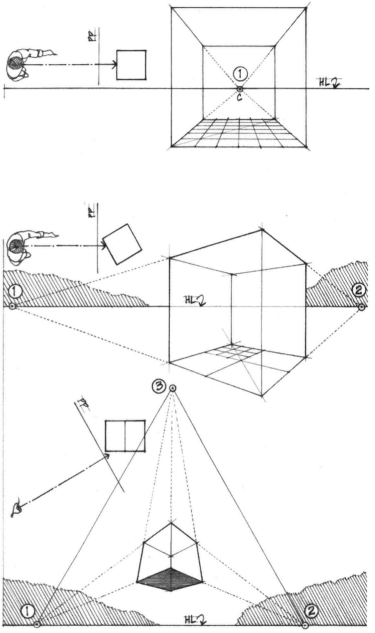

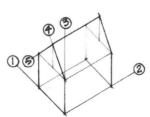

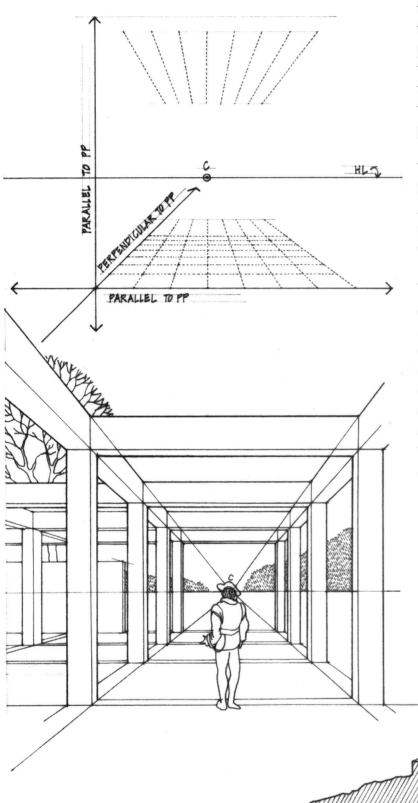

The one-point perspective system assumes that two of the three principal axes—one vertical and the other horizontal—are parallel to the picture plane. All lines parallel to these axes are also parallel to the picture plane (PP), and therefore retain their true orientation and do not appear to converge. For this reason, one-point perspective is also known as parallel perspective.

The third principal axis is horizontal, perpendicular to PP and parallel with the central axis of vision (CAV). All lines parallel to CAV converge on the horizon line (HL) at the center of vision (C). This is the particular vanishing point referred to in one-point perspective.

The one-point perspective system is particularly effective in depicting the interior of a spatial volume because the display of five bounding faces provides a clear sense of enclosure. For this reason, designers often use one-point perspectives to present experiential views of street scenes, formal gardens, courtyards, colonnades, and interior rooms. We can also use the presence of the central vanishing point to focus the viewer's attention and emphasize axial and symmetrical arrangements in space.

The diagonal point method for constructing a one-point perspective uses the geometry of a 45° right triangle and the principles of convergence to make depth measurements in perspective.

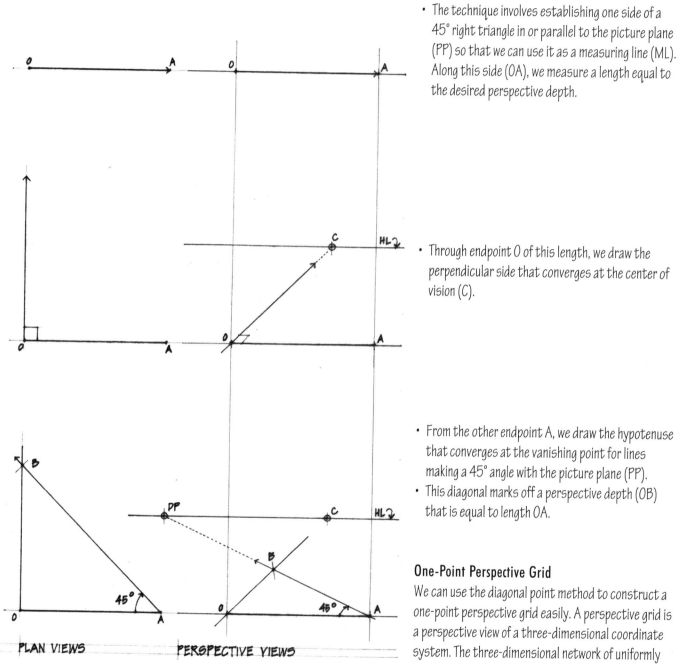

PLAN VIEWS   PERSPECTIVE VIEWS

• The technique involves establishing one side of a 45° right triangle in or parallel to the picture plane (PP) so that we can use it as a measuring line (ML). Along this side (OA), we measure a length equal to the desired perspective depth.

• Through endpoint O of this length, we draw the perpendicular side that converges at the center of vision (C).

• From the other endpoint A, we draw the hypotenuse that converges at the vanishing point for lines making a 45° angle with the picture plane (PP).
• This diagonal marks off a perspective depth (OB) that is equal to length OA.

One-Point Perspective Grid

We can use the diagonal point method to construct a one-point perspective grid easily. A perspective grid is a perspective view of a three-dimensional coordinate system. The three-dimensional network of uniformly spaced points and lines enables us to correctly establish the form and dimensions of an interior or exterior space, as well to regulate the position and size of objects within the space.

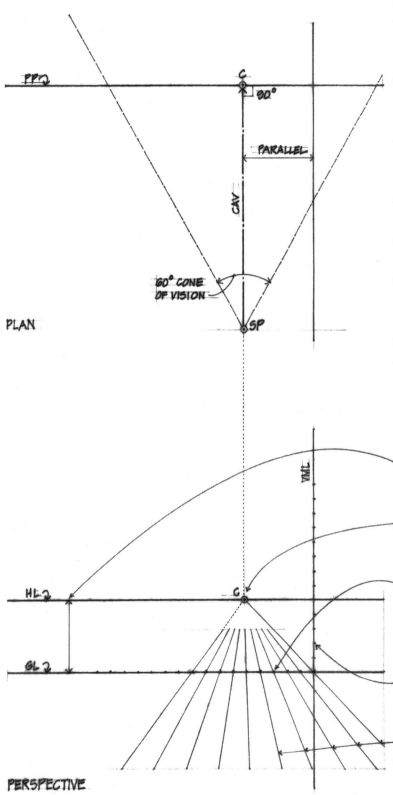

PLAN

PERSPECTIVE

Plan Setup

- Before beginning the construction of any perspective, we should first determine the desired point of view: What do we wish to illustrate in the perspective view and why?
- After we determine the space we are going to illustrate, we next establish the station point (SP) and the central axis of vision (CAV) in the plan view.
- Because this is a one-point perspective, CAV should be parallel to one major axis of the space and perpendicular to the other.
- We locate SP within the space but far enough back that the majority of the space lies within a 60° cone of vision.
- SP and CAV should be located off-center to avoid constructing a static, symmetrical perspective image.
- For ease of construction, we can locate PP coincidental with a major plane perpendicular to CAV.

Constructing the Perspective Grid

- We start by deciding on a scale for the picture plane (PP), taking into consideration both the dimensions of the space and the desired size of the perspective drawing. PP need not be drawn at the same scale as the plan setup.
- At the scale of PP, we establish the ground line (GL) and the horizon line (HL) at the height of the eye level of the observer, that is, the station point (SP) above the ground plane (GP).
- We establish the center of vision (C) on HL. The position of C can be determined from the plan setup.

- Along GL, we lay out to scale equal increments of measurement. The unit of measurement is typically one foot; we can, however, use smaller or larger increments depending on the scale of the drawing and the amount of detail desired in the perspective view.
- We do the same along a vertical measuring line (VML) drawn through one of the measured points at one end of GL.

- Through each of the measured points on GL, we draw receding lines that are perpendicular to PP and therefore converge at C.

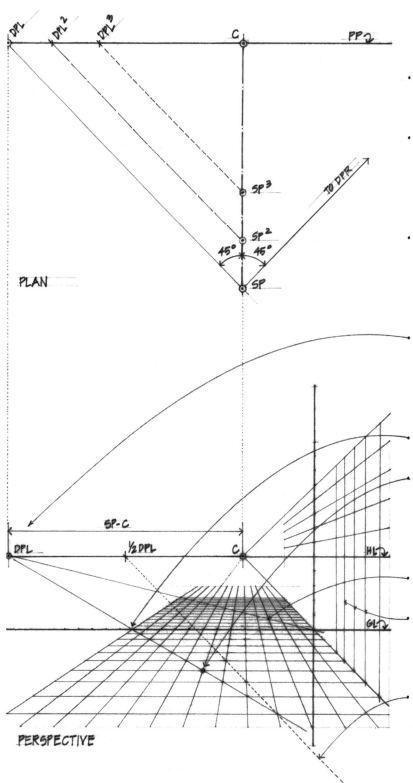

PLAN

PERSPECTIVE

Diagonal Points

- If we draw a 45° line from the station point (SP) in a plan view of the perspective setup, it will intersect the picture plane (PP) at the vanishing point for that diagonal and all lines parallel to it. We call this vanishing point a diagonal point (DP).

- There is one DP for horizontal diagonal lines receding to the left (DPL), and another for horizontal diagonal lines receding to the right (DPR).

- Both diagonal points lie on the horizon line (HL), equidistant from the center of vision (C). From the geometry of the 45° right triangle, we know that the distance from each DP to C is equal to the distance from SP to C in the plan setup.

- Note that if we move each DP toward C, this is equivalent to the observer moving closer to PP. If we shift each DP farther away from C, the observer also moves farther away from PP.

- Along HL, we establish DPL. Remember that the distance from DPL to C is equal to the distance of SP to C in the plan setup. Note that both DPL and DPR would serve the same purpose.

- From DPL, we draw a line through the left endpoint of the measurements along GL.

- Where this diagonal crosses the lines on the floor or ground plane that converge at C, we draw horizontal lines. The result is a perspective grid of one-foot squares on the floor or ground plane (GP).

- For depths beyond PP, we draw another diagonal to the other end of GL and follow a similar procedure.

- We can transfer these depth measurements and establish a similar grid along one or both receding sidewalls, as well as on a ceiling or overhead plane.

- A fractional distance point may be used if the drawing surface is too small to accommodate the normal distance point. A half-distance point will cut off two-foot increments in depth for every one-foot increment in width: $\frac{1}{2}$ DP = $\frac{1}{2}$ (SP − C) in plan.

DIAGONAL POINT METHOD

We can lay a piece of tracing paper over this perspective grid and draw in the major architectural elements of the space. With the same grid, we can also locate the positions and relative sizes of other elements within the space, such as furniture and lighting fixtures.

- We transfer measurements only along axial lines.
- For circles in perspective, see page 137.
- It's good practice to include people in our perspectives to indicate the function and scale of the space.

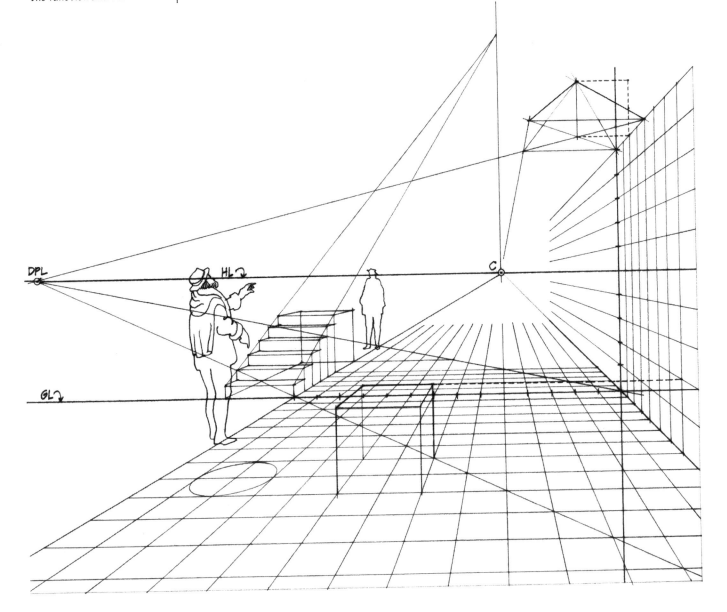

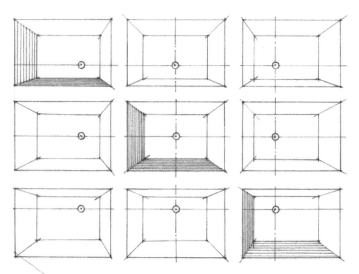

- When drawing a one-point perspective of a space, we notice that the observer's eye-level, equivalent to the height of the horizon line (HL) above the ground line (GL), as well as the location of the observer's center of vision (C), will determine which planes defining the space will be emphasized in the perspective view.

- The perspective drawing below uses the perspective grid shown on the facing page. Note that, particularly in interior views, properly cropped foreground elements can enhance the feeling that one is in a space rather than on the outside looking in. The center of vision (C) is closer to the lefthand wall so that the bending of the space to the right can be visualized. The change in scale between the righthand shelving and patio doors beyond, and a similar change between the foreground table and the window seat beyond, serve to emphasize the depth of the perspective.

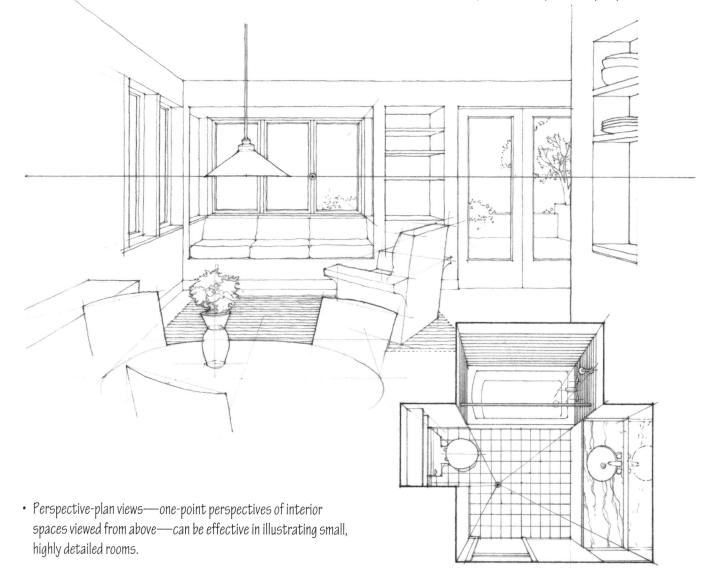

- Perspective-plan views—one-point perspectives of interior spaces viewed from above—can be effective in illustrating small, highly detailed rooms.

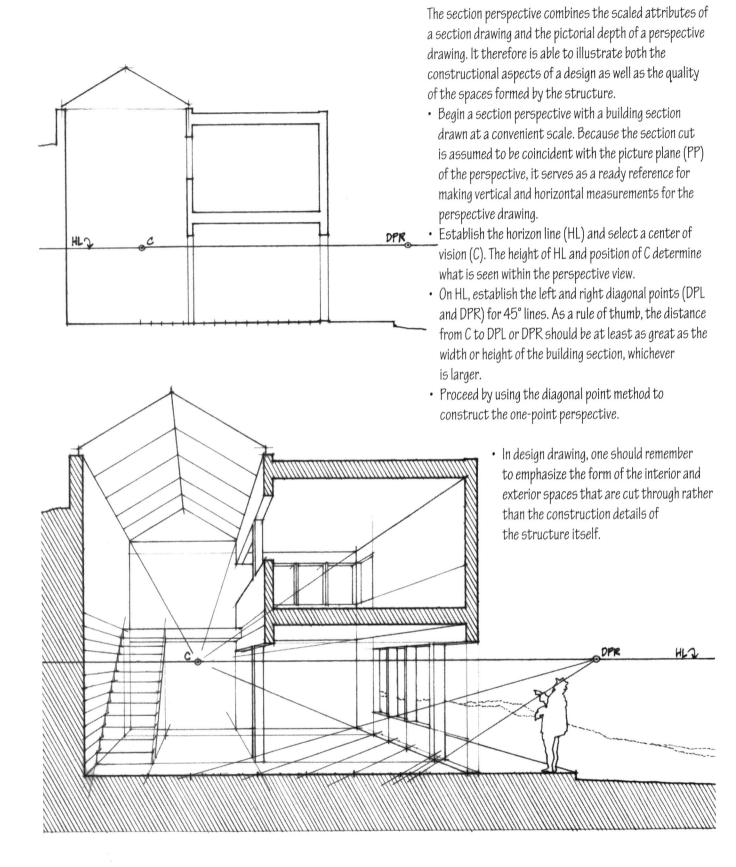

The section perspective combines the scaled attributes of a section drawing and the pictorial depth of a perspective drawing. It therefore is able to illustrate both the constructional aspects of a design as well as the quality of the spaces formed by the structure.

- Begin a section perspective with a building section drawn at a convenient scale. Because the section cut is assumed to be coincident with the picture plane (PP) of the perspective, it serves as a ready reference for making vertical and horizontal measurements for the perspective drawing.
- Establish the horizon line (HL) and select a center of vision (C). The height of HL and position of C determine what is seen within the perspective view.
- On HL, establish the left and right diagonal points (DPL and DPR) for 45° lines. As a rule of thumb, the distance from C to DPL or DPR should be at least as great as the width or height of the building section, whichever is larger.
- Proceed by using the diagonal point method to construct the one-point perspective.

- In design drawing, one should remember to emphasize the form of the interior and exterior spaces that are cut through rather than the construction details of the structure itself.

The two-point perspective system assumes that the observer's central axis of vision (CAV) is horizontal and the picture plane (PP) is vertical. The principal vertical axis is parallel to PP, and all lines parallel to it remain vertical and parallel in the perspective drawing. The two principal horizontal axes, however, are oblique to PP. All lines parallel to these axes therefore appear to converge to two vanishing points on the horizon line (HL), one set to the left and the other to the right. These are the two points referred to in two-point perspective.

Two-point perspective is probably the most widely used of the three types of linear perspective. Unlike one-point perspectives, two-point perspectives tend to be neither symmetrical nor static. A two-point perspective is particularly effective in illustrating the three-dimensional form of objects in space ranging in scale from a chair to the massing of a building.

- The pictorial effect of a two-point perspective varies with the spectator's angle of view. The orientation of the two horizontal axes to PP determines how much we will see of the two major sets of vertical planes and the degree to which they are foreshortened in perspective.
- In depicting a spatial volume, such as the interior of a room or an exterior courtyard or street, a two-point perspective is most effective when the angle of view approaches that of a one-point perspective.

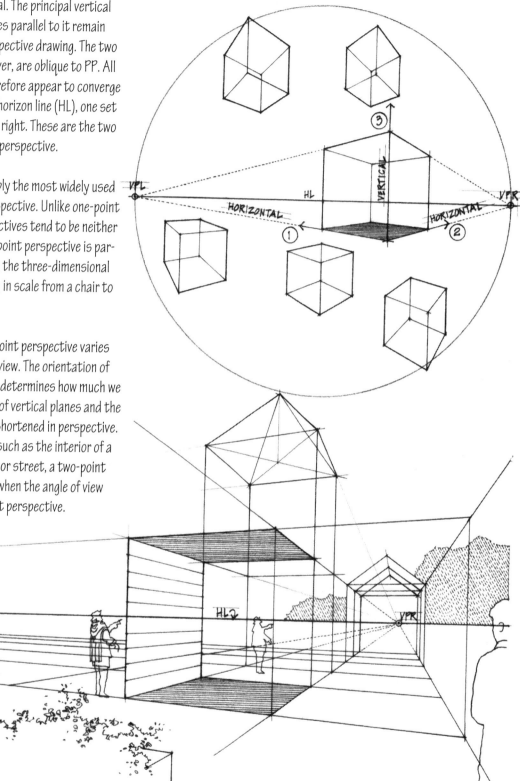

The following is a method for constructing a two-point perspective grid utilizing measuring points. As with the construction of a one-point perspective, you should first establish the observer's point of view. Determine what you wish to illustrate. Look toward the most significant areas and try to visualize from your plan drawing what will be seen in the foreground, middleground, and background. Review the perspective variables on pages 109–114.

Plan Setup

- At a convenient scale, construct a plan diagram of the perspective setup to determine the desired angle of view.
- Lay out the major baselines of the space.

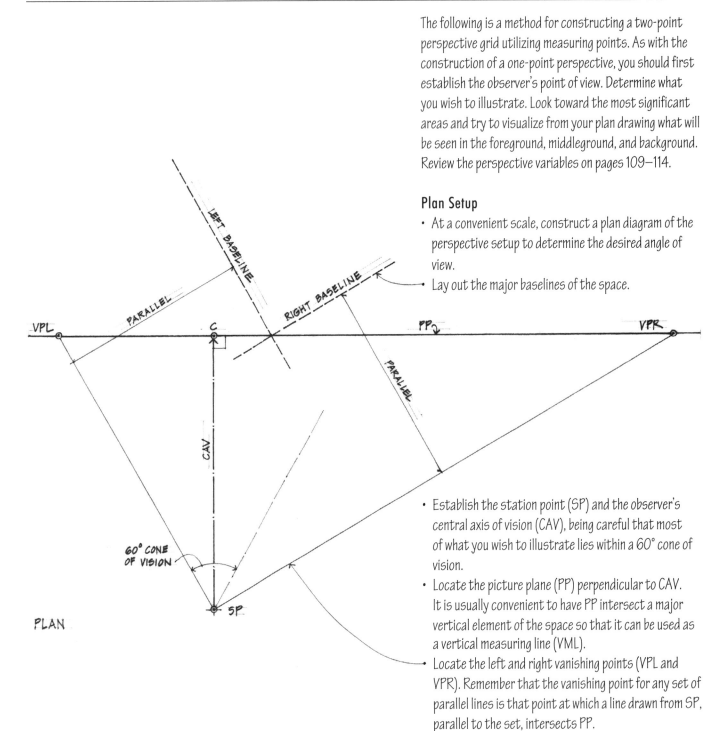

PLAN

- Establish the station point (SP) and the observer's central axis of vision (CAV), being careful that most of what you wish to illustrate lies within a 60° cone of vision.
- Locate the picture plane (PP) perpendicular to CAV. It is usually convenient to have PP intersect a major vertical element of the space so that it can be used as a vertical measuring line (VML).
- Locate the left and right vanishing points (VPL and VPR). Remember that the vanishing point for any set of parallel lines is that point at which a line drawn from SP, parallel to the set, intersects PP.

Measuring Points

A measuring point (MP) is a vanishing point for a set of parallel lines used to transfer true dimensions along a measuring line (ML) to a line receding in perspective. The diagonal point in one-point perspective is one example of such a measuring point.

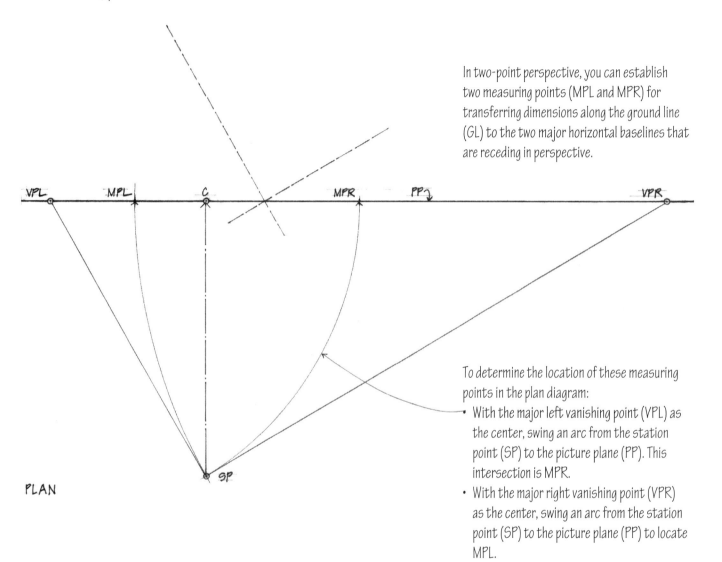

PLAN

In two-point perspective, you can establish two measuring points (MPL and MPR) for transferring dimensions along the ground line (GL) to the two major horizontal baselines that are receding in perspective.

To determine the location of these measuring points in the plan diagram:

• With the major left vanishing point (VPL) as the center, swing an arc from the station point (SP) to the picture plane (PP). This intersection is MPR.

• With the major right vanishing point (VPR) as the center, swing an arc from the station point (SP) to the picture plane (PP) to locate MPL.

• Include vanishing points for secondary lines that might be useful in constructing your perspective. For example, if you have a series of parallel diagonals in your design, establish their vanishing point as well.

Constructing the Perspective Grid

- Draw the horizon line (HL) and ground line (GL) at any convenient scale. This scale need not be the same as the scale of the plan setup.
- At the same scale, transfer the positions of the major left and right vanishing points (VPL and VPR) and the left and right measuring points (MPL and MPR) from the plan setup.

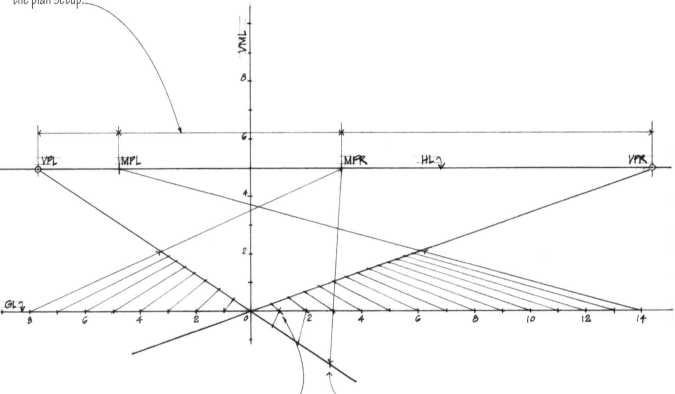

- Along GL, lay out equal increments of measurement to scale. The unit of measurement typically is one foot; we can use smaller or larger increments, however, depending on the scale of the drawing and the amount of detail desired in the perspective view.
- Establish the position of a vertical measuring line (VML) from the plan setup and lay out the same equal increments of measurement.
- From VPL and VPR draw baselines through the intersection of VML and GL.

- Transfer the units of measurements on GL to the left baseline in perspective by drawing lines to MPR. Transfer scale measurements on GL to the right baseline by drawing lines to MPL. These are construction lines used only to transfer scaled measurements along GL to the major horizontal baselines in perspective.

- A fractional measuring point can be used to reduce the length of measurements along GL. For example, you can use $1/2$ MPR to transfer a 5-foot measurement to a point 10 feet beyond the picture plane along the left baseline.

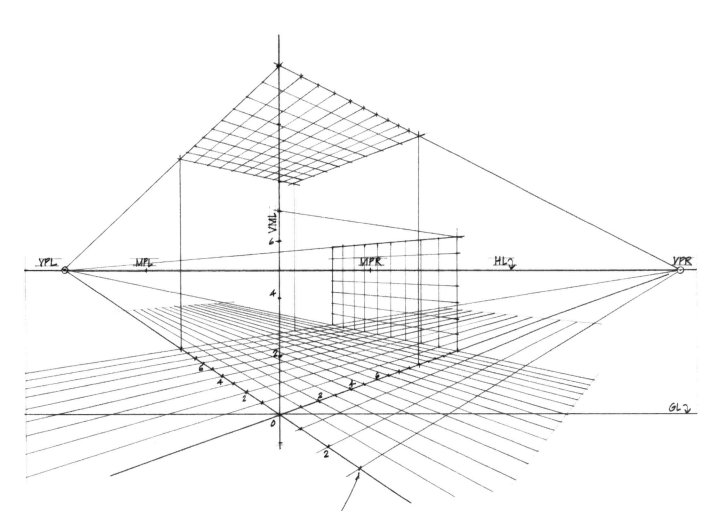

- From the major left and right vanishing points (VPL and VPR), draw lines through the transferred measurements along the major horizontal baselines in perspective.
- The result is a perspective grid of one-foot squares on the floor or ground plane. When one-foot squares become too small to draw accurately, use two-foot or four-foot squares instead.
- From VPL and VPR, draw lines through the scaled measurements along VML to establish a similar vertical grid.

- Over this perspective grid, you can lay tracing paper and draw a perspective view. It is important to see the perspective grid as a network of points and lines defining transparent planes in space rather than solid, opaque walls enclosing space. The grid of squares facilitates the plotting of points in three-dimensional space, regulates the perspective width, height, and depth of objects, and guides the drawing of lines in proper perspective.

Once constructed, a perspective grid should be saved and reused to draw perspective views of interior and exterior spaces of similar size and scale. Each unit of measurement can represent a foot, four feet, a hundred yards, or even a mile. Rotating and reversing the grid can also vary the point of view. Therefore, you can use the same grid to draw an interior perspective of a room, an exterior perspective of a courtyard, as well as an aerial view of a city block or neighborhood.

- To draw an object within a space, begin by laying out its plan or footprint on the grid of the ground or floor plane.
- Then elevate each of the corners to its perspective height using either a vertical grid or the known height of the horizon line (HL) above the ground line (GL).
- Complete the object by drawing its upper edges, using the principles of convergence and the grid lines to guide their direction.
- Remember to transfer all measurements only along axial lines.

- You can use the grid to plot inclined and curved lines as well.

- For circles in perspective, see page 137.
- For inclined lines in perspective, see pages 134–35.

These three perspectives use the perspective grid shown on the preceding page. In each case, however, the height of the observer's station point (SP) above the ground plane (GP) has been selected to portray a specific point of view, and the scale of the grid has been altered to suit the scale of the structure.

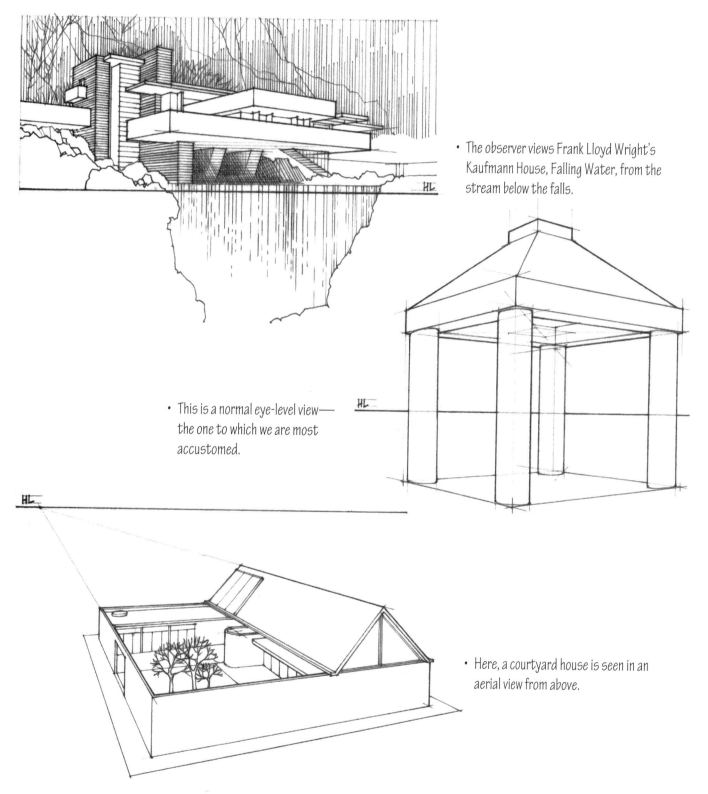

- The observer views Frank Lloyd Wright's Kaufmann House, Falling Water, from the stream below the falls.

- This is a normal eye-level view— the one to which we are most accustomed.

- Here, a courtyard house is seen in an aerial view from above.

This interior perspective also uses the grid shown on page 128. Note that the left vanishing point (VPL) lies within the drawing, enabling three sides of the space to be shown and a greater sense of enclosure to be felt. Because VPL lies within the drawing, greater emphasis is placed on the right-hand portion of the space. If the left-hand side of the space is to be emphasized, use a reverse image of the grid.

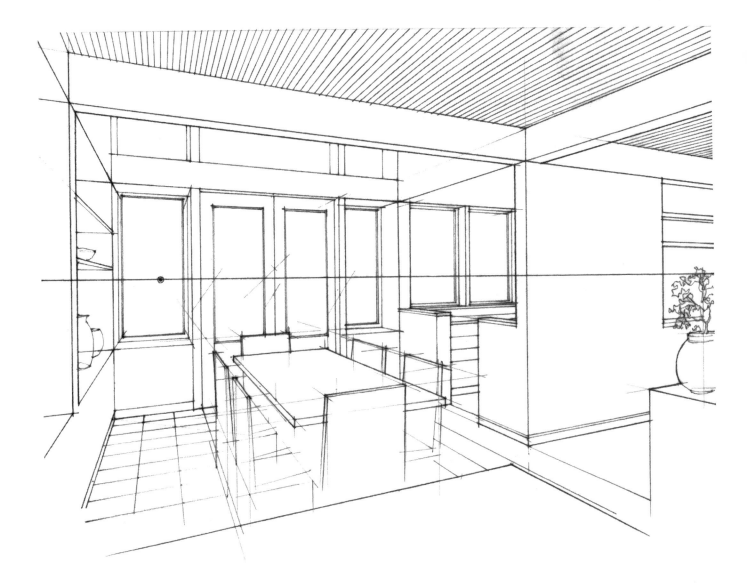

The combined effects of convergence and diminishing size make it more difficult to establish and draw measurements in linear perspective than in the other two drawing systems. But there are techniques we can use to determine the relative heights, widths, and depths of objects in the pictorial space of a perspective drawing.

Measuring Height and Width

In linear perspective, any line in the picture plane (PP) displays its true direction and true length at the scale of the picture plane. We can therefore use any such line as a measuring line (ML) to scale dimensions in a perspective drawing. While a measuring line may have any orientation in the picture plane, it typically is vertical or horizontal and used to measure true heights or widths. The ground line (GL) is one example of a horizontal measuring line.

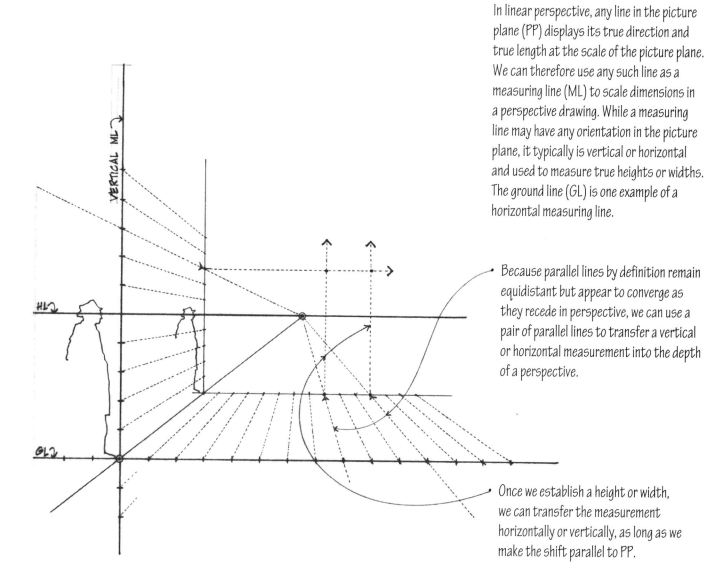

Because parallel lines by definition remain equidistant but appear to converge as they recede in perspective, we can use a pair of parallel lines to transfer a vertical or horizontal measurement into the depth of a perspective.

Once we establish a height or width, we can transfer the measurement horizontally or vertically, as long as we make the shift parallel to PP.

Digital Measurements

Perspective measurements are not a major issue in 3D-modeling programs because the software uses mathematical formulas to process the three-dimensional data we have already entered.

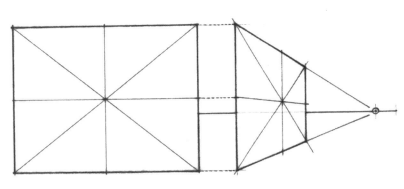

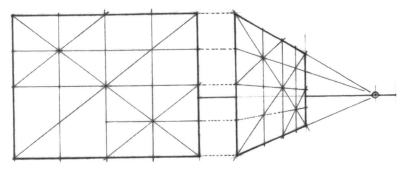

Measuring Depth

Measuring perspective depth is more difficult than gauging heights and widths in linear perspective. Various methods of perspective construction establish depth in different ways. Once we establish an initial depth judgment, however, we can make succeeding depth judgments in proportion to the first.

Subdividing Depth Measurements

There are two methods for subdividing depth measurements in linear perspective: the method of diagonals and the method of triangles.

Method of Diagonals

In any projection system, we can subdivide a rectangle into four equal parts by drawing two diagonals.

- For example, if we draw two diagonals across a rectangular plane in perspective, they will intersect at the geometric center of the plane. Lines drawn through this midpoint, parallel to the edges of the plane, will subdivide the rectangle and its receding sides into equal parts. We can repeat this procedure to subdivide a rectangle into any even number of parts.

To subdivide a rectangle into an odd number of equal parts, or to subdivide its receding edges into a series of unequal segments, its forward edge must be parallel to the picture plane (PP) so that it can be used as a measuring line (ML).

- On the forward edge of the rectangle, we mark off the same proportional subdivisions to be made in the depth of the perspective.
- From each of the marked points, we draw parallel lines that converge at the same point as the receding edges of the plane.
- Then we draw a single diagonal.
- At each point where this diagonal crosses the series of receding lines, we draw lines parallel to the forward edge. These mark off the desired spaces, which diminish as they recede in perspective.
- If the rectangle is a square, then the subdivisions are equal; otherwise, the segments are proportional but not equal.

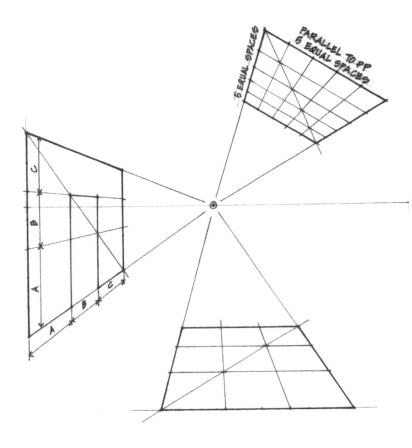

Method of Triangles

Because any line parallel to the picture plane (PP) can be subdivided proportionately to scale, we can use such a parallel line as a measuring line (ML) to subdivide any intersecting line into equal or unequal parts.

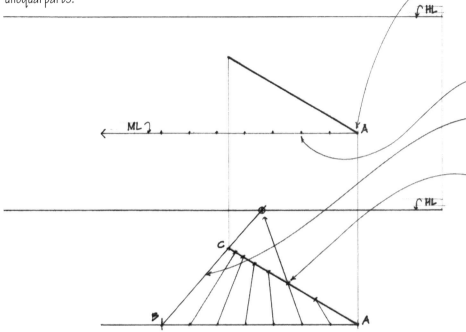

- From one end (A) of the receding line to be subdivided, we draw a measuring line (ML) parallel to PP. If the receding line is horizontal in space, then ML will be a horizontal line in the drawing.
- At an appropriate scale, we mark off the desired subdivisions on ML.
- We define a triangle by connecting the end (B) of ML and the end (C) of the receding line.
- From each of the scaled subdivisions, we draw lines that are parallel to BC and therefore converge at the same vanishing point. These lines subdivide the receding line into the same proportional segments.

Extending a Depth Measurement

If the forward edge of a rectangular plane is parallel to the picture plane (PP), we can extend and duplicate its depth in perspective.

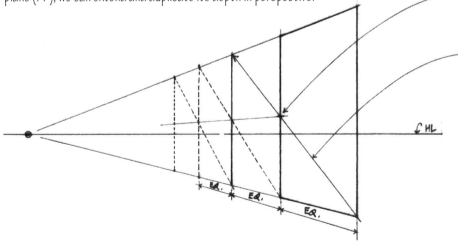

- First, we establish the midpoint of the rear edge opposite the forward edge of the rectangle.
- Then we extend a diagonal from a forward corner through this midpoint to meet an extended side of the rectangle.
- From this point, we draw a line parallel to the forward edge. The distance from the first to the second edge is identical to the distance from the second to the third edge, but the equal spaces are foreshortened in perspective.
- We can repeat this procedure as often as necessary to produce the desired number of equal spaces in the depth of a perspective drawing.

- Note that it is usually better to subdivide a larger measurement into equal parts than it is to multiply a smaller measurement to arrive at a larger whole. The reason for this is that, in the latter procedure, even minute errors can accumulate and become visible in the overall measurement.

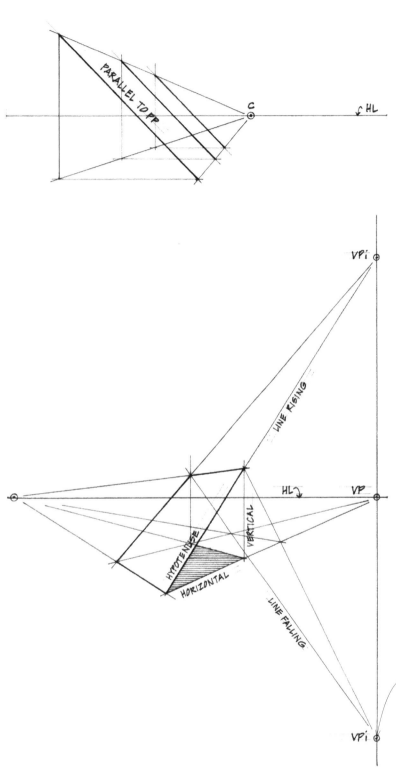

Once we are familiar with how lines parallel to the three principal axes of an object converge in linear perspective, we can use this rectilinear geometry as the basis for drawing perspective views of inclined lines, circles, and irregular shapes.

- Inclined lines parallel to the picture plane (PP) retain their orientation but diminish in size according to their distance from the spectator. If perpendicular or oblique to PP, however, an inclined set of lines will appear to converge at a vanishing point above or below the horizon line (HL).

- We can draw any inclined line in perspective by first finding the perspective projections of its end points and then connecting them. The easiest way to do this is to visualize the inclined line as being the hypotenuse of a right triangle. If we can draw the sides of the triangle in proper perspective, we can connect the end points to establish the inclined line.

- If we must draw a number of inclined parallel lines, as in the case of a sloping roof, a ramp, or a stairway, it is useful to know where the inclined set appears to converge in perspective. An inclined set of parallel lines is not horizontal and therefore will not converge on HL. If the set rises upward as it recedes, its vanishing point will be above HL; if it falls as it recedes, it will appear to converge below HL.

- An expedient method for determining the vanishing point for an inclined set of lines (VPi) is to extend one of the inclined lines until it intersects a vertical line drawn through the vanishing point (VP) for a horizontal line lying in the same vertical plane. This intersection is the vanishing point (VPi) for the inclined line and all other lines parallel to it.

A more precise method for determining the vanishing point for an inclined set of parallel lines is as follows:

- In the plan view of the perspective setup, we determine the vanishing point (VP) for a horizontal line in the same vertical plane as one of the inclined lines.
- With VP as the center, we swing an arc from the station point (SP) to the picture plane (PP). Mark this point A.
- In the perspective view, we mark point A along the horizon line (HL).

- A vanishing trace (VT) is a line along which all sets of parallel lines within a plane will appear to converge in linear perspective. The horizon line, for example, is the vanishing trace along which all horizontal sets of parallel lines converge.
- We establish a vertical vanishing trace (VT) through VP. This is the vanishing trace for the vertical plane containing the inclined set of parallel lines.
- From point A, we draw a line at the true slope (α) of the inclined set.
- The point at which this line intersects VT is the vanishing point (VPi) for the inclined set of parallel lines.

- The steeper the inclined set of parallel lines, the farther up or down on its vanishing trace (VT) will be its vanishing point (VPi).
- Note that if an inclined set of parallel lines rises upward and another set in the same vertical plane falls at the same but opposite angle to the horizontal, the distances of their respective vanishing points (VPi[1] and VPi[2]) above and below the horizon line (HL) are equal.

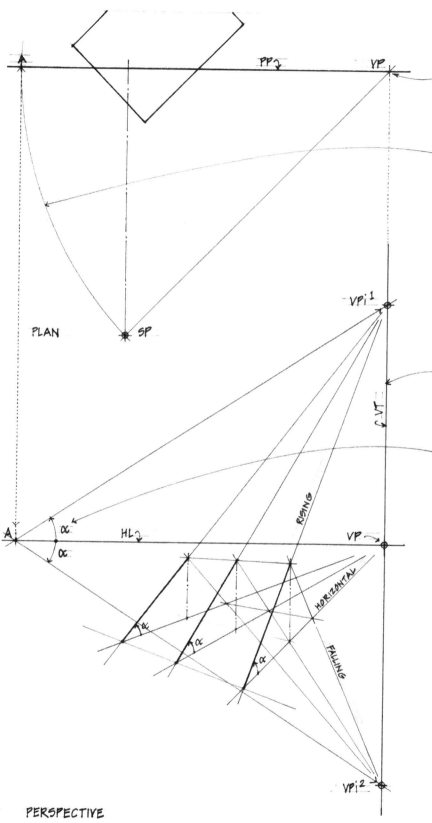

PLAN

SP

A

α

α

HL

VP

VPi[1]

VT

RISING

HORIZONTAL

FALLING

α

α

α

VPi[2]

PP

VP

PERSPECTIVE

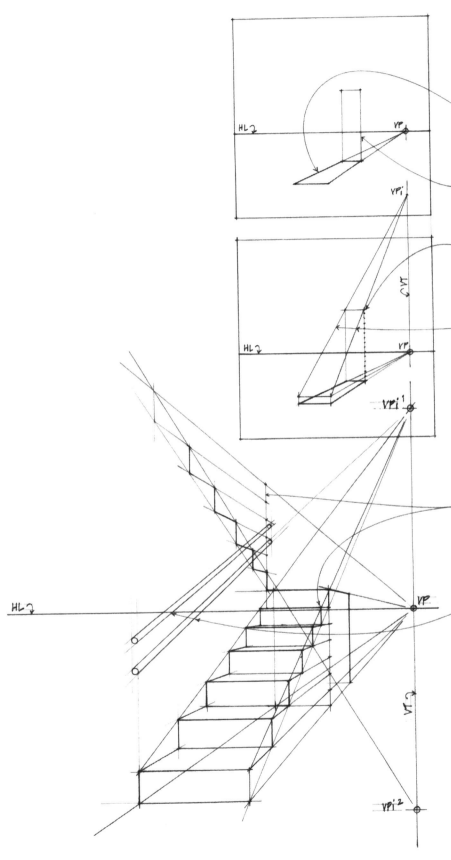

Drawing stairs in perspective is easiest when we can determine the vanishing point for the inclined lines that connect the stair nosings.

• We first lay out the perspective view of the horizontal stair run on the floor plane. We are not concerned yet with the individual treads of the stairway.
• We then extend a vertical plane to the height of the stair landing or next floor level.
• Next we divide one side of this plane into the number of equal risers in the stair run.
• We can determine the height of the first riser in perspective.
• We draw an inclined line from the top of the first riser to the top of the landing or upper floor level.

• This inclined line is subdivided by extending horizontal lines from the riser markings.
• From these points, we draw the risers and treads as vertical and horizontal planes in perspective.
• We can use the vanishing points for inclined lines to draw other elements parallel to the inclined lines, such as stair stringers and railings.

The circle is the essential basis for drawing cylindrical objects, arches, and other circular forms.

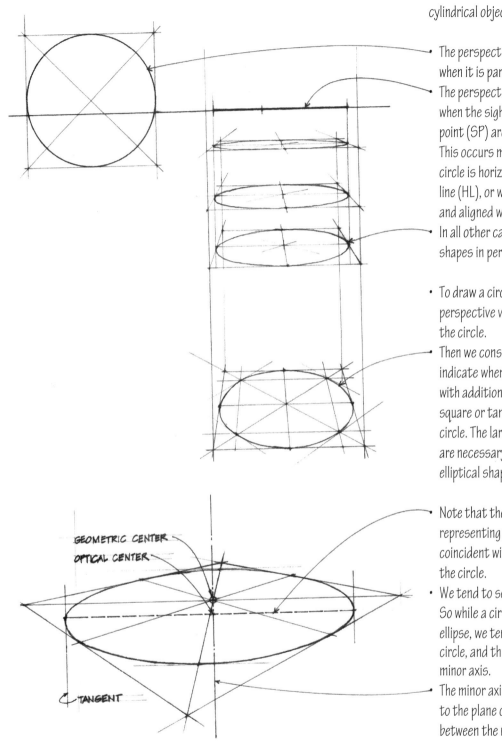

- The perspective view of a circle remains a circle when it is parallel to the picture plane (PP).
- The perspective view of a circle is a straight line when the sightlines radiating from the station point (SP) are parallel to the plane of the circle. This occurs most frequently when the plane of the circle is horizontal and at the height of the horizon line (HL), or when the plane of the circle is vertical and aligned with the central axis of vision (CAV).
- In all other cases, circles appear as elliptical shapes in perspective.

- To draw a circle in perspective, we first draw a perspective view of a square that circumscribes the circle.
- Then we construct the diagonals of the square and indicate where the circle crosses the diagonals with additional lines parallel to the sides of the square or tangent to the circumference of the circle. The larger the circle, the more subdivisions are necessary to ensure smoothness of the elliptical shape.

GEOMETRIC CENTER
OPTICAL CENTER

TANGENT

- Note that the major axis of the ellipse representing the circle in perspective is not coincident with the geometric diameter of the circle.
- We tend to see things as we believe them to be. So while a circle in perspective appears to be an ellipse, we tend to see it in the mind's eye as a circle, and thus exaggerate the length of its minor axis.
- The minor axis should appear to be perpendicular to the plane of the circle. Checking the relationship between the major and minor axes of elliptical shapes helps to ensure accuracy of the foreshortening of circles in perspective.

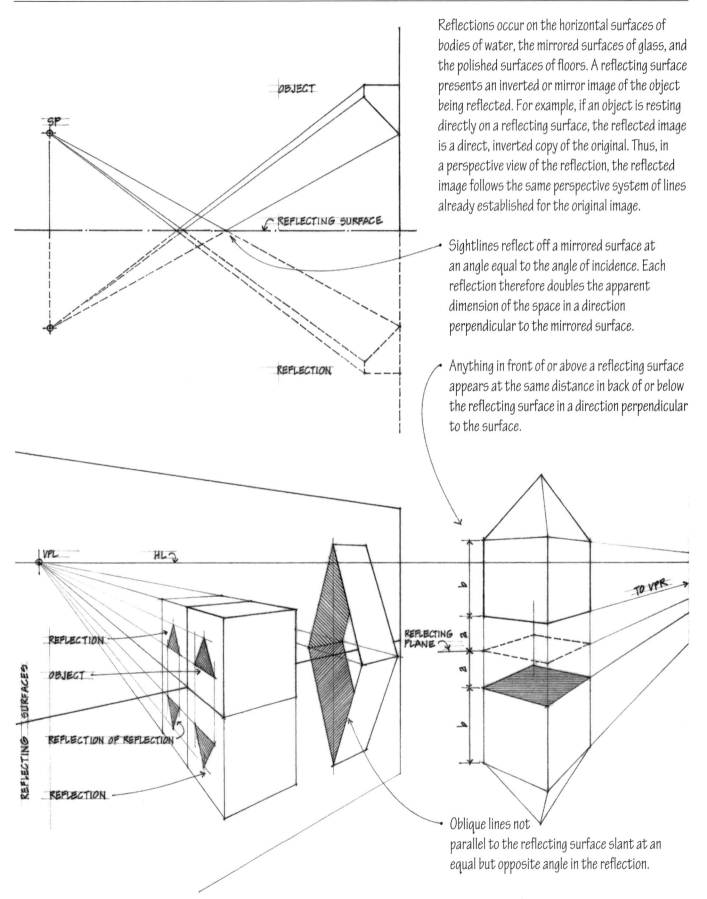

Reflections occur on the horizontal surfaces of bodies of water, the mirrored surfaces of glass, and the polished surfaces of floors. A reflecting surface presents an inverted or mirror image of the object being reflected. For example, if an object is resting directly on a reflecting surface, the reflected image is a direct, inverted copy of the original. Thus, in a perspective view of the reflection, the reflected image follows the same perspective system of lines already established for the original image.

Sightlines reflect off a mirrored surface at an angle equal to the angle of incidence. Each reflection therefore doubles the apparent dimension of the space in a direction perpendicular to the mirrored surface.

Anything in front of or above a reflecting surface appears at the same distance in back of or below the reflecting surface in a direction perpendicular to the surface.

Oblique lines not parallel to the reflecting surface slant at an equal but opposite angle in the reflection.

SP

OBJECT

REFLECTING SURFACE

REFLECTION

VPL

HL

TO VPR

REFLECTION

OBJECT

REFLECTION OF REFLECTION

REFLECTION

REFLECTING SURFACES

REFLECTING PLANE

Any reflecting planar surface parallel to one of the three major axes extends the perspective system of the subject. Therefore, the major sets of parallel lines in the reflection appear to converge to the same vanishing points as do the corresponding sets of lines in the subject.

When the subject is in front of or above a reflecting surface, first reflect its distance to the reflecting surface, then draw its mirror image. The plane of the reflecting surface should appear to be halfway between the subject and its reflected image. For example, the waterline establishes the horizontal reflecting plane. Point o lies in this plane. Therefore, oa = oa' and ab = a'b'.

Reflections of lines perpendicular to the reflecting surface extend the original lines.

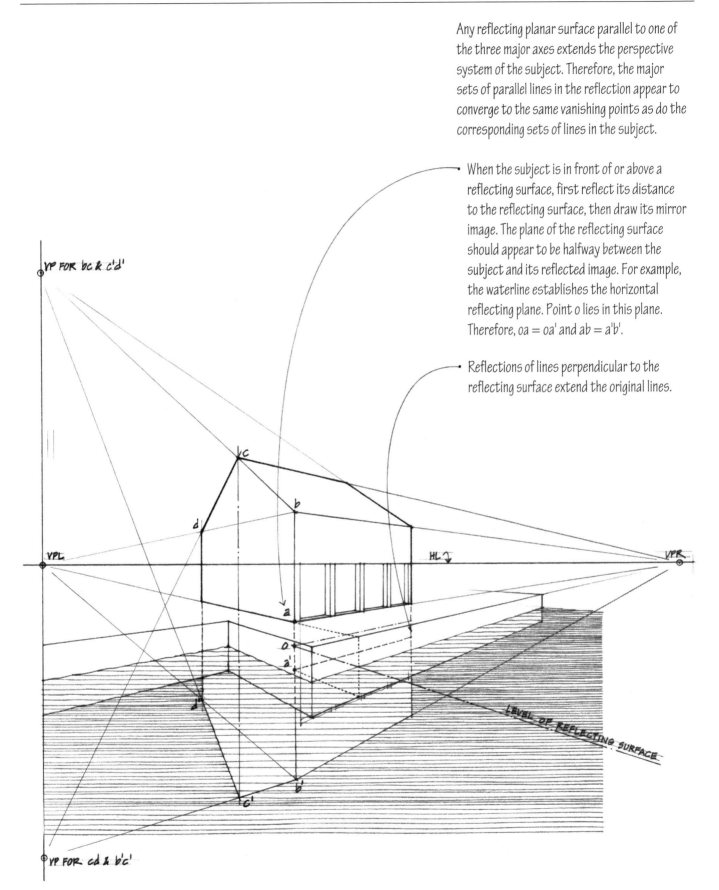

When drawing a perspective of an interior space having a mirrored surface on one or more of its major planes, we extend the perspective system in the manner described on the previous page.

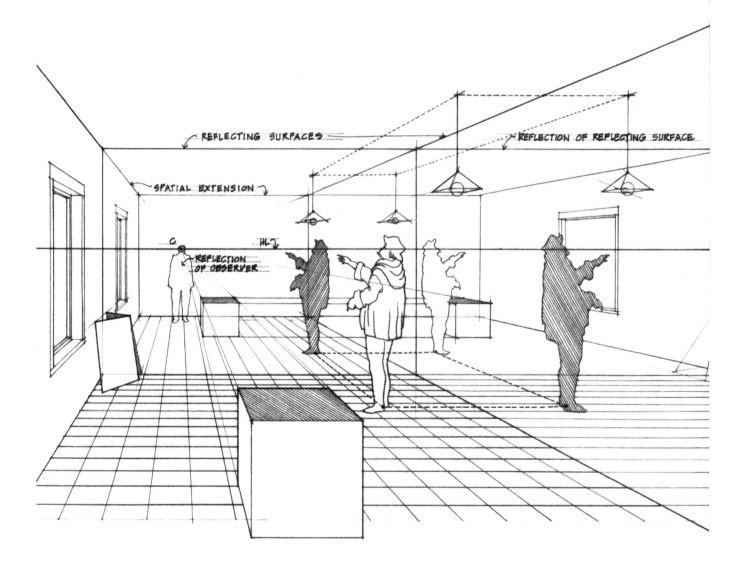

REFLECTING SURFACES

REFLECTION OF REFLECTING SURFACE

SPATIAL EXTENSION

C

HL

REFLECTION OF OBSERVER

7
Rendering Tonal Values

This chapter focuses on the principles that regulate how well a composition of lines and shapes conveys the illusion of a three-dimensional construction or spatial environment on a two-dimensional surface, be it a sheet of paper, an illustration board, or a computer monitor. While lines are essential to the task of delineating contour and shape, there are also visual qualities of light, texture, mass, and space that cannot be fully described by line alone. In order to model the surfaces of forms and convey a sense of light, we rely on the rendering of tonal values.

Vision results from the stimulation of nerve cells in the retina of the eye, signaling patterns of light intensity and color. Our visual system processes these patterns of light and dark, and is able to extract specific features of our environment—edges, contours, size, movement, and color. If seeing patterns of light and dark is essential to our perception of objects, then establishing contrasts in value discernible to the eye is the key to the graphic definition of light, form, and space.

Through the interplay of tonal values we are able to:

• Describe how light reveals the form of objects.

• Clarify the arrangements of forms in space.

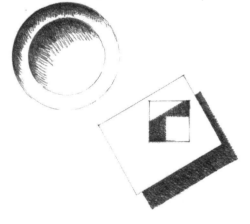

• Depict the color and texture of surfaces.

Using the traditional media of pencil and pen-and-ink to make dark marks on a light surface, there are several basic techniques for creating tonal values.

- Hatching
- Crosshatching
- Scribbling
- Stippling

These shading techniques all require a gradual building up or layering of strokes or dots. The visual effect of each technique varies according to the nature of the stroke, the medium, and the texture of the drawing surface. Regardless of the shading technique we use, we must always be fully aware of the tonal value being depicted.

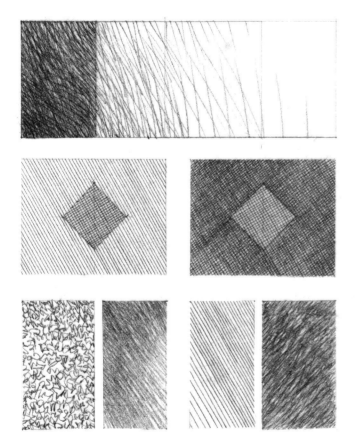

- Because tonal value is expressed primarily through the relative proportion of light to dark areas on the drawing surface, the most important characteristic of these techniques is the spacing and density of the strokes or dots.

- The law of simultaneous contrast states that the stimulation of one tonal value is projected instantaneously on a juxtaposed value. For example, a tonal value superimposed upon a darker tone will appear lighter than the same value set against a lighter tone.

- Secondary characteristics include the visual texture, grain, and direction of the strokes.
- When rendering the darkest values, we should be careful not to lose the white of the paper. Covering the paper surface entirely can cause a drawing to lose depth and vitality.

Hatching

Hatching consists of a series of more or less parallel lines. The strokes may be long or short, mechanically ruled or drawn freehand, and executed with either a pen or a pencil on smooth or rough paper. When spaced close enough together, the lines lose their individuality and merge to form a tonal value. We therefore rely primarily on the spacing and density of lines to control the lightness or darkness of a value. While thickening the linear strokes can serve to deepen the darkest values, using too thick of a line can result in an unintentional coarseness and heaviness of texture.

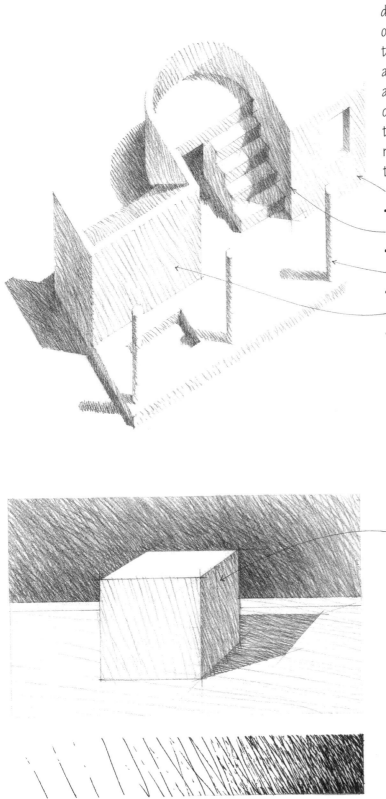

- The most flexible freehand technique for hatching utilizes relatively short diagonal strokes.
- To define a precise edge, fix the beginning of each stroke with slight pressure.
- Feather the ends of the strokes to depict curved surfaces, a texture gradient, or subtleties of light and shade.
- When extending a tonal value over a large area, avoid the effect of banding by softening the edges and overlapping each set of strokes in a random manner.
- By applying additional layers of diagonal strokes at only slightly different angles to the preceding sets, we can build up the density, and therefore the tonal value, of an area. Maintaining the diagonal direction of the strokes in this manner avoids confusion with the underlying drawing and unifies the various tonal areas of a drawing composition.

- The direction of hatching can also follow the contours of a form and emphasize the orientation of its surfaces. Remember that direction alone, however, has no impact on tonal value. With texture and contour, the series of lines can also convey material characteristics, such as the grain of wood, the marbling of stone, or the weave of fabric.

- Do not attempt to produce a range of values by varying the grade of lead. Be careful not to use too dense a grade of lead or press so hard that the pencil point embosses the drawing surface.
- Unlike a pencil line, the tonal value of an ink line remains constant. You can only control the spacing and density of the hatching.

Crosshatching

Crosshatching utilizes two or more series of parallel lines to create tonal values. As with hatching, the strokes may be long or short, mechanically ruled or drawn freehand, and executed with either a pen or a pencil on smooth or rough paper.

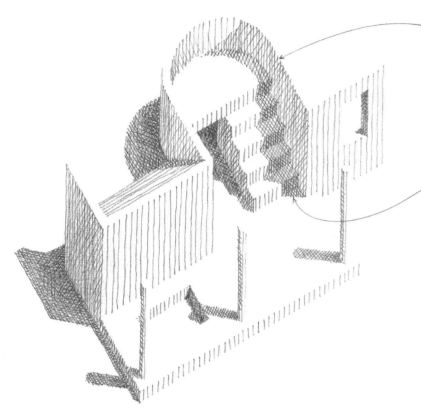

• The simplest crosshatching consists of two intersecting sets of parallel lines.
• While the resulting weave may be appropriate for describing certain textures and materials, the pattern can also produce a stiff, sterile, and mechanical feeling, especially when the lines are ruled and widely spaced.

Using three or more sets or layers of hatching provides more flexibility in generating a greater range of tonal values and surface textures. The multidirectional nature of the hatching also makes it easier describe the orientation and curvature of surfaces.

• In practice, hatching and crosshatching are often combined into a single technique. While simple hatching creates the lighter range of values in a drawing, crosshatching renders the darker range.

Scribbling

Scribbling is a shading technique that involves drawing a network of random, multidirectional lines. The freehand nature of scribbling gives us great flexibility in describing tonal values and textures. We can vary the shape, density, and direction of the strokes to achieve a wide range of tonal values, textures, and visual expression.

The strokes may be broken or continuous, relatively straight or curvilinear, jagged or softly undulating.

By interweaving the strokes, we create a more cohesive structure of tonal value.

• By maintaining a dominant direction, we produce a grain that unifies the various areas and shades of value.

• As with hatching, we have to pay attention to both the scale and density of the strokes, and be aware of the qualities of surface texture, pattern, and material they convey.

Stippling

Stippling is a technique for shading by means of very fine dots. Applying stippling is a slow and time-consuming procedure that requires the utmost patience and care in controlling the size and spacing of the dots. The best results occur when using a fine-tipped ink pen on a smooth drawing surface.

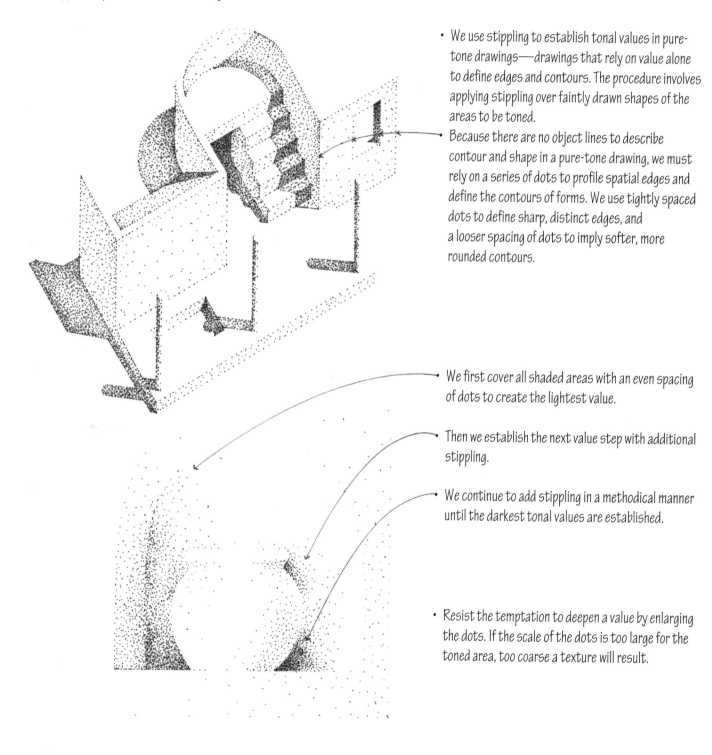

- We use stippling to establish tonal values in pure-tone drawings—drawings that rely on value alone to define edges and contours. The procedure involves applying stippling over faintly drawn shapes of the areas to be toned.
- Because there are no object lines to describe contour and shape in a pure-tone drawing, we must rely on a series of dots to profile spatial edges and define the contours of forms. We use tightly spaced dots to define sharp, distinct edges, and a looser spacing of dots to imply softer, more rounded contours.

We first cover all shaded areas with an even spacing of dots to create the lightest value.

Then we establish the next value step with additional stippling.

We continue to add stippling in a methodical manner until the darkest tonal values are established.

- Resist the temptation to deepen a value by enlarging the dots. If the scale of the dots is too large for the toned area, too coarse a texture will result.

Digital Tonal Values

2D drawing and 3D modeling programs usually permit colors and tonal values to be selected from a menu or palette and assigned to the surfaces of forms. Image-processing software further allows the creation and application of visual textures, some of which mimic the traditional techniques outlined on the previous pages.

Shown on this and the facing page are two digital examples using simple gray tones and gradients. The first illustrates a line-and-tone technique to model the forms.

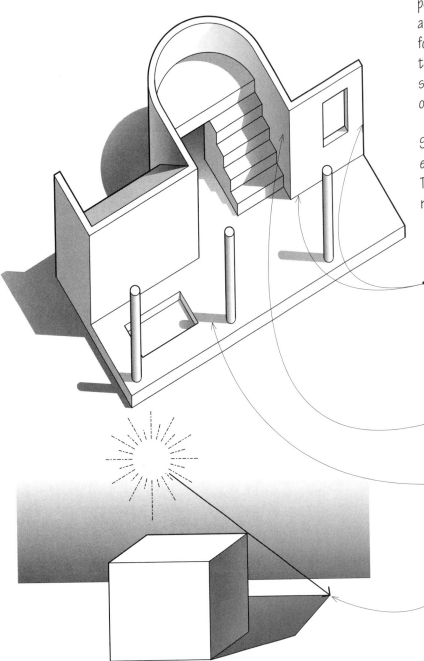

The use of lines to define planar corners and spatial edges lessens the need for the tonal values to model the forms. Instead, the range of tonal values serves primarily to define the orientation of the surfaces relative to an assumed light source.

Surfaces that face away from the assumed light source and are in shade receive one set of values.

Shadows cast by the forms receive a slightly darker set of values to maintain contrast along spatial edges.

See pages 164–178 for more information on casting shadows.

This example of a pure tone drawing relies primarily on the selection and arrangement of tonal values to model the three-dimensional qualities of forms.

• Because there are no lines in the drawing, we must rely on discernible contrasts in tonal value to define the planar corners and spatial edges of the forms.

• Sharply contrasting tonal values should occur along spatial edges to separate a form from its background, and along planar corners to define where a break in plane occurs.

• Curved surfaces require soft transitions from dark to light tonal values.

• Even where the corner or edge of a form is incomplete, our visual system is often able to complete the contour in its search for continuity, regularity, and stability.

• Because of the way light is reflected and refracted within a space, few surfaces have a consistent tonal value across their surface.

• A lighter area often occurs within an area of shade or shadow due to indirect, reflected illumination from adjacent or nearby surfaces.

White represents the lightest possible value and black the darkest. In between exists an intermediate range of grays. A familiar form of this range is represented by a value or gray scale having ten equal gradations from white to black. It is worthwhile to practice producing both a stepped series and a graduated scale of tonal values using a variety of media and techniques.

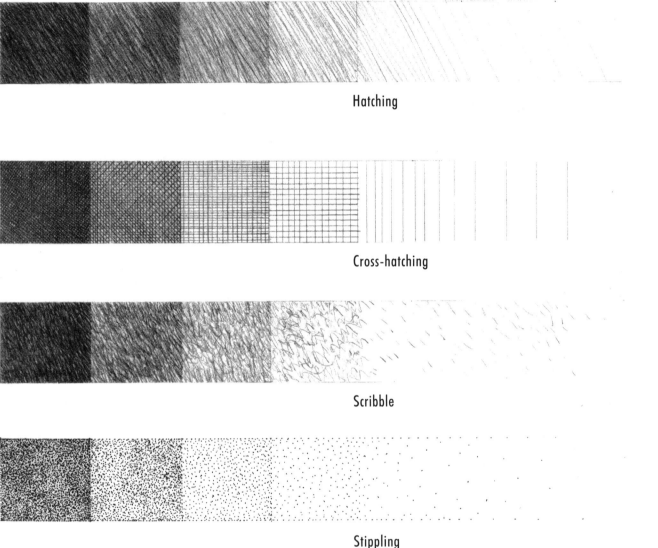

Hatching

Cross-hatching

Scribble

Stippling

- Note that a series of dots rather than a line defines the edge of the field.

- It is also possible to execute a gray scale on a tinted or colored surface, using a black pencil to define values darker than the tone of the surface and a white pencil to establish the lighter values.

We use the term "texture" most often to describe the relative smoothness or roughness of a surface. It can also describe the characteristic surface qualities of familiar materials, as the hewn appearance of stone, the grain of wood, and the weave of a fabric. This is tactile texture that can be felt by touch.

Our senses of sight and touch are closely intertwined. As our eyes read the visual texture of a surface, we often respond to its apparent tactile quality without actually touching it. We base these physical reactions on the textural qualities of similar materials we have experienced in the past.

• Whenever we use hatching or stippling to create a tonal value, we simultaneously create visual texture.

• Likewise, as soon as we begin to describe the nature of a material with lines, we simultaneously create a tonal value.

• We should always be aware of this relationship between tonal value and texture, whether smooth or rough, hard or soft, polished or dull. In most cases, tonal value is more critical than texture to the representation of light, shade, and the way they model forms in space.

"Modeling" refers to the technique of rendering the illusion of volume, solidity, and depth on a two-dimensional surface by means of shading. Shading with tonal values extends a simple drawing of contours into the three-dimensional realm of forms arranged in space.

Since the definition of edges gives rise to shape recognition, we look to edges to discover the configuration of the surfaces of a three-dimensional form. We must therefore be careful how we define the nature of the edge or boundary wherever two shapes of contrasting values meet. The skillful manipulation of tonal edges is critical to defining the nature and solidity of a surface or object.

- Hard edges delineate sharp, angular breaks in form or describe contours that are separated from the background by some intervening space. We define hard edges with an abrupt and incisive shift in tonal value.

- Soft edges describe indistinct or vague background shapes, gently curving surfaces and rounded forms, and areas of low contrast. We create soft edges with a gradual change in tonal value or diffuse tonal contrast.

While tonal values can imply depth on a flat drawing surface, we turn to light to more vividly describe the three-dimensional qualities of forms and spaces in our environment. Light is the radiant energy that illuminates our world and enables us to see three-dimensional forms in space. We do not actually see light but rather the effects of light. The way light falls on and is reflected from a surface creates areas of light, shade, and shadow, which give us perceptual clues to the surface's three-dimensional qualities.

The light-and-dark patterns we see emanate from the interaction of light with the objects and surfaces around us. Within these patterns of light and dark shapes, we can recognize the following elements:

- Light values occur on any surface turned toward the light source.

- Tonal values shift as a surface turns away from the light source, with intermediate values occurring on surfaces that are tangent to the direction of the light rays.

- Highlights appear as luminous spots on smooth surfaces that directly face or mirror the light source.

- Shade refers to the comparatively dark values of surfaces that are turned away from the light source.

- Shadows are the dark values cast by an object or part of an object upon a surface that would otherwise be illuminated by the light source.

- Areas of reflected light—light cast back from a nearby surface—lighten the tonal value of a portion of a shaded surface or a shadow.

- Tonal value is the graphic equivalent of shade and shadow, and can only indicate light by describing its absence.

Digital Lighting
A range of digital techniques exist for modeling and simulating the lighting of three-dimensional forms and spaces. The simplest approach is ray casting.

Ray Casting
Ray casting is a technique that analyzes the three-dimensional geometry of forms and determines the illumination and shading of surfaces based on their orientation to an assumed light source. The primary advantage of ray casting is the speed with which an illuminated three-dimensional image or scene can be generated, often in real-time. This makes ray casting a useful tool in preliminary design to study the solar consequences of the massing and composition of building forms and the shadows they cast. See pages 166–167 for examples.

Ray casting, however, does not take into account the way light travels after intersecting a surface and therefore cannot accurately render reflections, refractions, or the natural fall off of shadows. For this, ray tracing is necessary.

Basic shading model without lighting

Ray casting with direct light

Local illumination: ray tracing with direct and approximated ambient light

Ray Tracing

As a ray of light travels from its source to a surface that interrupts its progress, it may be absorbed, reflected, or refracted in one or more directions, depending on the material, color, and texture of the surface. Ray tracing is a digital technique for tracing these paths to simulate the optical effects of illumination.

Local illumination is a basic level of ray tracing that is limited to direct illumination and the specular reflections of light rays. While local illumination does not take into account the diffuse inter-reflection of light among the surfaces in a three-dimensional space or scene, some ray tracing programs can approximate this ambient light in their lighting algorithms.

Global illumination: ray tracing with direct and ambient light

A better predictor of how a space would be illuminated by any number of light sources is global illumination. Global illumination techniques use sophisticated algorithms to more accurately simulate the illumination of a space or scene. These algorithms take into account not only the light rays that are emitted directly from one or more sources. They also track the light rays as they are reflected or refracted from one surface to another, especially the diffuse inter-reflections that occur among the surfaces in a space or scene. This enhanced level of simulation comes at a cost, however. The process requires time and is computationally intensive, and should therefore be used only when appropriate to the design task at hand.

The drawings on this and the following ten pages illustrate how we can use tonal values to enhance spatial depth and focus attention in various types of architectural drawing.

- We use tonal values in site plan drawings to define the relationship between the form of a building and its spatial context. These two drawings of the Piazza San Marco in Venice illustrate how the tonal contrast can be achieved either by rendering the building as a dark figure against a light background or by reversing the figure-ground relationship and rendering the tonal values of the site.
- See also the site plans illustrated on pages 61 and 62.

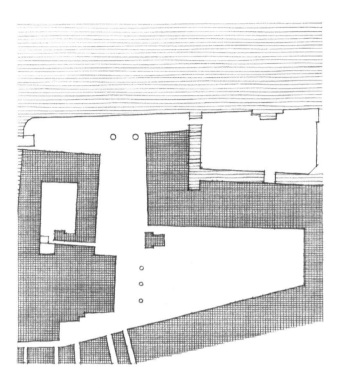

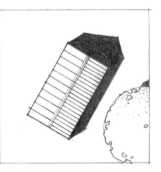

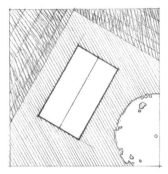

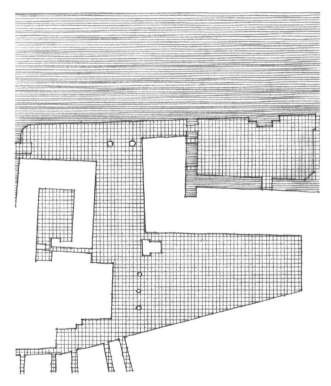

The principal use of tonal values in floor plans is to emphasize the shape and arrangement of cut elements.

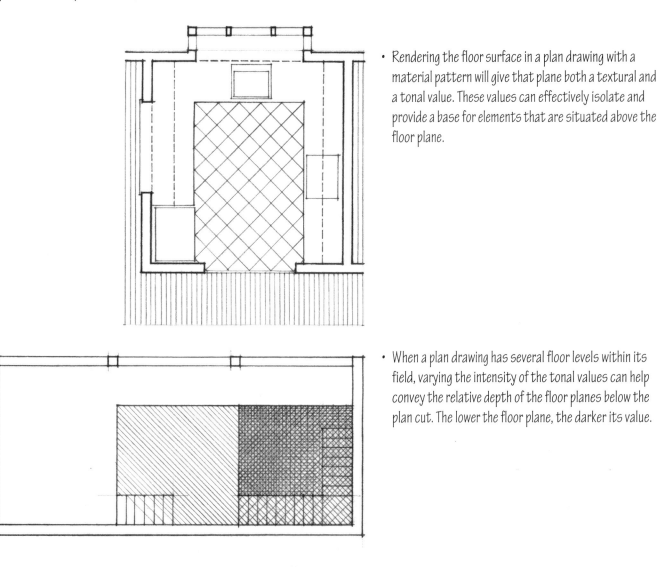

- Rendering the floor surface in a plan drawing with a material pattern will give that plane both a textural and a tonal value. These values can effectively isolate and provide a base for elements that are situated above the floor plane.

- When a plan drawing has several floor levels within its field, varying the intensity of the tonal values can help convey the relative depth of the floor planes below the plan cut. The lower the floor plane, the darker its value.

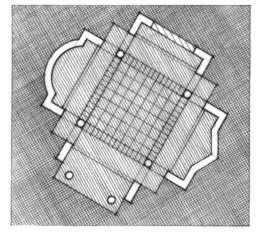

- If the space defined in a plan drawing is given a tonal value along with the surrounding field, the cut elements can be left white or be given a very light value. Be sure, however, that there is sufficient contrast to emphasize the dominance of the cut elements. If necessary, outline the cut elements with a heavy line weight.

- For more examples of how tonal values can be used in floor plans, see pages 49–51.

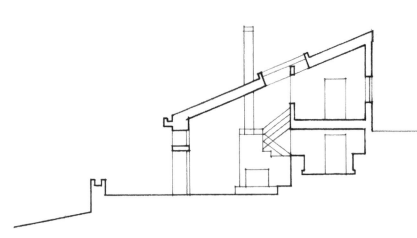

We use tonal values in section drawings to establish contrast between the cut elements and what is seen in elevation beyond the plane of the cut.

• The top drawing uses a heavy line weight to outline the cut elements.

• The center drawing projects the cut elements forward with a dark value.

• The bottom drawing reverses the value system and renders the cut elements as light figures against a dark field.

• Note that in the latter two cases, the relationship of the building to the supporting ground mass is clearly indicated by the manner in which the ground is given a value similar to that of the cut elements of the building.

• For more examples of how tonal values can be used in building sections, see pages 67–69.

We use contrasting tonal values in elevation drawings to define layers of spatial depth. The most important distinctions to establish are between the cut through the ground plane in front of the building elevation and the building itself, and between the building elevation and its background.

- First, contrasting values for the foreground and background are established.

- Elements are projected forward by having their tonal contrasts defined more sharply and by having their materials, textures, and details drawn more distinctly.

- Areas are pushed into the background by diminishing contrast and detail.

- See pages 164–170 for using shade and shadows to clarify the relative depth of projections and recesses within the massing of a building.

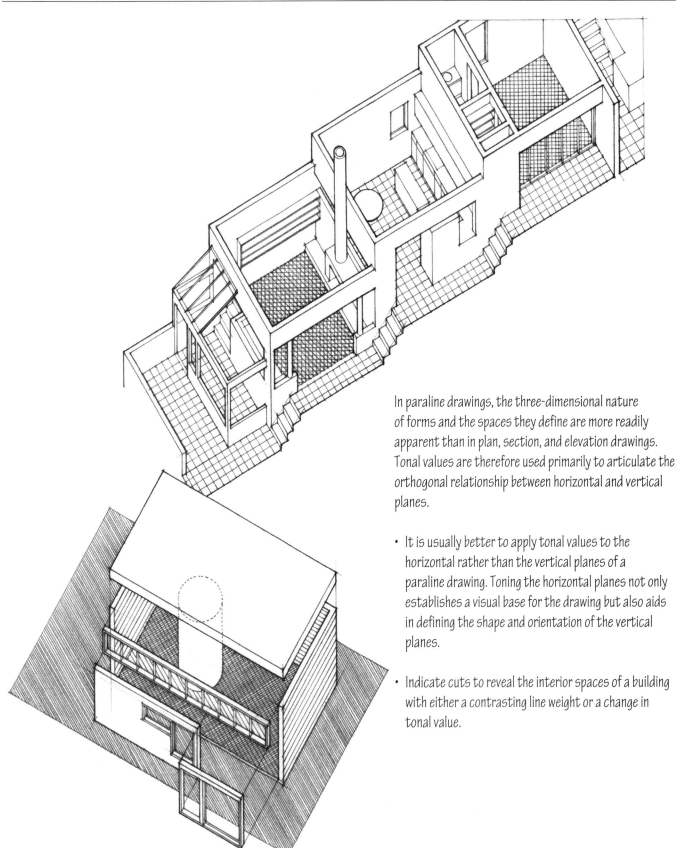

In paraline drawings, the three-dimensional nature of forms and the spaces they define are more readily apparent than in plan, section, and elevation drawings. Tonal values are therefore used primarily to articulate the orthogonal relationship between horizontal and vertical planes.

• It is usually better to apply tonal values to the horizontal rather than the vertical planes of a paraline drawing. Toning the horizontal planes not only establishes a visual base for the drawing but also aids in defining the shape and orientation of the vertical planes.

• Indicate cuts to reveal the interior spaces of a building with either a contrasting line weight or a change in tonal value.

In perspective drawings, we use tonal values to enhance spatial depth, define the drawing field, and develop focus.

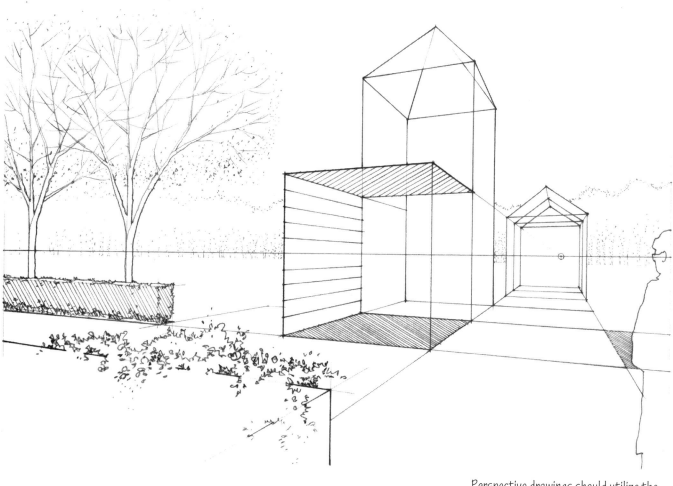

Perspective drawings should utilize the principles of atmospheric perspective to enhance the sense of spatial depth.

• Values are lightened and tonal contrasts are softened to push elements back.
• Values are darkened and tonal contrasts are sharpened to bring elements forward.

These exterior perspectives employ a value system similar to that used in elevation drawings.

- Above, the contour drawing of the building and foreground contrasts with the darker field of the background.
- In the drawing below, the building and foreground are rendered in some detail to contrast with a lighter, more diffuse background.

- Turn to page 122 to see how contrasting the cut elements of a section perspective helps to isolate and frame the space seen beyond in perspective.

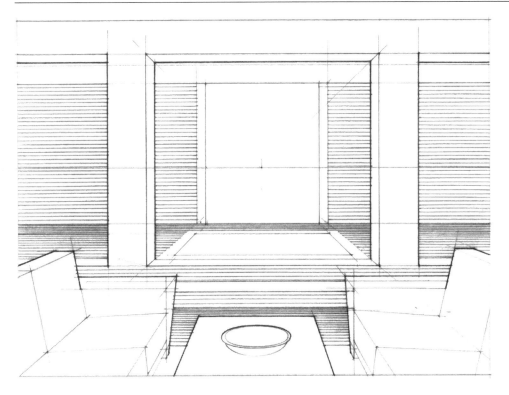

- The depth of the interior perspective above is enhanced by contrasting light foreground elements with a continuous darker wall in the background.

- In the drawing to the right, dark foreground elements help frame what is seen beyond.

Digital Rendering

Although improvements continue to be made, the rendering of atmospheric and texture perspective remains problematic in many graphics programs. Image-processing software, however, allows us to modify digital drawings and simulate the pictorial effects of atmospheric and texture perspective.

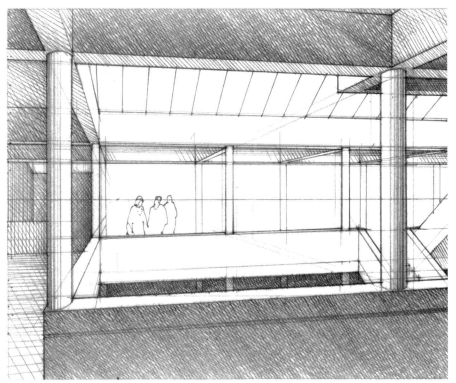

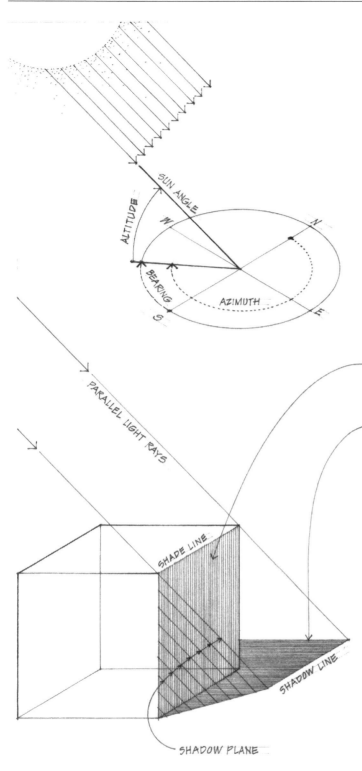

"Shade and shadows" refers to the technique of determining areas in shade and casting shadows on surfaces by means of projection drawing. The depiction of light, shade, and shadow can model the surfaces of a design, describe the disposition of its masses, and articulate the depth and character of its details.

- The light source for architectural shade and shadows is assumed to be the sun. The sun is so large and distant a source that its light rays are considered to be parallel.
- The sun angle is the direction of the sun's rays, measured in terms of either bearing or azimuth and altitude.
- Bearing is a horizontal angular direction expressed in degrees east or west of a standard north or south direction.
- Azimuth is a horizontal angular distance, measured clockwise, of a bearing from due north.
- Altitude is the angular elevation of the sun above the horizon.

Shade refers to the relatively dark area on those parts of a solid that are tangent to or turned away from a theoretical light source.

Shadows are the relatively dark figures cast upon a surface by an opaque body or part of a body intercepting the rays from a theoretical light source.

- A shade line or casting edge separates an illuminated surface from one in shade.
- A shadow line is the shadow cast by a shade line on a receiving surface.
- A shadow plane is a plane of light rays that passes through adjacent points of a straight line.

- Every part of an object in light must cast a shadow. The corollary to this is that any point that is not in light cannot cast a shadow because light does not strike it.
- A shadow is visible only when there is an illuminated surface to receive the shadow. A shadow can never be cast on a surface in shade, nor can it exist within another shadow.

Multiview Drawings

The casting of shade and shadows is especially useful to overcome the flatness of multiview drawings and enhance the illusion of depth. It generally requires two related views—either a plan and elevation or two related elevations—and the transferring of information back and forth from one view to the other.

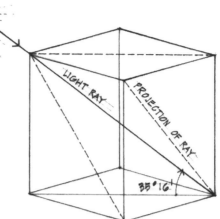

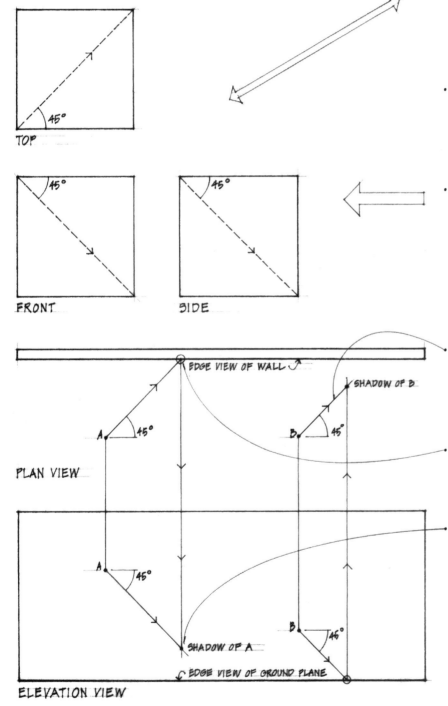

- In multiview drawings, we assume the conventional direction of sunlight to be parallel to the diagonal of a cube from the upper left front corner to the lower right rear corner.

- While the true altitude of this diagonal is 35° 16', in plan and elevation views, this direction is seen as the 45° diagonal of a square. This convention produces shadows of width or depth equal to the width or depth of the projections that cast the shadows.

The process of determining the shape of a cast shadow begins with drawing a 45° light ray through a point along the casting edge in both views.

In the view showing the edge view of the receiving surface, the ray is extended until it intersects the receiving surface.

- We project this intersection to the related view. The intersection of this transferred line with the ray in the adjacent view marks the shadow of the point.

Digital Shade and Shadows

While the drafting of architectural shade and shadows in multiview drawings assumes the conventional direction of sunlight to be the diagonal of a cube, 3D modeling software typically includes the ability to specify the direction of sunlight according to the hour of the day and the time of the year, and to cast shade and shadows automatically. This feature can be especially useful in the schematic design phase to study the form of a building or the massing of a building complex on a site and to evaluate the impact of the shadows they cast on adjacent buildings and outdoor areas.

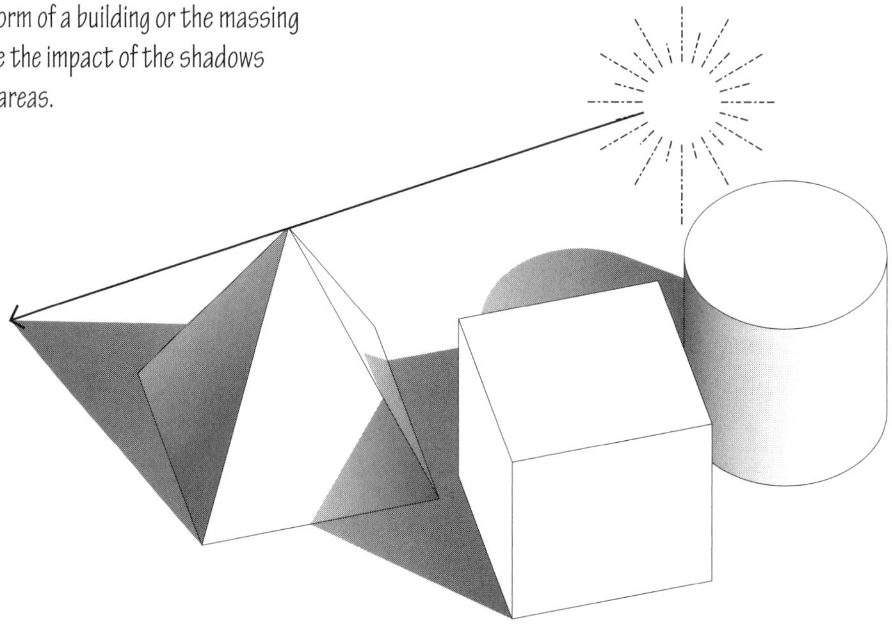

• Late spring morning

• Early spring morning

The digital technique for determining what surfaces are in shade and the shapes of the shadows cast in a three-dimensional image or scene is referred to as ray casting. While efficient and useful for preliminary design studies, ray casting does not take into account the way the light rays from an illuminating source are absorbed, reflected, or refracted by the surfaces of forms and spaces. For a visual comparison of digital lighting methods, see pages 154–155.

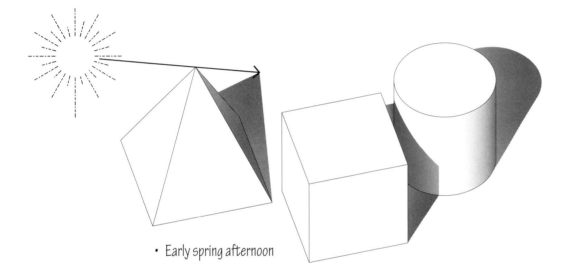

• Early spring afternoon

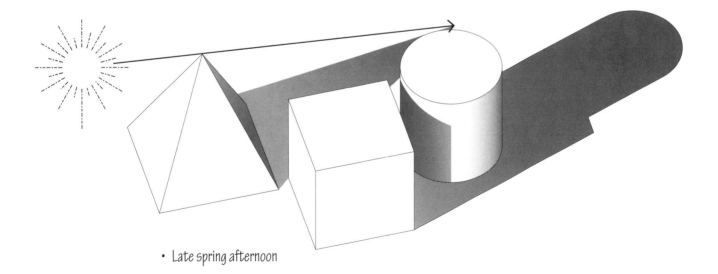

• Late spring afternoon

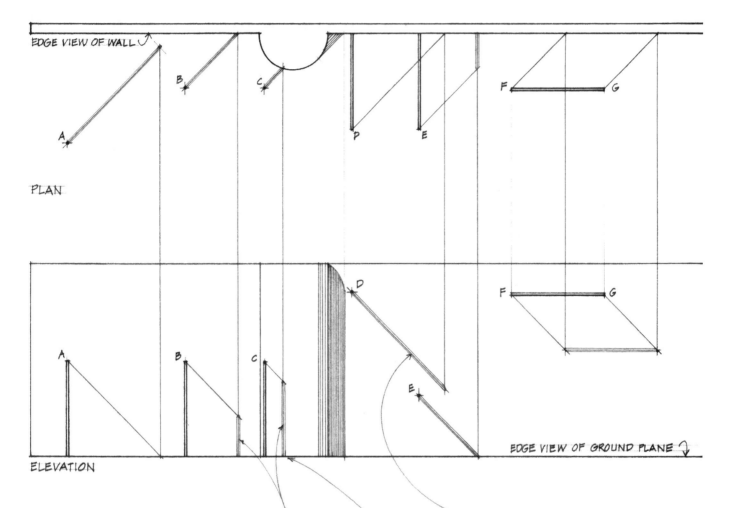

EDGE VIEW OF WALL

PLAN

A B C D E F G

ELEVATION

A B C D E F G

EDGE VIEW OF GROUND PLANE

• The shadow of a straight line is the intersection of its shadow plane with the surface receiving the shadow. The hypotenuse of the triangular shadow plane establishes the direction of the light rays, and its base describes their bearing.

The shadow of a straight line on a flat surface is the line that connects the shadows of its end points. If the line intersects the surface, its shadow must begin at that juncture.

A shadow line changes direction where it crosses a corner, edge, or other break in the continuity of a surface.

A straight line casts onto a parallel plane a shadow that is parallel to itself. This is also true when the line is parallel to the straight lines in a curved surface receiving the shadow.

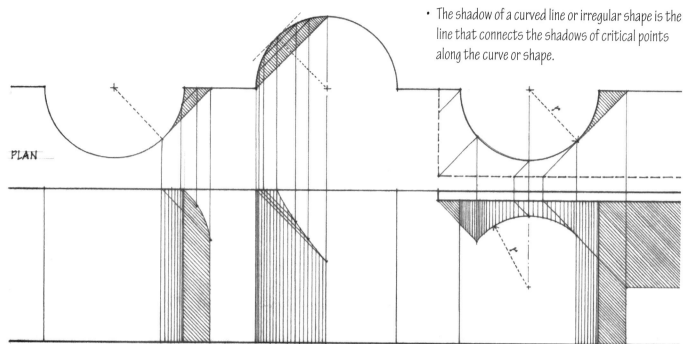

PLAN

ELEVATION

• The shadow of a curved line or irregular shape is the line that connects the shadows of critical points along the curve or shape.

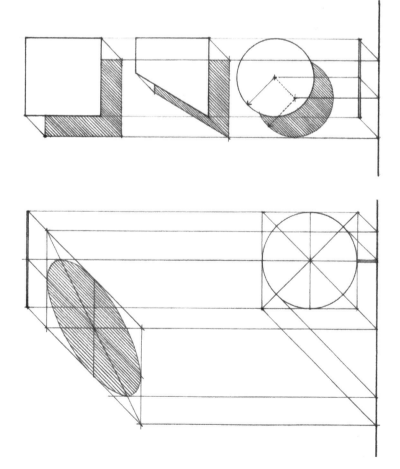

• The shadow of a plane figure on a parallel plane is identical in size and shape to the figure.

• The shadow of any polygonal figure on a plane is circumscribed by the shadows of its shade lines.
• The shadow of a circle is the intersection of the cylinder of light rays passing through adjacent points of the circle and the surface receiving the shadow. The shape of the shadow is elliptical since the section of a cylinder cut by any plane oblique to its axis is an ellipse. The most convenient method of determining the shadow of a circle is to determine the shadow of the square or octagon circumscribing the given circle, and then to inscribe within it the elliptical shadow of the circle.

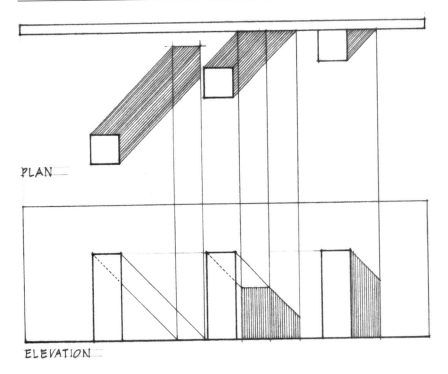

PLAN

ELEVATION

- The shadow cast by a solid is bound by the shadows of the shade lines of the object. It is usually best to begin by determining the shadows of significant points in the form, such as the end points of straight lines and the tangent points of curves.

- Note that shadows of parallel lines are parallel when they fall on the same plane or on parallel planes.
- The orthographic projection of a straight line perpendicular to the plane of projection is a point. The shadow of the line will appear to be straight regardless of the shape of the surface receiving the shadow.

In clarifying the relative depth of projections, overhangs, and recesses within the massing of a building, shade and shadows can also model the relief and texture of surfaces.

- Most often simply use a flat or slightly textured field of gray to indicate shade and shadows.
- An alternate method is to intensify the texture or pattern of a material so that we do not lose a sense of the material that is in shade or receiving the shadow.

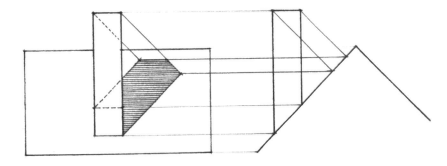

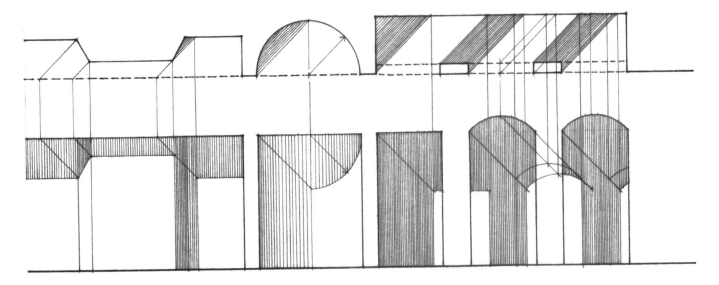

We use shade and shadows in site plans to convey the relative heights of building masses as well as to reveal the topographical nature of the ground plane on which the shadows are cast.

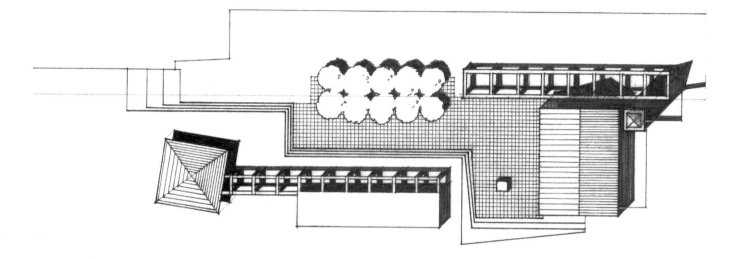

- The intent of cast shadows is not to render the actual condition of sunlight at a specific point in time. Rather, they merely indicate the relative heights of the parts of a building above the ground plane.
- A change in shadow depth can indicate either an increase in building height or a rise in the ground slope.

- Shade and shadows are not usually employed in floor plans and building sections. However, they may be used to emphasize the cut elements and the relative heights of objects within the space.
- In a building section, shadows clarify the projection of cut elements beyond surfaces seen in elevation.

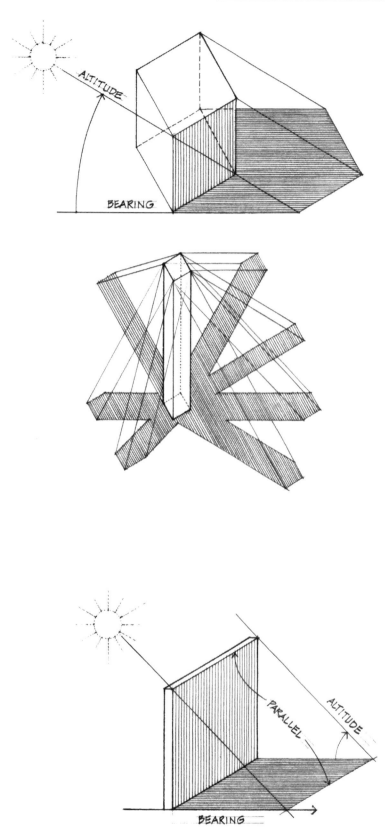

Paraline Views

Shade and shadows are not often used in paraline drawings. However, they can be used effectively to distinguish between horizontal and vertical elements, and the three-dimensional nature of their forms.

- It is relatively easy to visualize the three-dimensional relationships between light rays, shade lines, and cast shadows in paraline views because they are pictorial in nature and display the three major spatial axes simultaneously.
- Parallel light rays and their bearing directions remain parallel in a paraline drawing.

To construct shade and shadows in a paraline drawing, it is necessary to assume a source and direction of light. Deciding on a direction of light is a problem in composition as well as communication. It is important to remember that cast shadows should clarify rather than confuse the nature of forms and their spatial relationships.

There are occasions when it may be desirable to determine the actual conditions of light, shade, and shadow. For example, when studying the effects of solar radiation and shadow patterns on thermal comfort and energy conservation, it is necessary to construct shades and shadows using the actual sun angles for specific times and dates of the year.

- For ease of construction, the bearing direction of the light rays is often parallel with the picture plane, and they emanate from either the left or the right.
- Consequently, the altitude of the light rays appears true in the drawing, and their bearing direction remains horizontal.
- While the desired depth of shadows should determine the altitude of the light rays, we often use 45°, 30°, or 60° angles when drafting with 45° and 30°-60° triangles.

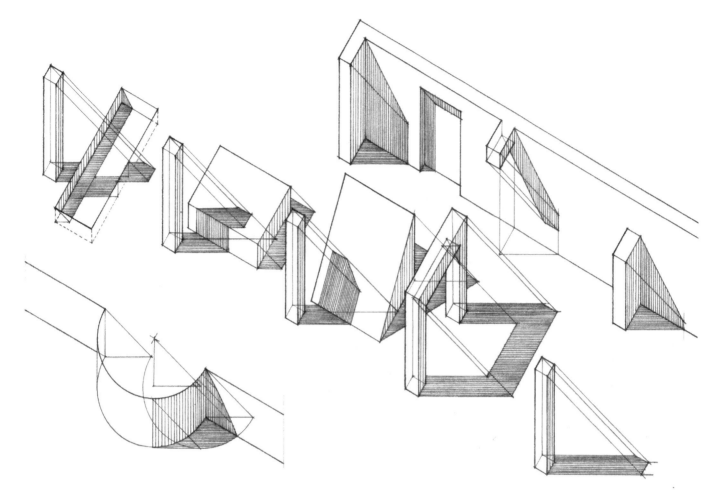

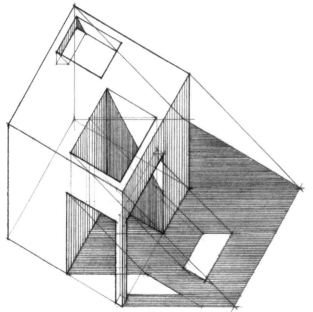

- A shadow's profile is continuous, except where interrupted by a surface in light.
- A shadow's profile changes direction with every change in form that receives the shadow.

- Cast shadows anchor an object to the surface on which it sits.
- Cast shadows reveal the distance between a form and the surface upon which it is cast.
- Cast shadows clarify the form of the surface upon which they are cast.

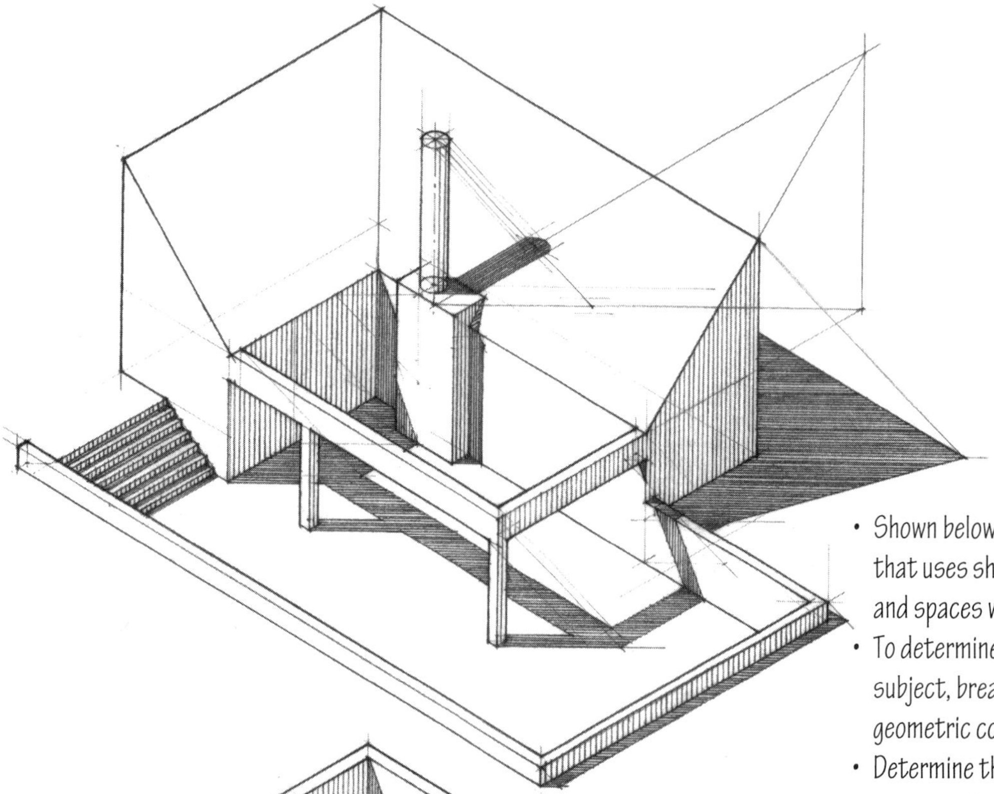

- Shown below is an example of a paraline drawing that uses shade and shadows to reveal the forms and spaces within the interior of a building.
- To determine the shadow cast by a complex subject, break down the form into its simplest geometric components.
- Determine the shadows cast by these components.
- The overall shadow pattern will be a composite of these shadows.

- Note that the sharpest contrast in value should be along the line between the shade or shadow and the adjacent lit surface. Within the shadow or area in shade, there is usually some variation in value due to the reflected light from adjacent lit surfaces.

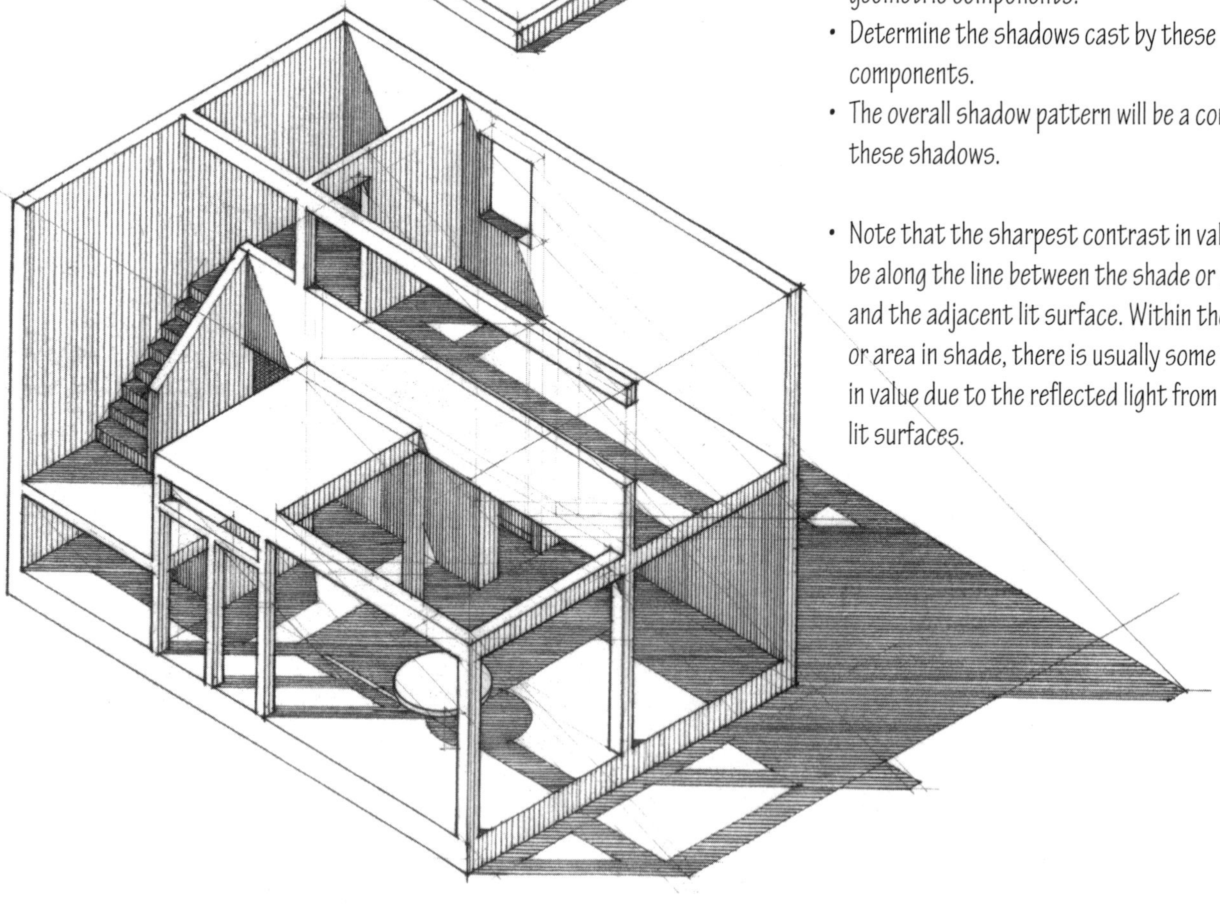

Perspective Views

The casting of shade and shadows in linear perspective is similar to their construction in paraline drawings, except that the sloping lines representing the conventional or actual light rays appear to converge when oblique to the picture plane.

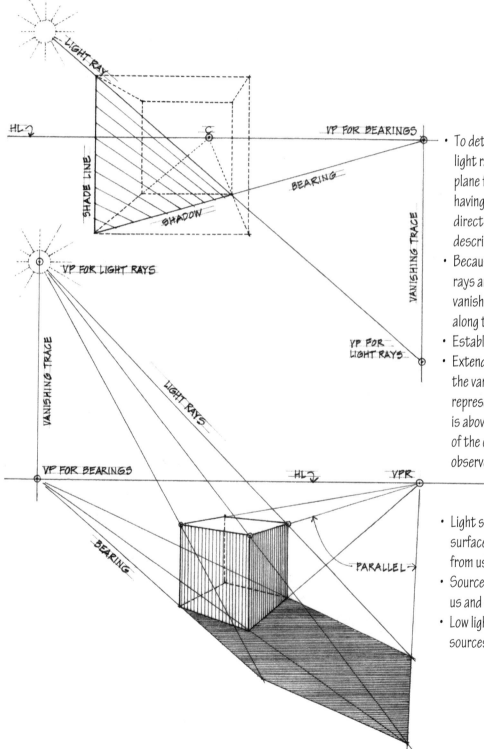

- To determine the vanishing point for inclined light rays, construct a triangular shadow plane for a vertical shade line in perspective, having a hypotenuse establishing the direction of the light rays and a base describing their bearing direction.
- Because the bearing directions of light rays are described by horizontal lines, their vanishing point (VP) must occur somewhere along the horizon line (HL).
- Establish a vanishing trace through VP.
- Extend the hypotenuse until it intersects the vanishing trace. This intersection represents the source of the light rays, and is above HL when the light source is in front of the observer and below HL when behind the observer.

- Light sources behind us illuminate the surfaces we see and cast shadows away from us.
- Sources in front of us cast shadows toward us and emphasize backlit surfaces in shade.
- Low light angles lengthen shadows, while high sources shorten them.

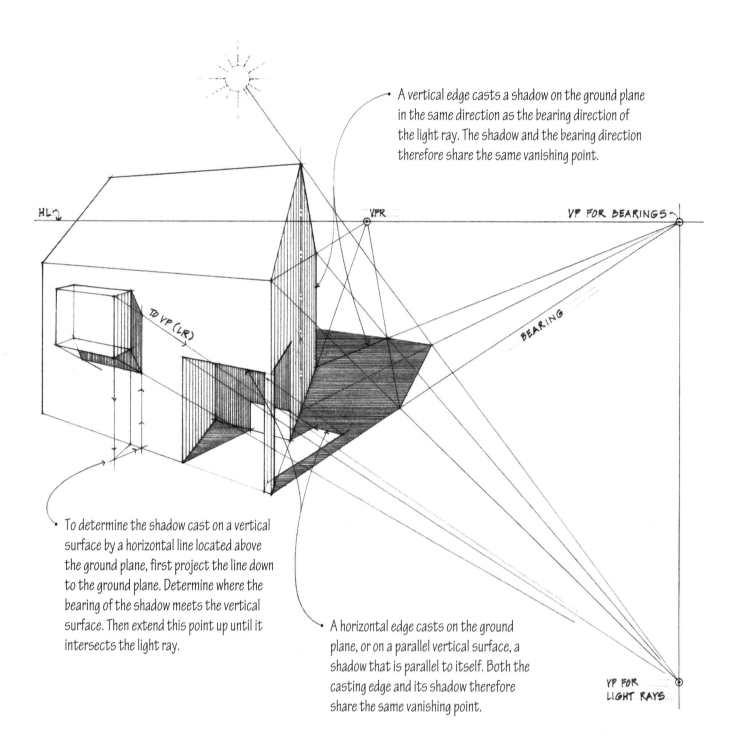

A vertical edge casts a shadow on the ground plane in the same direction as the bearing direction of the light ray. The shadow and the bearing direction therefore share the same vanishing point.

HL

VPR

VP FOR BEARINGS

TO VP (LR)

BEARING

To determine the shadow cast on a vertical surface by a horizontal line located above the ground plane, first project the line down to the ground plane. Determine where the bearing of the shadow meets the vertical surface. Then extend this point up until it intersects the light ray.

A horizontal edge casts on the ground plane, or on a parallel vertical surface, a shadow that is parallel to itself. Both the casting edge and its shadow therefore share the same vanishing point.

VP FOR LIGHT RAYS

In two-point perspective, the simplest method for casting shadows is to assume that the bearing direction for the light rays originates from either the left or right and is parallel to the picture plane. You can then use 45° triangles to determine the direction of the light rays and the shadows cast by vertical elements in perspective.

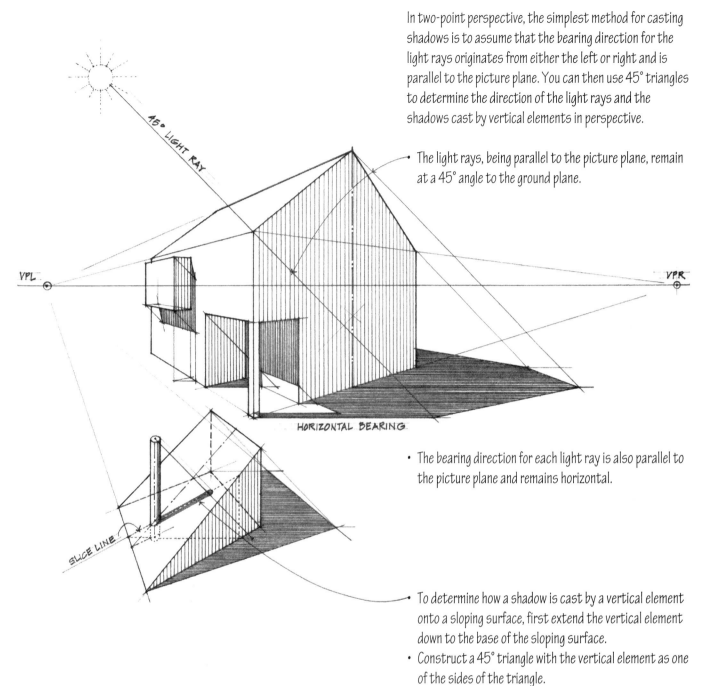

- The light rays, being parallel to the picture plane, remain at a 45° angle to the ground plane.

- The bearing direction for each light ray is also parallel to the picture plane and remains horizontal.

- To determine how a shadow is cast by a vertical element onto a sloping surface, first extend the vertical element down to the base of the sloping surface.
- Construct a 45° triangle with the vertical element as one of the sides of the triangle.
- Slice the sloping surface along the plane of the triangle.
- The shadow falls along this slice line and terminates at the hypotenuse of the 45° triangle.

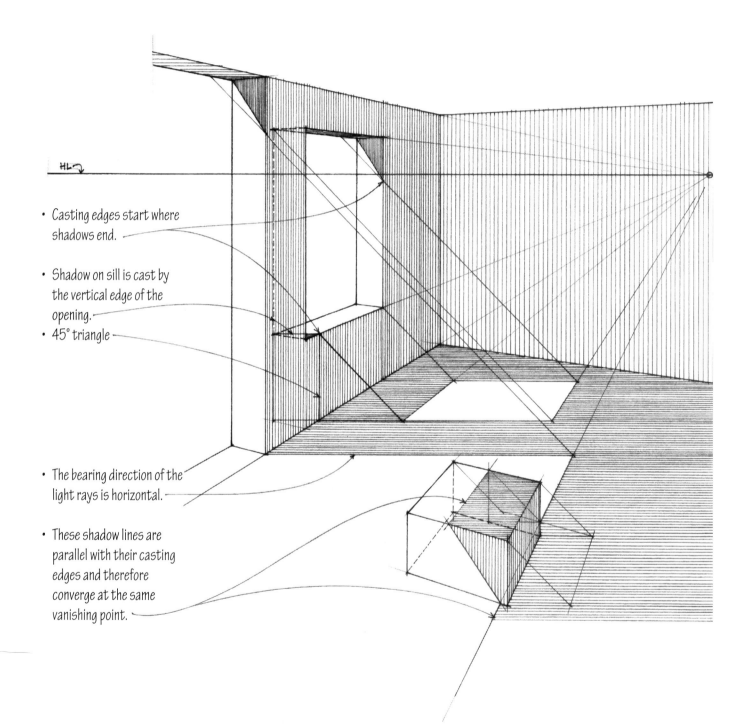

HL

• Casting edges start where shadows end.

• Shadow on sill is cast by the vertical edge of the opening.

• 45° triangle

• The bearing direction of the light rays is horizontal.

• These shadow lines are parallel with their casting edges and therefore converge at the same vanishing point.

8

Rendering Context

Because we design and evaluate architecture in relation to its environment, it is important to incorporate the context in the drawing of a design proposal. In each of the major drawing systems, we do this by extending the ground line and plane to include adjacent structures and site features. In addition to the physical context, we should indicate the scale and intended use of spaces by including human figures and furnishings. We can also attempt to describe the ambience of a place by depicting the quality of light, the colors and textures of materials, the scale and proportion of the space, or the cumulative effect of details.

The viewer of a drawing relates to the human figures within it and is thus drawn into the scene. Therefore, in the drawing of architectural and urban spaces, we include people to:

• Express the scale of a space.
• Indicate the intended use or activity of a space.
• Convey spatial depth and changes of level.

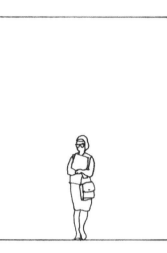

Important aspects to consider in the drawing of human figures are:
• Size
• Proportion
• Activity

Size

• In orthographic projection, the height and width of elements remain constant regardless of the elements' depth within the projected view. We can therefore simply scale the normal height of people in elevations and section drawings.
• We can also scale the height of human figures in paraline views. Since the view is three-dimensional, however, the figures should have some degree of roundness to indicate their volume.

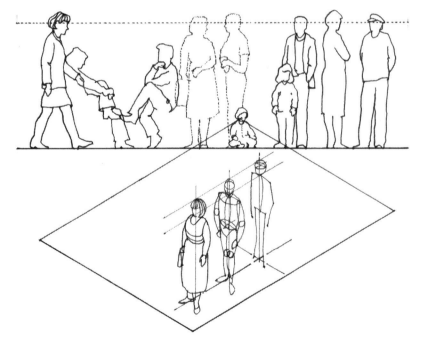

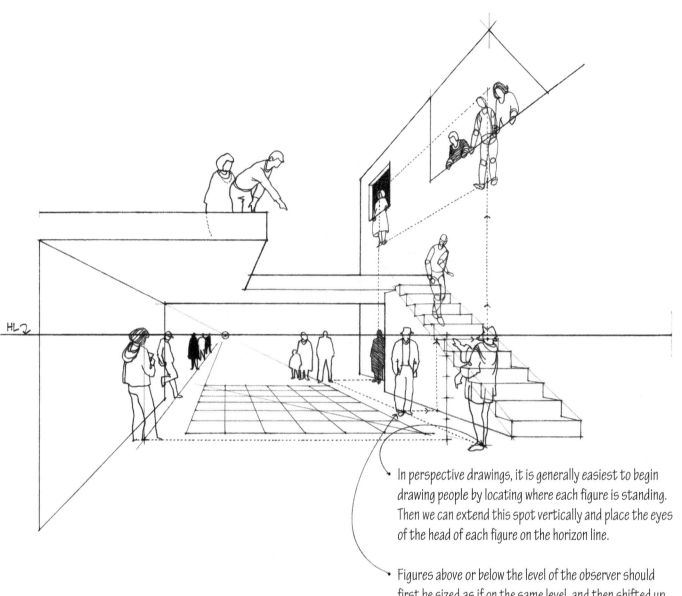

HL

In perspective drawings, it is generally easiest to begin drawing people by locating where each figure is standing. Then we can extend this spot vertically and place the eyes of the head of each figure on the horizon line.

Figures above or below the level of the observer should first be sized as if on the same level, and then shifted up or down as required. The principles of linear perspective can be used to shift the figure right or left, up or down, or into the depth of the perspective.

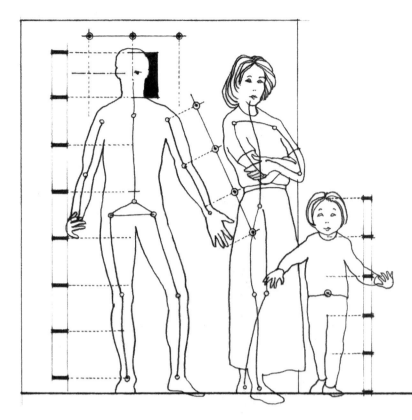

Proportion

The people we use to populate a drawing should be in scale with the environment. We therefore need to draw human figures in proper size and proportion.

- First, we establish the height of each figure and then the proportions of the parts, the most critical being the size of the head. If we can divide the standing human figure into seven or eight equal parts, the head is between $1/7$ and $1/8$ of the total body height.

- We should avoid drawing outlined frontal views of people that appear like flat, cardboard cutouts. Instead, figures should be given a sense of volume, especially in paraline and perspective views.
- When drawing a person sitting on a bench or chair, it is usually best to first draw a figure standing alongside the bench or chair. Then the established proportions are used to draw the same person sitting down.
- The attitude of each human figure can be established by paying particular attention to the contour of the spine and support points for the body.

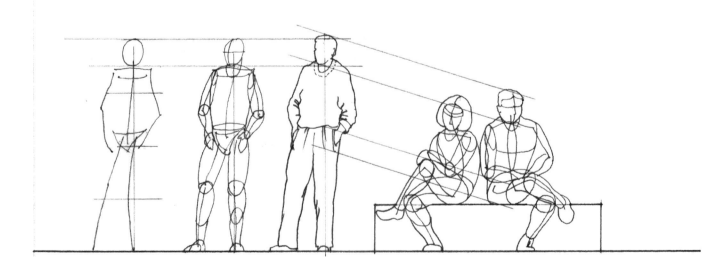

Activity

The figures in a drawing should convey the nature of the
activity in a space and be appropriate to the setting.
The manner in which we draw them should answer the
fundamental question: What activity should occur in
this room or space?

- Both groups and solitary figures should be appropriate to the
  scale and activity of the space.
- People should not be placed where they might conceal
  important spatial features or distract from the focus of
  a drawing.
- Use the principle of overlap, however, to convey spatial depth.

- Figures should be clothed appropriately, avoiding unnecessary
  details that might distract from the focus of the drawing.
- People should be depicted in a manner consistent with the
  style of the rest of the drawing.
- Where appropriate, people should be shown gesturing with
  their arms and hands.

- It's important to be patient; each one of us inevitably develops
  our own style of drawing.

Digital Figures

We can create digital figures from photographs using image-processing software as well as retrieve them from online resources. The same principles that govern the scale, clothing, placement, and gesturing in hand drawing should apply to the use of digital images of people in architectural settings.

The ability to produce photorealistic images of people is seductive. Keep in mind that the graphic style with which we populate architectural drawings should not distract or detract from the architectural subject matter. The figures should have a similar level of abstraction and be compatible with the graphic style of the drawn setting.

The type and arrangement of furnishings are important indicators of use and activity in a space. Their placement should remind us that there should be places on which to sit, lean, rest our elbow or foot, or simply touch.

• Drawing furniture in conjunction with people helps establish their scale and maintain the proper proportion of their parts.

• Except when furniture is the subject of a design proposal, well-designed, commercially available examples should be used as models.

• We should proceed from the geometric basis of each piece.
• Once the structural framework for the form is established, we can add indications of material, thickness, and details.

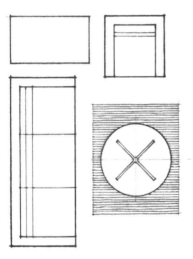

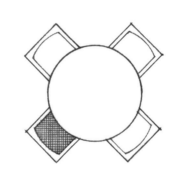

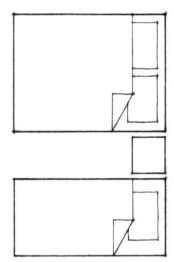

- Furniture should be drawn simply in plan views so as not to obscure the essential pattern of solid matter and spatial void.

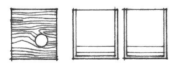

Digital Libraries

Many CAD and modeling programs include ready-made libraries or templates of furniture elements. These can be easily copied, resized, and placed directly into drawings.

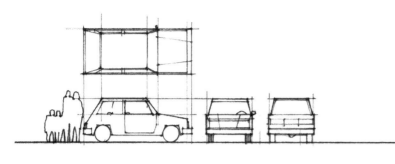

We include a variety of vehicles—cars, trucks, buses, even bicycles—to indicate roadways and parking areas in exterior scenes.

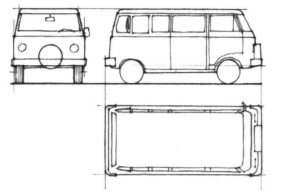

- The placement and scale of vehicles must be realistic.
- Drawing vehicles in conjunction with people helps establish their scale.
- Actual models should be used whenever possible.
- As in the drawing of furniture, we proceed from the geometric basis of the vehicular forms.
- If we draw vehicles with too much detail, they can easily become unintended distractions and detract from the focus of a drawing.

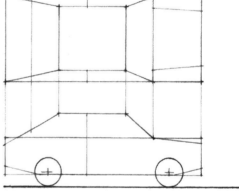

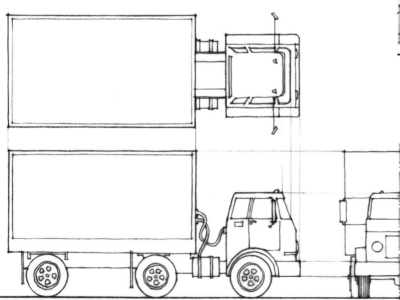

LANDSCAPING

Another opportunity to convey the context for a design is in the drawing of landscaping elements. These include:

• Natural plant materials, such as trees, shrubs, and ground covers.
• Exterior construction, such as decks, pavements, and retaining walls.

With these landscaping elements, we can:

• Convey the geographic character of a site

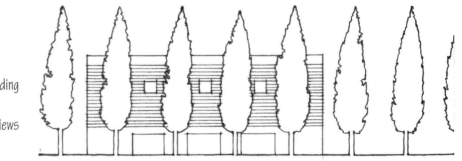

• Indicate the scale of a building

• Frame views

• Define outdoor spaces

• Direct movement

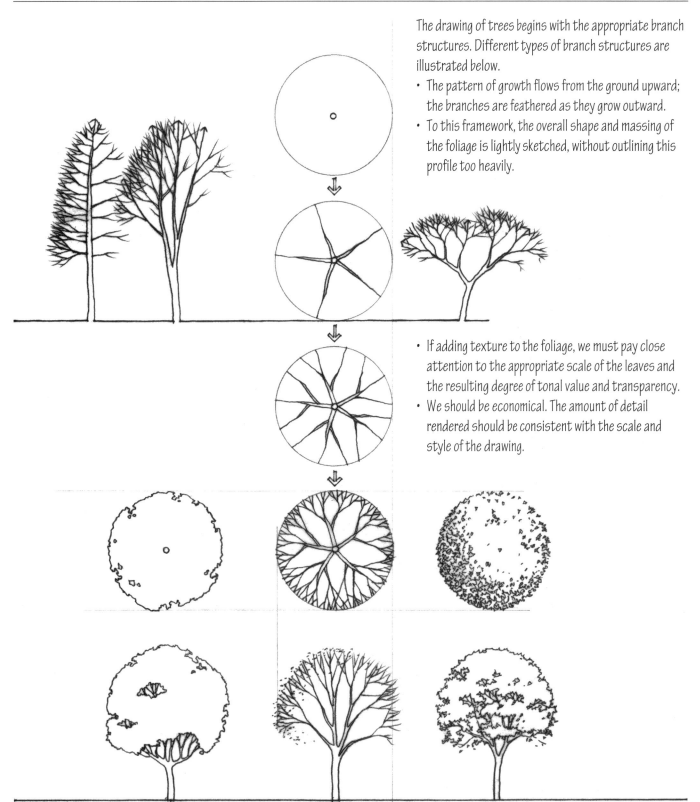

The drawing of trees begins with the appropriate branch structures. Different types of branch structures are illustrated below.

- The pattern of growth flows from the ground upward; the branches are feathered as they grow outward.
- To this framework, the overall shape and massing of the foliage is lightly sketched, without outlining this profile too heavily.

- If adding texture to the foliage, we must pay close attention to the appropriate scale of the leaves and the resulting degree of tonal value and transparency.
- We should be economical. The amount of detail rendered should be consistent with the scale and style of the drawing.

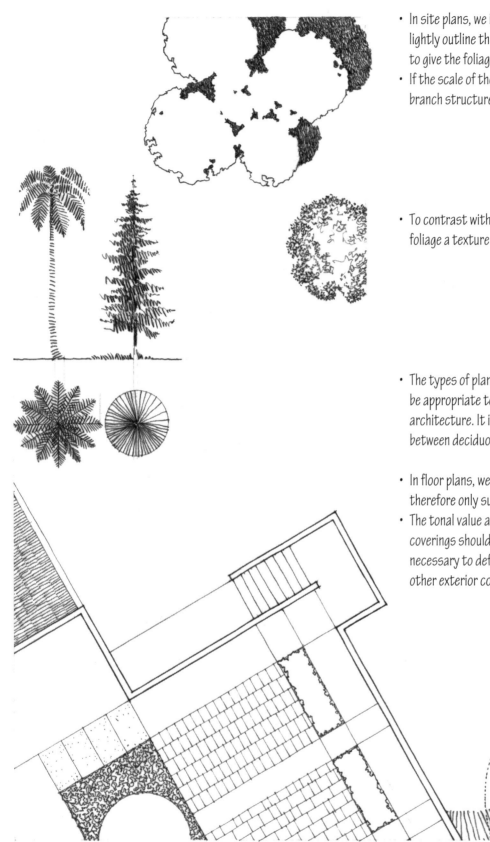

- In site plans, we indicate the positions of tree trunks and lightly outline their foliage. Draw these outlines freehand to give the foliage a textural quality.
- If the scale of the site plan permits, we can also show the branch structures of the trees.

- To contrast with a light ground surface, we can give the foliage a texture and tonal value.

- The types of plants we use in a drawing should be appropriate to the geographic location of the architecture. It is therefore necessary to differentiate between deciduous trees, conifers, and palms.

- In floor plans, we cut through the trunks of trees and therefore only suggest the extent of their foliage.
- The tonal value and texture of shrubs and ground coverings should provide the degree of contrast necessary to define adjacent pavements, decks, and other exterior construction.

We should pay careful attention to the appropriate scale of the trees we draw in elevations and section drawings. As always, the type of trees selected should be appropriate to the geographic location of the architecture.

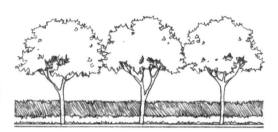

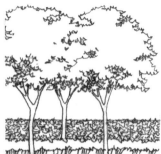

- In small-scale elevations, we draw the portion of tree trunks that are visible and simply outline the foliage. Draw these outlines freehand to give the foliage a textural quality.
- To contrast with the light values of adjacent, overlapping, or background forms, we can give the foliage a contrasting texture and tonal value.

- If the scale of the drawing permits and a high degree of transparency is desired, we can simply draw the branch structures of trees. The outline of foliage can be suggested with dotted or lightly drawn freehand lines.

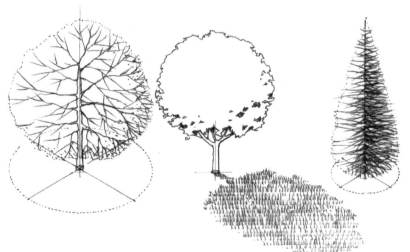

- In paraline drawings, trees should have a three-dimensional quality in order to comply with the principles of paraline drawing.

In perspective views, we apply the principles of atmospheric perspective to the drawing of trees and landscaping elements. Foreground elements typically possess dark, saturated colors and sharply defined contrasts in value. As elements move farther away, their colors become lighter and more subdued, and their tonal contrasts more diffuse. In the background, we see mainly shapes of grayed tones and muted hues.

- The contrast of trees and other landscape elements in the foreground is sharpened. This can sometimes be accomplished simply with an articulated profile line.
- The middleground is typically the focus of a perspective scene. This area therefore requires more detail and sharp contrasts in tonal value.
- The background of a perspective has diminished details, lightened tonal values, and softened contrasts. Trees and landscaping are shown merely as shapes of tonal value and texture.

Image-processing software provides the means to manipulate photographic images of an existing site and landscape and adapt them for use in describing the context for an architectural design.

As with digital images of people, the ability to produce photorealistic images of trees and other landscape elements can be seductive. Keep in mind that the graphic style of site and contextual elements should not distract or detract from the architectural subject matter. Their graphic description should have the same level of abstraction and be compatible with the graphic style of the drawn setting.

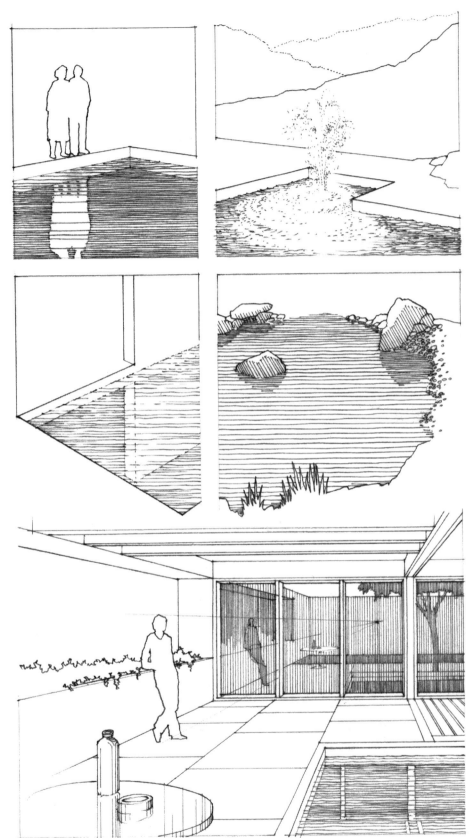

- Water should be rendered as a horizontal planar surface.
- We use horizontal lines: drafted lines for still water and freehand, wavy lines for ripply water.
- Surfaces that are light in value appear lighter than the value of the water.
- Likewise, darker surfaces appear darker in reflection than the value of the water's surface.

- The actual values we use for the reflecting surface, as well as the reflections within the surface area, should be determined relative to the range of values for the rest of the drawing.

9

Architectural Presentations

Presentation drawings are those we typically think of when the term "design drawing" is used or mentioned. These drawings describe a design proposal in a graphic manner intended to persuade an audience of its value. The audience may be a client, a committee, or merely someone browsing for an idea. Whether produced to assist the client's imagination or to obtain a commission, either privately or through a competition, presentation drawings should communicate as clearly and accurately as possible the three-dimensional qualities of a design. Although the drawings that comprise a presentation may be excellent two-dimensional graphics worthy of an exhibition, they are merely tools for communicating a design idea, never ends in themselves.

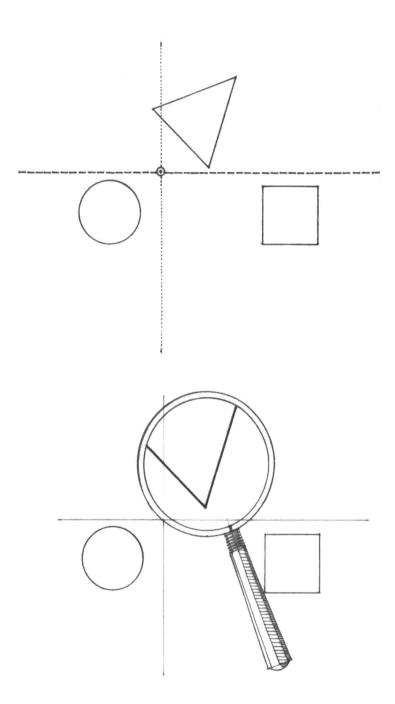

Unless presentation drawings are comprehensible and persuasive—their conventions understood and their substance meaningful—a presentation will be weak and ineffective. An effective presentation, however, also possesses important collective characteristics.

Point of View

Be clear about design intent. A presentation should communicate the central idea or concept of a design scheme. Graphic diagrams and text are effective means of articulating and clarifying the essential aspects of a design scheme, especially when they are visually related to the more common types of design drawing.

Efficiency

Be economical. An effective presentation employs economy of means, utilizing only what is necessary to communicate an idea. Any graphic elements of a presentation that are distracting and ends in themselves can obscure the intent and purpose of the presentation.

Clarity

Be articulate. At a minimum, presentation drawings should explain a design clearly and in enough detail so that viewers unfamiliar with it will be able to understand the design proposal. Eliminate unintended distractions, such as those caused by ambiguous figure-ground relationships or inappropriate groupings of drawings. Too often, we can be blind to these glitches, because we know what we want to communicate and therefore cannot read our own work in an objective manner.

Accuracy

Avoid presenting distorted or incorrect information. Presentation drawings should accurately simulate a possible reality and the consequences of future actions so that any decisions made based on the information presented are sound and reasonable.

Unity

Be organized. In an effective presentation, no one segment is inconsistent with or detracts from the whole. Unity, not to be confused with uniformity, depends on:

- A logical and comprehensive arrangement of integrated graphic and verbal information;
- A synthesis of format, scale, medium, and technique appropriate to the design as well as to the place and audience for which the presentation is intended.

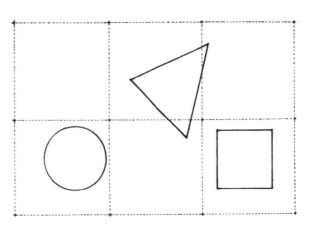

Continuity

Each segment of a presentation should relate to what precedes it and what follows, reinforcing all the other segments of the presentation.

The principles of unity and continuity are mutually self-supporting; one cannot be achieved without the other. The factors that produce one invariably reinforce the other. At the same time, however, we can bring into focus the central idea of a design through the placement and pacing of the major and supporting elements of the presentation.

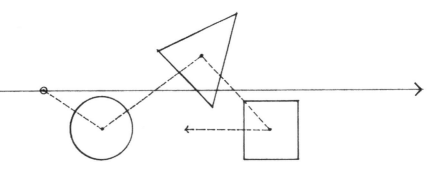

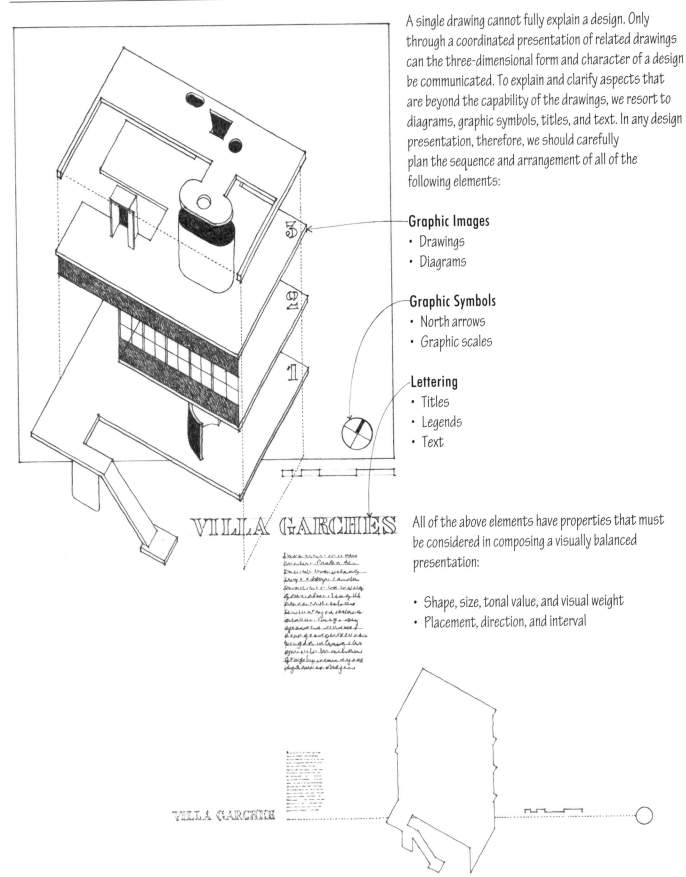

A single drawing cannot fully explain a design. Only through a coordinated presentation of related drawings can the three-dimensional form and character of a design be communicated. To explain and clarify aspects that are beyond the capability of the drawings, we resort to diagrams, graphic symbols, titles, and text. In any design presentation, therefore, we should carefully plan the sequence and arrangement of all of the following elements:

Graphic Images
- Drawings
- Diagrams

Graphic Symbols
- North arrows
- Graphic scales

Lettering
- Titles
- Legends
- Text

VILLA GARCHES

All of the above elements have properties that must be considered in composing a visually balanced presentation:

- Shape, size, tonal value, and visual weight
- Placement, direction, and interval

We generally read design presentations
from left to right and from top to bottom.
Slide and computerized presentations
involve a sequence in time. In either case, the
subject matter presented should progress
in sequence from small-scale to large-scale
graphic information, and from the general or
contextual view to the specific.

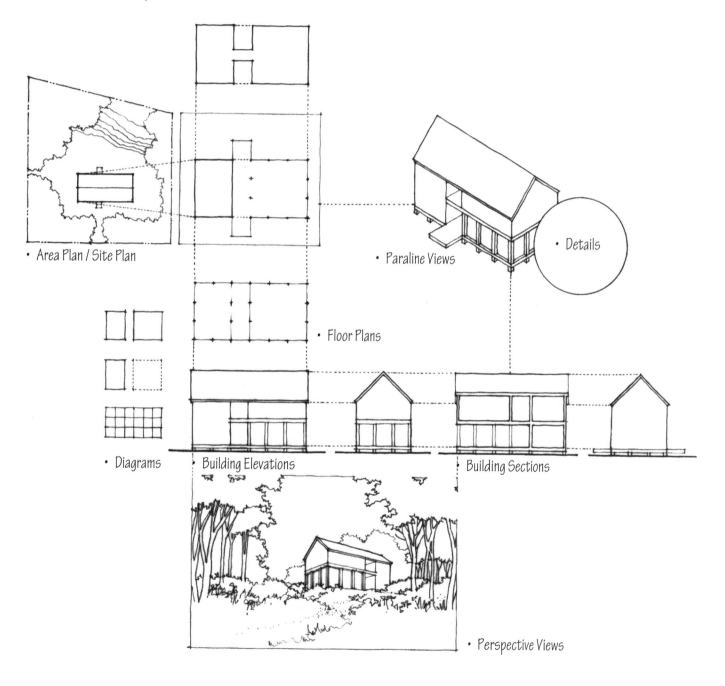

• Area Plan / Site Plan

• Paraline Views

• Details

• Floor Plans

• Diagrams

• Building Elevations

• Building Sections

• Perspective Views

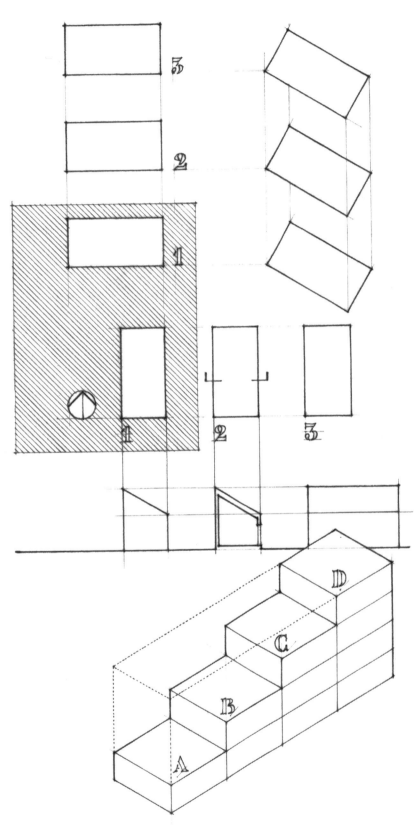

The sequence and alignment of the drawings should reinforce their projected relationships.

• Orient all plans in a similar manner. Whenever possible, orient plan drawings with north up or upward on the sheet.
• The first- or ground-floor plan may extend out to include adjacent outdoor spaces and features, such as courtyards, landscaping, and garden structures.

• Relate floor plans of multistory buildings either vertically above one another, or horizontally side by side.
• Vertical arrangements should begin with the lowest floor level at the bottom and rise to the highest level at the top.
• Horizontal arrangements should begin with the lowest floor level on the left and proceed to the upper levels on the right.
• Whenever possible, relate floor plans along their longer dimensions.

• Arrange building elevations either vertically or horizontally, correlating them whenever possible to corresponding floor plans.
• Likewise, organize building sections either vertically or horizontally and relate them whenever possible to the floor plans or building elevations.

• Lay out a related series of paraline drawings vertically or horizontally. When each drawing successively builds on the preceding one, work from the bottom up or proceed from left to right.
• Relate paraline and perspective drawings as directly as possible to the plan drawing that best shows their context or point of view.

• Include people and furniture to show the scale and use of spaces in all drawings.

Design drawings are usually presented as a related set or group of figures. Typical examples include a series of floor plans for a multistory building or a sequence of building elevations. The spacing and alignment of these individual drawings, as well as similarity of shape and treatment, are the key factors in determining whether we read these drawings as a set of related information or as individual figures.

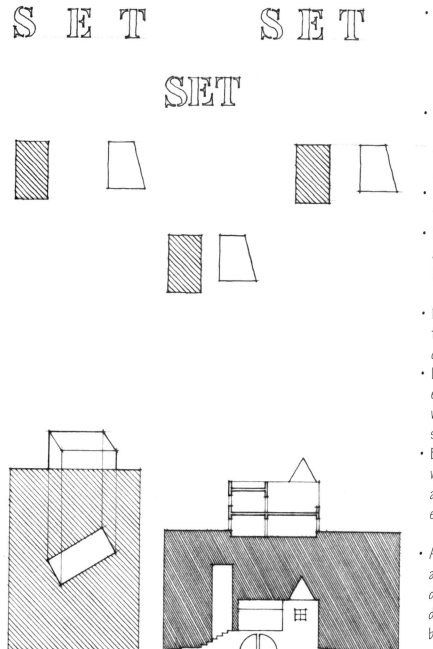

- Use white space and alignment to reinforce the organization of the graphic and verbal information of a presentation. Do not fill up white space unless absolutely necessary.

- If you want two drawings to be read as individual figures, the space between them should be equal to the space between each drawing and the nearest edge of the field.
- Moving the two drawings closer together causes them to be read as a related group.
- If you move the drawings closer still, they will appear to be a single view rather than two related but individual views.

- Properly related drawings that form a visual set can themselves define the edge of a field for another drawing or set of figures.
- Lines can serve to separate as well as to unify, emphasize, and outline. Avoid using lines, however, when spacing or alignment can achieve the same purpose.
- Boxes can establish a field within a larger field or within the boundaries of the sheet or board. Be aware, however, that using too many frames can establish ambiguous figure-ground relationships.

- A tonal value can be used to define a field within a large field. A darker background for an elevation drawing, for example, can merge with a section drawing. The foreground for a perspective can become the field for a plan view of the building.

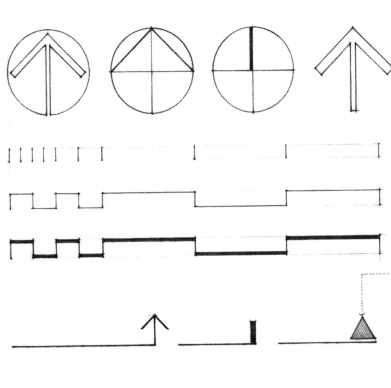

Graphic symbols help the viewer identify the various aspects and features of a drawing or presentation.

- North arrows indicate the major compass points on architectural plans so that the viewer is able to grasp the orientation of a building and its site.

- Graphic scales are graduated lines or bars representing proportionate size. These scales are especially useful because they remain proportional when a drawing is enlarged or reduced.

- Section arrows indicate the location of section cuts on plan drawings.

Graphic symbols rely on conventions to convey information. To be easily recognizable and readable, keep them simple and clean—free of extraneous detail and stylistic flourishes. In enhancing the clarity and readability of a presentation, these devices also become important elements in the overall composition of a drawing or presentation. The impact of graphic symbols and lettering depends on their size, visual weight, and placement.

Size
The size of a graphic symbol should be in proportion to the scale of the drawing and readable from the anticipated viewing distance.

Visual Weight
The size and tonal value of a graphic symbol determines its visual weight. If a large symbol or typeface is required for readability but a low value is mandatory for a balanced composition, then use an outline symbol or letter style.

Placement
Place graphic symbols as close as possible to the drawing to which they refer. Whenever possible, use spacing and alignment instead of boxes or frames to form visual sets of information.

GROUND FLOOR PLAN

A wealth of well-designed and legible typefaces is available in the form of pressure-sensitive, dry-transfer sheets as well as in digital typography. You should therefore spend time on the appropriate selection and use of fonts rather than attempt to design new ones.

HELVETICA IS A VERY LEGIBLE TYPEFACE.

HELVETICA NARROW
is useful when space is tight.

TIMES IS A CLASSIC EXAMPLE OF A TYPEFACE WITH SERIFS.

PALATINO has broader proportions than Times.

Serifs enhance the recognition and readability of letter forms.

Lowercase lettering is particularly appropriate for bodies of text.

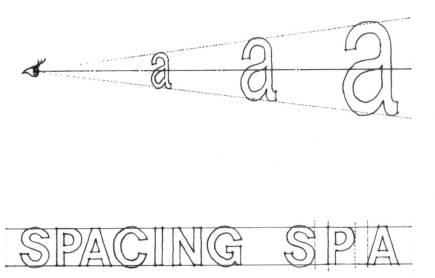

- The most important characteristic of lettering is legibility.
- The character of the typeface we use should be appropriate to the design being presented and not detract from the drawings themselves.

- Serifs enhance the recognition and readability of letter forms. Avoid mixing serif and nonserif typefaces in a single title or body of text.

- Lowercase lettering is appropriate if executed consistently throughout a presentation.
- The differences among lowercase characters are more distinct, making lowercase lettering generally easier to read than text composed of all capitals.

- Determine the range of lettering sizes by judging the distance from which the audience will view the presentation. Keep in mind that we may read different portions of a presentation—project overviews, diagrams, details, text, and so on—at different distances.

- Space letters by optically equalizing the areas between the letter forms rather than by mechanically measuring the distance between the extremities of each letter.
- Word processing and page layout programs incorporate the ability to adjust both tracking, the spacing of letters, as well as leading, the spacing of lines of type, in any body of text.

ABCDEFGHIJKLMNOPQRSTUVWXYZ   &   1234567890

ABCDEFGHIJKLMNOPQRSTUVWXYZ   &   1234567890

MNPTEIIII O →

- Guidelines are required to control the height and line spacing of handlettering. The maximum size for a handlettering is $3/16$ of an inch. Beyond this size, the letters require a width beyond what a single pen or pencil stroke is capable of producing.

- Use a small triangle to maintain the verticality of vertical lettering strokes. The visual movement of slanted lettering can be distracting in a rectilinear drawing scheme.

BROAD PROPORTIONS A

NORMAL PROPORTIONS ABCI

NARROW PROPORTIONS ABCDEFGHI

- Maintain similar proportions among the characters of a title or line of text.

- Everyone inevitably develops an individual style of handlettering. The most important characteristics of a lettering style are readability and consistency in both style and spacing.

ABCDEFGHIJKLMNOPQRST

UVWXYZ   &   1234567890

Lettering in a design presentation should be carefully integrated into the composition of drawings on each sheet or board.

Drawing Titles

Arrange titles and graphic symbols into visual sets that identify and explain the contents of a drawing. By convention, we always place titles directly below a drawing. In this position, titles can help stabilize drawing fields, especially irregularly shaped ones. Use symmetrical layouts with symmetrical drawings and designs. In all other cases, it is usually easier to justify—align vertically—a drawing title with either the drawing itself or its field.

Text

Organize text into visual sets of information and relate these sets directly to the portion of the drawing to which they refer. The line spacing of text should be more than one-half of the letter height used, but no more than the letter height itself. The space between blocks of text should be equal to or greater than the height of two lines of text.

Project Title

The project title and associated information should relate to the overall sheet or board, not to any single drawing within the field of the panel.

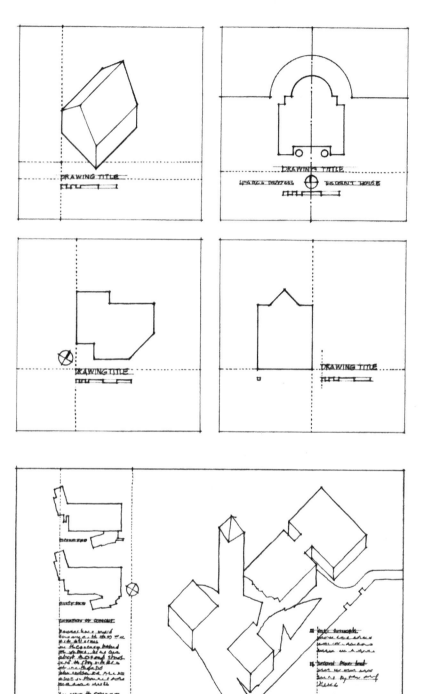

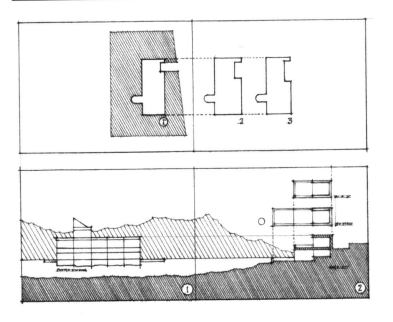

A set of related drawings may be laid out in a vertical, horizontal, or grid format. In planning the layout for a presentation, first identify the essential relationships you want to achieve. Then use a storyboard or small-scale mockup of the presentation to explore alternative drawing arrangements, alignments, and spacing prior to beginning the final presentation drawings.

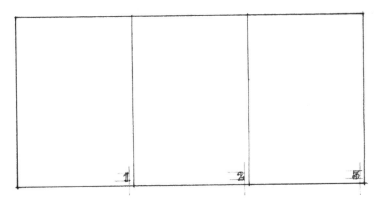

- Remember to explore potential relationships between the sheets or panels.
- Maintain horizontal continuity across sheets with a ground line or by the alignment of drawing titles.

- Do not include unnecessary dimensions or employ borders and title blocks; we reserve these conventions for construction or working drawings.

- When a presentation consists of more than one sheet or board, identify each panel by a number. This information should be in the same relative position on each panel.

- If the panels of a presentation are to be displayed in a specific manner, you can use more graphic means to identify the relative position of each panel in the display.

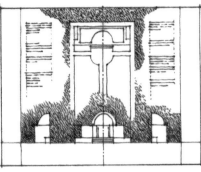

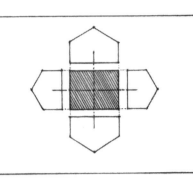

- A symmetrical layout works best in presenting symmetrical designs.

- Centralized formats are suitable when presenting a plan surrounded by elevation views, an expanded paraline drawing, or a key drawing surrounded by detailed portions drawn at a larger scale.

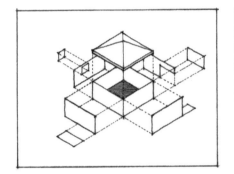

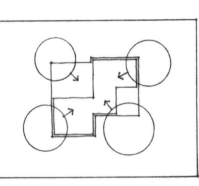

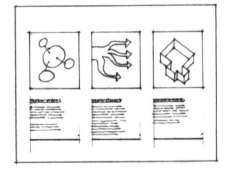

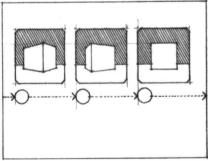

- If a series of drawings are treated in different ways or are of different types, you can unify them by framing or boxing them in a uniform manner.
- We can display drawings horizontally with text below each drawing to form related columns.

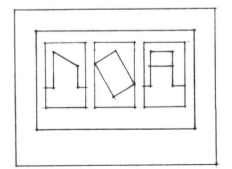

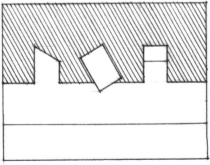

- Avoid using a double or triple frame around a drawing. Doing so can create the impression of a figure on a background that itself has a background. Attention would be diverted from the figure, where it belongs, to the frame around it.

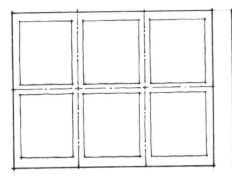

- A grid provides the most flexibility for laying out a series of drawings and text blocks on a panel or series of boards. The underlying sense of order created by the grid allows a great variety of information to be presented in a uniform manner.

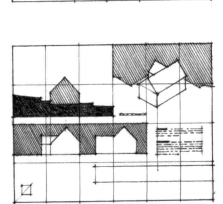

- The grid may be square or rectangular, uniform or irregular.
- We can display drawings, diagrams, and text in individual boxes or frames.
- An important drawing may take up more than one box or frame.

- Graphics and text may be integrated in an organic manner.

Digital Formatting

Drawing and page layout programs give us the ability to try out different ways to arrange the elements of a presentation. However, because what we see on a monitor may not necessarily match the output from a printer or plotter, a trial layout should always be printed or plotted to ensure that the results are satisfactory.

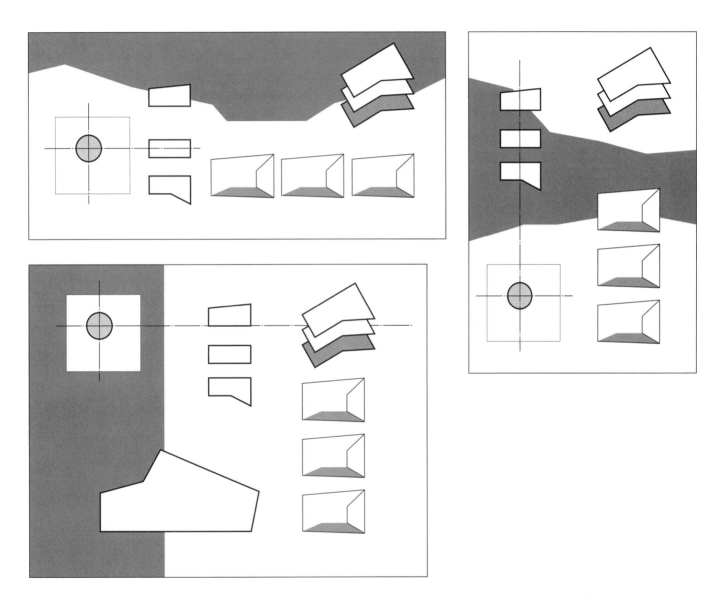

PRESENTATION FORMATS

Digital Presentations

Digital technology has introduced the elements of time and motion into architectural presentations. Presentation software enables us to plan and present slide shows of static graphic images as well as animations. Whereas we can roam and ponder a series of drawings displayed on a wall of a room, our viewing of a computer-based presentation is sequential and controlled by the presenter.

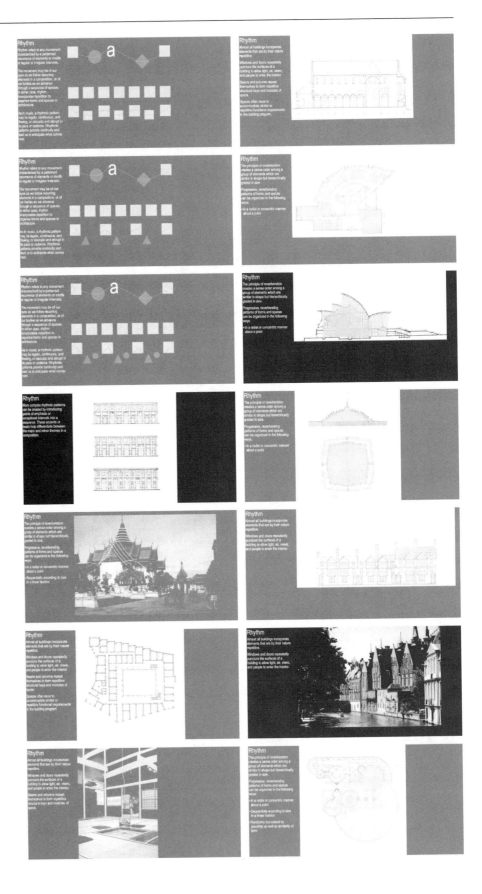

10
Freehand Drawing

Despite rapid and continuing advances in digital imaging technology, drawing with a free hand holding a pen or pencil remains the most intuitive means we have for graphically recording observations, thoughts, and experiences. The tactile, kinesthetic nature of freehand drawing in direct response to sensory phenomena sharpens our awareness in the present and enables us to collect visual memories of the past. Freehand drawing also empowers us to initiate and freely work through ideas of a possible future that we imagine in the mind's eye. During the design process itself, the freehand drawing of diagrams allows us to further explore these ideas and develop them into workable concepts.

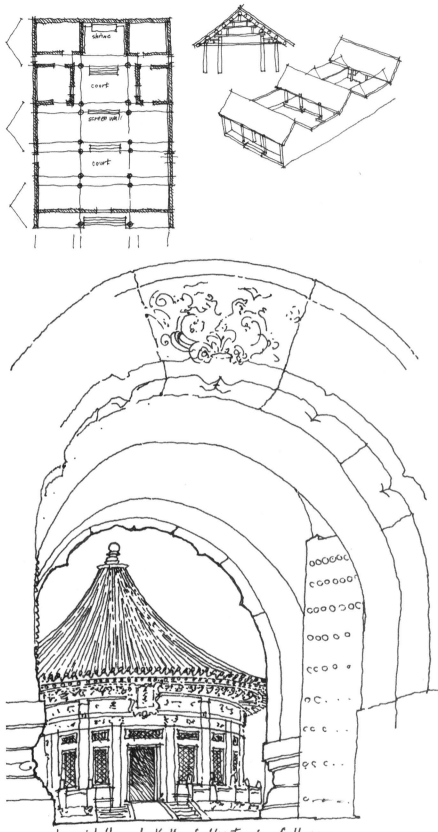

Imperial Heavenly Vault of the Temple of Heaven
8·30·93

Drawing from observation sharpens your awareness of environmental settings, enhances your ability to retain visual memories, and helps build up your design vocabulary.

• Drawing from observation is most meaningful and rewarding when you draw what interests you. If assigned a subject to draw, consider what aspect or quality of the subject attracts your attention.
• Possible subject matter includes the relationship between interior and exterior or public and private spaces, spatial sequences, and urban patterns.
• Other worthwhile explorations include studies of proportion, scale, light, and color, how materials meet in construction assemblies, details, and other sensible qualities that contribute to the character of a place.
• Do not neglect to look at architecture in relation to the landscape.

The process for drawing from observation is to look, respond, and record.
• First pay careful attention to the subject.
• Respond by recording not simply the optical image but also your thoughts and impressions.
• The constant challenge is to select a point of view, medium, and technique appropriate to describing the selected aspect, characteristic, or quality of the subject.
• Do not be overly concerned with technique; each one of us inevitably develops a personal style of drawing.

Drawing from observation requires simple equipment: a pen or pencil and a pad of paper or sketchbook suitable for both dry and wet media.

You may want to experiment with the feel and capabilities of other media, such as charcoal pencils and markers. Try to determine the limits of expression of which each is capable and how its characteristics affect the nature of a drawing. For example, you should find that a fine-tipped pen or pencil encourages you to focus on minute details. Because it takes innumerable fine lines to cover a given area, many line drawings end up smaller than intended or, if large in size, weak in intensity. On the other hand, sketching with a broad-tipped pencil or marker fosters a broader view and the omission of details.

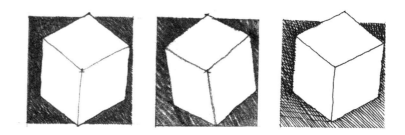

Campidoglio 11:45am 10/17 2000

Freehand sketches may consist purely of lines or be a combination of lines and tones. The line, however, remains the single most essential drawing element, one that is capable of a wide range of expression. It can define shape and form and even imply a sense of depth and space. A line can portray hard as well as soft materials; it can be light or heavy, limp or taut, bold or tentative.

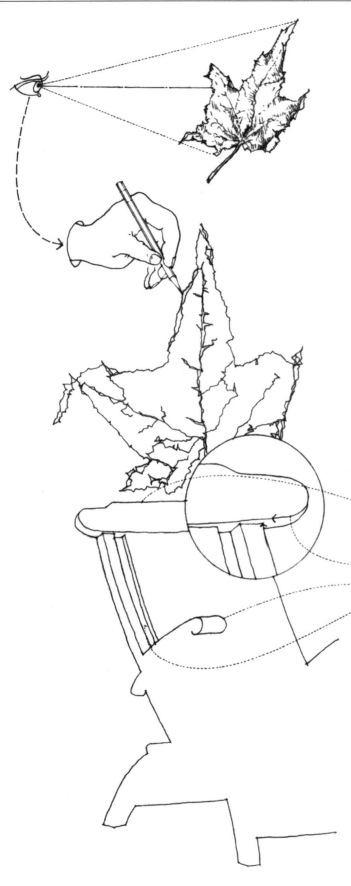

Contour drawing is one approach to drawing from observation. Its primary purpose is to develop visual acuity and sensitivity to qualities of surface and form. The process of contour drawing suppresses the symbolic abstraction we normally use to represent things. Instead, it compels us to pay close attention, look carefully, and experience a subject with both our visual and tactile senses.

- Contour drawing is best done with either a soft, well-sharpened pencil or a fine-tipped pen that is capable of producing a single incisive line. This fosters a feeling of precision that corresponds to the acuity of vision that contour drawing requires.

- Imagine the pencil or pen is in actual contact with the subject as you draw.
- As the eye carefully traces the contours of a subject, the hand moves the drawing instrument at the same slow and deliberate pace, and responds to every indentation and undulation of form.
- Avoid the temptation to move the hand faster than the eye can see; examine the shape of each contour you see in the subject without considering or worrying about its identity.

- The most noticeable contours are those that circumscribe an object and define the outer boundary between the figure and its background.
- Some contours travel inward at folds or breaks in a plane.
- Others are formed by overlapping or projecting parts.
- Still other contours describe the shapes of spaces and shadows within the form.

We are conditioned to see the shapes of things rather than the shapes of the spaces between them. While we normally perceive spatial voids as having no substance, they share the same edges as the objects they separate or envelop. The positive shapes of figures and the shapeless spaces of backgrounds share the same boundaries and combine to form an inseparable whole—a unity of opposites.

In drawing, also, negative shapes share the contour lines that define the edges of positive shapes. The format and composition of a drawing consists of positive and negative shapes that fit together like the interlocking pieces of a jigsaw puzzle. In both seeing and drawing, we should raise the shapes of negative spaces to the same level of importance as the positive shapes of figures and see them as equal partners in the relationship. Since negative shapes do not always have the easily recognizable qualities of positive shapes, they can be seen only if we make the effort.

- We should carefully observe the interconnected nature of positive and negative shapes.
- As we draw the edges of positive shapes, we should also be aware of the negative shapes we are creating.
- Focusing on the shapes of these negative spaces prevents us from thinking consciously about what the positive shapes represent, and we are free to draw them purely as two-dimensional figures.

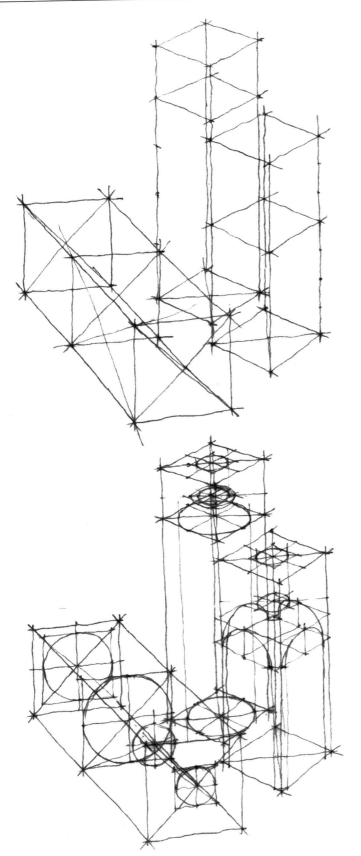

In drawing analytically, we seek to merge two approaches—describing the outer configuration of surfaces of an object and explaining its inner structural nature and the way its parts are arranged and joined in space. Unlike contour drawing, in which we proceed from part to part, analytical drawing proceeds from the whole to the subordinate parts and finally the details. Subordinating parts and details to the structure of the overall form prevents a piecemeal approach that can result in faulty proportional relationships and a lack of unity.

- Begin an analytical drawing with light, freely drawn lines. Draw these lines in an exploratory manner to block out and establish a transparent volumetric framework for a form or composition.
- These exploratory lines are diagrammatic in nature, serving to establish and explain the underlying geometry and structure of the subject.
- These initial traces are also called regulating lines because they can be used to locate points, measure size and distance, find centers, express perpendicular and tangential relationships, and establish alignments and offsets.
- Regulating lines represent visual judgments to be confirmed or adjusted. Do not erase any previously drawn lines. If necessary, restate a line—correcting basic shapes and checking the relative proportions between the parts.
- Always strive for incremental improvement over the last line drawn.

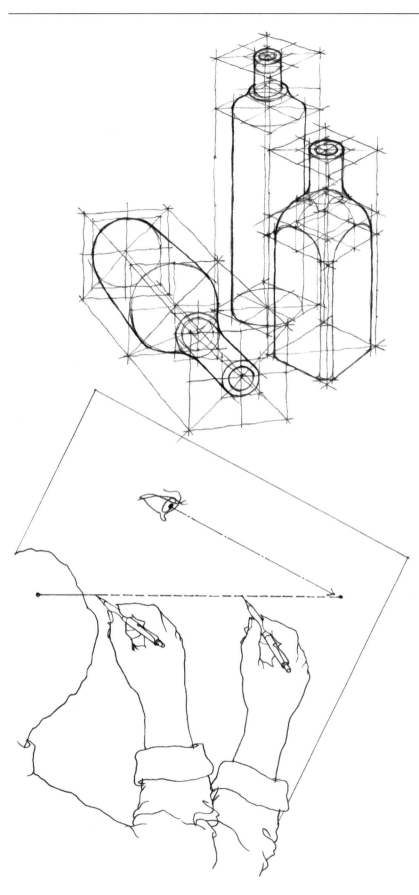

- Because of their constructive nature, regulating lines are not limited by the physical boundaries of objects. They can cut through forms and extend through space as they link, organize, and give measure to the various parts of an object or composition.
- Drawing both unseen and visible parts of the subject makes it easier to gauge angles, control proportions, and see the optical appearance of shapes. The resulting transparency also conveys a convincing sense of volume occupied by the form. Working in this way prevents the appearance of flatness that can result from concentrating too much on surface rather than volume.
- Through a continual process of elimination and intensification, gradually build up the density and weight of the final object lines, especially at critical points of intersection, connection, and transition.
- Having all lines remain visible in the final drawing intensifies the depth of the image and reveals the constructive process by which it was generated and developed.

- The closest analogy to analytical drawing is the wireframe model produced by 3D CAD and modeling software.

- Before actually drawing a line, practice the eye-mind-hand movement by marking the beginning and end of the intended line with dots. Avoid scratching in lines with short, feeble strokes. Instead, draw lines as smoothly and continuously as possible.
- For short strokes or when applying considerable pressure, swing the hand at the wrist or let the fingers perform the necessary motions.
- For longer strokes, swing the entire forearm and hand freely from the elbow, with a minimum of wrist and finger movement. Only as you approach the end of the stroke should you bring the wrist and fingers into motion to control where the line ends.

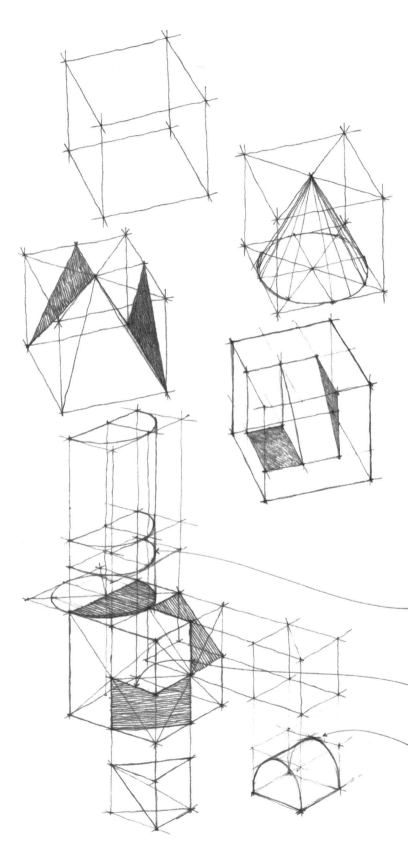

In the analytical process of drawing, we build on geometry. If we are able to break down what we see into regular geometric volumes or a geometric arrangement of parts, we can more easily draw them. We can reorganize the forms in an additive manner or transform them in a subtractive manner. The resulting structure can then serve as a framework for the development and refinement of the forms and intervening spaces.

- The cube is a convenient three-dimensional unit with which to begin.
- From the cube, we can use geometric principles to derive other basic geometric volumes, such as the pyramid, cylinder, and cone. Mastery of drawing these simple forms is a prerequisite for drawing a variety of derivative compositions.

- We can extend a cube horizontally, vertically, as well as into the depth of a drawing. A number of cubic volumes or derivative forms can link, extend, or grow into centralized, linear, symmetrical, or clustered compositions.
- Working from a cubic form, we can selectively remove or carve out portions to generate a new form. In this subtractive process, we use the solid-void relationship between form and space to guide us as we draw the proportion and development of the parts.

In drawing complex forms, keep the following points in mind:

- Use cross-sectional contours to develop the form of complicated shapes. These imaginary slices strengthen the three-dimensional effect of the drawing and show the volume of the object.
- Pay close attention to overlapping forms and negative spaces in the composition.
- Distinguish overlapping forms with linear accents.
- Use scattered lines to indicate the transitional surfaces of curved forms.
- Subordinate details to the overall form.

Every drawing evolves over time. Knowing where to begin, how to proceed, and when to stop are crucial to the process of drawing. Building up a drawing in a systematic way is an important concept. We should advance by progressive stages and construct a drawing from the ground up. Each successive iteration or cycle through the drawing process should first resolve the relationships between the major parts, then resolve the relationships within each part, and finally readjust the relationships between the major parts once again.

Tediously finishing one part of a drawing before going on to the next can easily result in distorting the relationships between each part and the rest of the composition. Maintaining a consistent level of completeness or incompleteness across the entire surface of a drawing is important to preserving a unified, balanced, and focused image.

The following procedure prescribes a way of seeing as well as drawing. It involves building up a drawing in the following stages:

• Composing a view and establishing structure

• Layering tonal values and textures

• Adding significant details

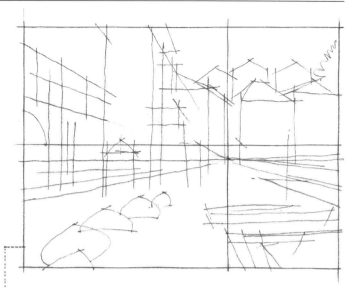

Composing a View

We normally select out from what we see what is of interest to us. Since our perception is discriminating, we should also be selective in what we draw. How we frame and compose a view, and what we emphasize with our drawing technique, will tell others what attracted our attention and what visual qualities we focused on. In this way, our drawings will naturally communicate our perceptions with an economy of means.

Composing a perspective view of a scene involves positioning ourselves at a particular point in space and deciding how to frame what we see.

• To convey the sense that the viewer is within a space rather than on the outside looking in, we must establish three pictorial regions: a foreground, a middleground, and a background. All three should not have equal emphasis; one should dominate to heighten the pictorial space of the drawing.

• When portraying a specific aspect of an object or scene, a closer viewpoint may be necessary so that the size of the drawing can accommodate the rendering of tonal value, texture, and light.

Establishing Structure

Without a cohesive structure to hold it together, the composition of a drawing collapses. Once the composition for a view is established, we use the analytical process of drawing to establish its structural framework.

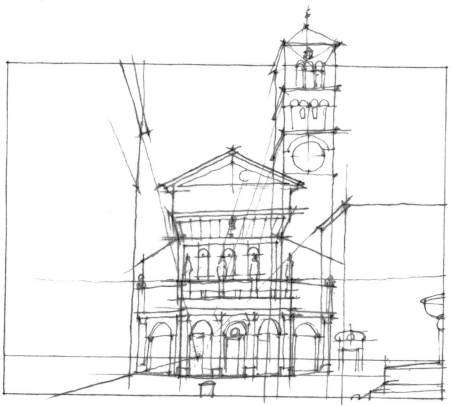

In drawing an environmental setting—an outdoor space or an interior room—we view the scene from a fixed position in space. The structure must therefore be regulated by the principles of linear perspective. We are concerned here principally with the pictorial effects of linear perspective—the convergence of parallel lines and the diminishing size of objects with depth. Our mind interprets what we see and presents an objective reality based on what we know of an object. In drawing a perspective view, we attempt to illustrate an optical reality. These two are often at odds, and the mind usually wins out.

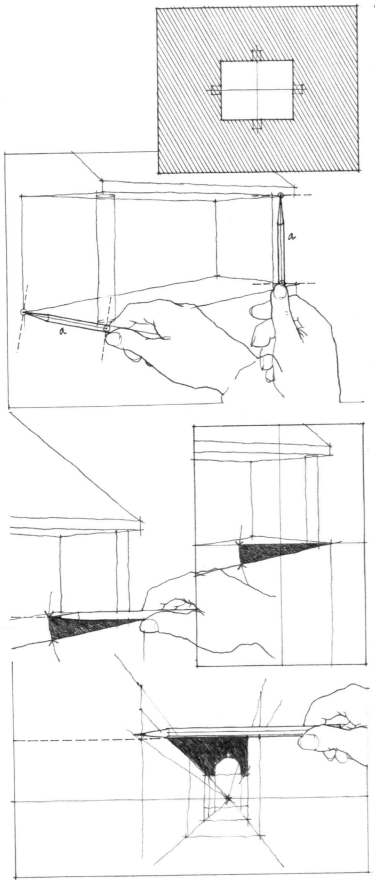

- To help us frame and compose a view as well as gauge the relative lengths and angles of lines, we can construct a viewfinder out of dark gray or black cardboard.
- Another convenient sighting device is the shaft of the pencil or pen with which we are drawing.

- We hold the pen or pencil out at arm's length, in a plane parallel with our eyes and perpendicular to our line of sight.
- To make a linear measurement, we can align the tip of the pen or pencil with one end of an observed line and use our thumb to mark the other end. Then we shift the pencil to another line and use the initial measurement to gauge the length of the second line.

- To gauge the apparent slope of a line, we can align one end of an inclined line with the shaft of the pen or pencil held vertically or horizontally. We gauge the angle between the two visually. Then we transfer this angular measurement to the drawing, using as guides the edges of the drawing surface that correspond to the vertical or horizontal reference line.

- We can use the same reference lines to see which points in the image align vertically or horizontally with other points. Checking alignments in this way effectively controls the proportions and relations of both positive and negative shapes.

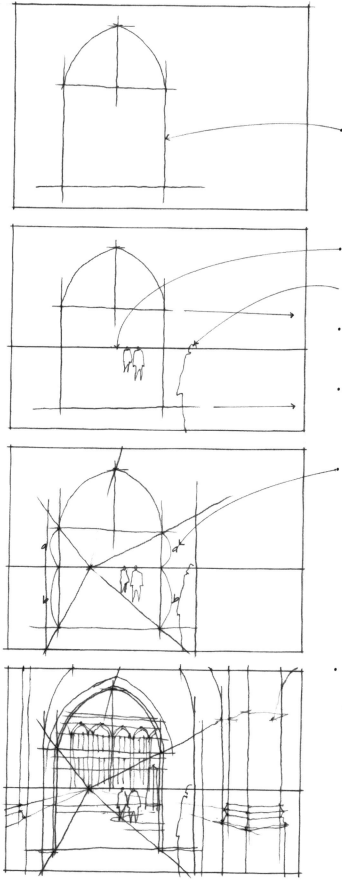

We begin by drawing the perceived shape of a vertical plane that we face. This plane may be the wall of a room, the facade of a building, or an implied plane defined by two vertical elements, such as the corners of two buildings.

We need to establish our eye level relative to the vertical plane we have chosen. We focus on a specific point and draw a horizontal, or horizon line, through that point.

• Notice that horizontal elements situated above our eye level slope downward toward the horizon, whereas horizontal elements that are below rise upward.
• We can establish human figures in the foreground, middleground, and background to establish a vertical scale.

If the vanishing points for a set of horizontal lines lie off the sheet of the drawing, we can draw the front and rear vertical edges of a receding face and judge what proportion of the vertical leading edge lies above the horizon line and what lies below. We can then reproduce the same proportions for the rear vertical edge.

• We use the established points to guide the drawing of the inclined lines in perspective. These receding lines along with the horizon line then serve as visual guides for any other lines that converge at the same point.

Layering Tonal Values

In composing and establishing the structure of a drawing, we create a framework of lines. To this scaffolding, we add tonal values to represent light and dark areas of the scene, define planes in space, model their form, describe surface color and texture, and convey spatial depth.

Work from light to dark by layering shapes of tonal value over preceding areas of value. If an area is too light, we can always darken it. But once an area has been darkened too much and becomes muddy, it is difficult to correct. The freshness and vitality of a drawing is fragile and easily lost.

- Shaded surfaces and cast shadows are neither opaque nor uniform in value. Avoid employing large areas of solid dark tones, which obliterate detail and disrupt our reading of the form of a surface.
- Light reflecting back from nearby surfaces illuminates surfaces in shade or on which shadows are cast. To depict the modifying effects of reflected light, we vary the tonal value of surfaces in shade and those on which shadows are cast. The effects of reflected light, however, should be suggested in a subtle way, so as not to disrupt the nature of the surface in shade or shadow.
- Shades and shadows can be applied as transparent tones that belong to the form and through which we can read the texture and local color of the surface.
- The boundaries of cast shadows are distinct in brilliant light, but softer in diffuse light. In either case, we can define the outer edges of shadows with a contrast in value, never with a drawn line.

- The way light illuminates a color and makes it visible affects its apparent value. A highlight on a colored surface will appear much lighter than the same hue seen in shade or within a shadow.

Adding Details

The final stage in the building of a drawing is the addition of those details that help us identify the various elements of an object or scene. It is through these details that we sense and communicate the inherent qualities of a subject or uniqueness of a place. The smaller parts and details of a drawing must join in a way that further explains the whole.

via Giotto looking north 10/6/00

- Details must be placed within a structured pattern to make sense. This structure provides a framework for a particular area or feature to be worked on in greater detail and more elaborately.
- At the same time, a drawing needs contrast with areas of little or no detail. By this contrast, those areas with detail will naturally be given more emphasis.

- Remember to be selective. We can never include every detail in a drawing. Some editing is necessary as we attempt to communicate particular qualities of form and space, and this often means tolerating a degree of incompleteness.
- The very incompleteness of a drawn image involves and invites the viewer to participate in its completion. Even our perception of optical reality is usually incomplete, being edited by the knowledge we bring to the act of seeing and our momentary needs and concerns.

On this and the next three pages are examples of travel sketches. They illustrate the fact that one does not always have to draw the grand perspective view typified by travel postcards, although this is indeed the most tempting to replicate. It can be just as satisfying to draw a simple detail that attracts your attention, or an analytical diagram that attempts to explain the proportions of a pleasing space or the pattern of solids and voids in an attractive urban setting.

A key benefit of sketching is that the very act of drawing engages the eye and the mind in the travel experience, focusing attention on the present and creating vivid visual memories that can be recalled at a later time.

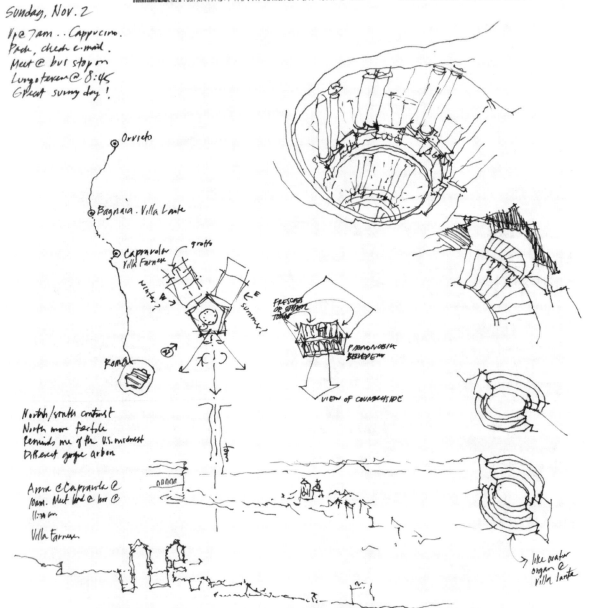

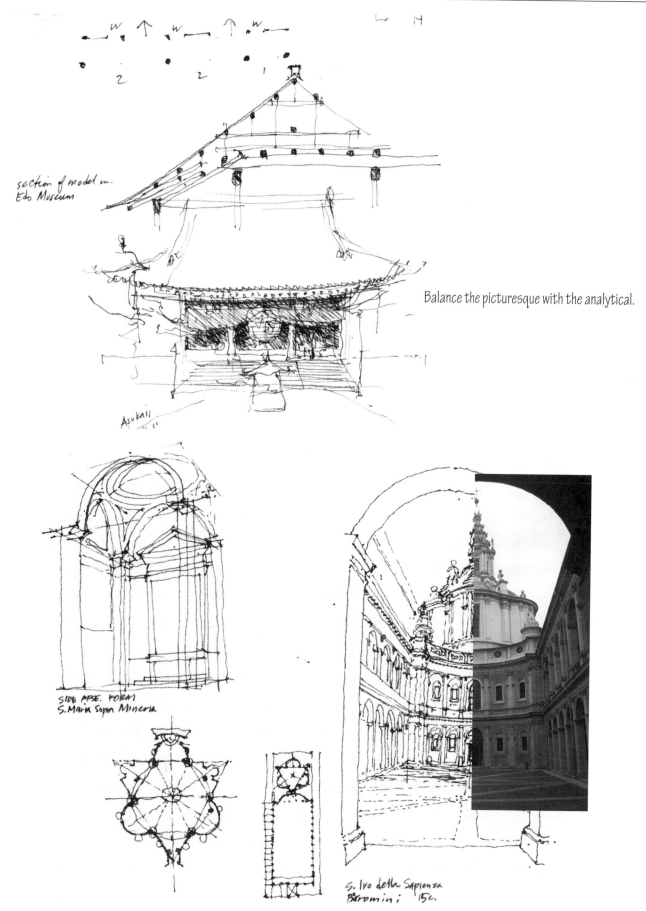

section of model in.
Edo Museum

Asukaii

Balance the picturesque with the analytical.

SIDE APSE. FORM
S. Maria Sopra Minerva

S. Ivo della Sapienza
Borromini 15c.

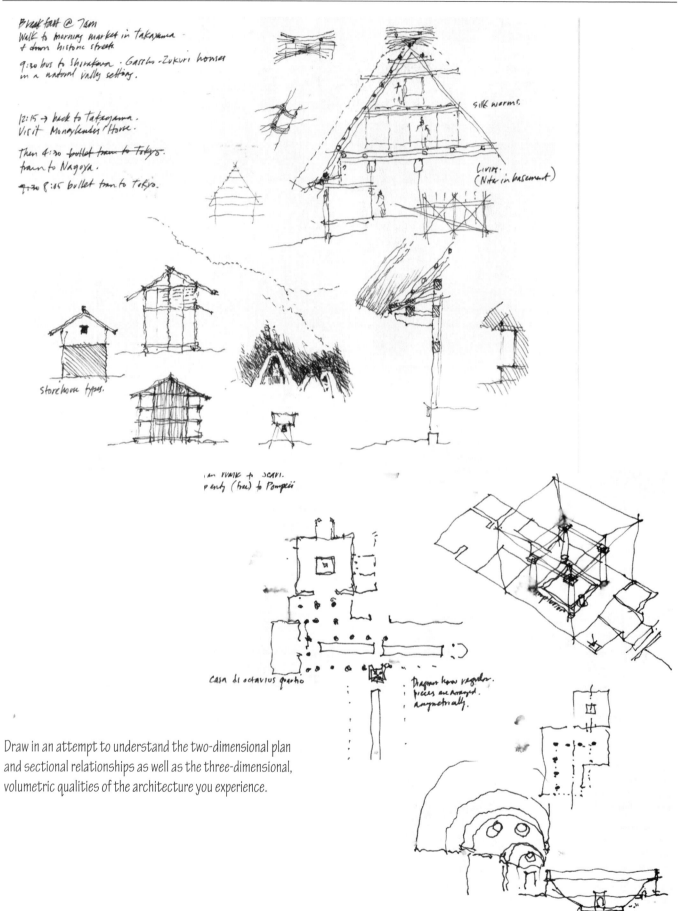

Breakfast @ 7am
Walk to morning market in Takayama
+ down historic streets

9:30 bus to Shirakawa · Gassho-Zukuri houses
in a natural valley setting.

12:15 → back to Takayama.
Visit Monaykentus' House.

Then 4:30 bullet train to Tokyo.
train to Nagoya.

4:30 8:05 bullet train to Tokyo.

silk worms.

Living.
(Note in basement)

Storehouse types.

from PVNTK to SCAFI.
p enty (tree) to Pompeii

casa di octavius quarho

Diagram how regular.
pieces are arranged.
anymetrically.

Draw in an attempt to understand the two-dimensional plan
and sectional relationships as well as the three-dimensional,
volumetric qualities of the architecture you experience.

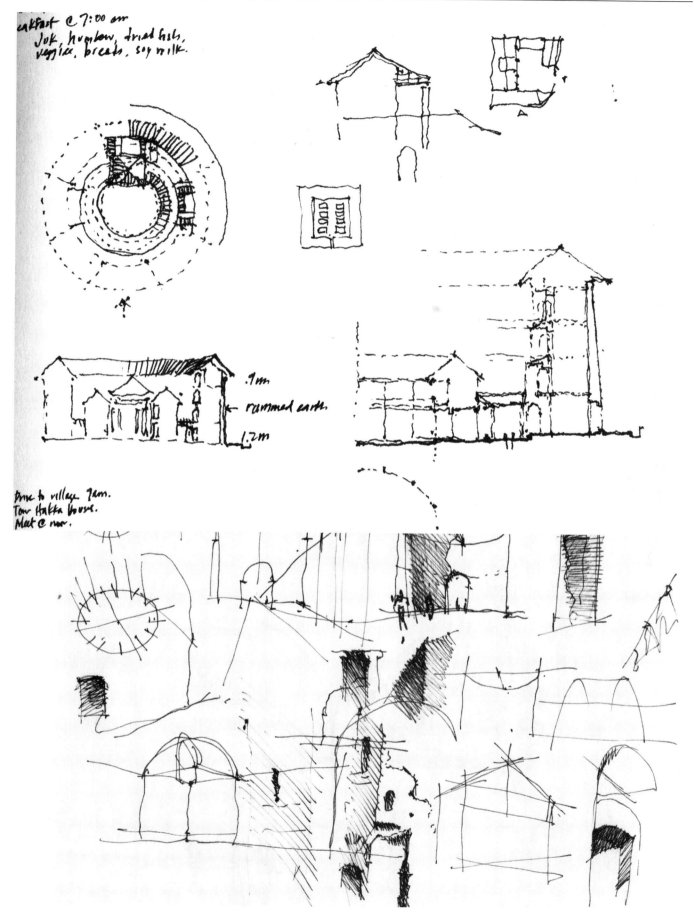

eakfast @ 7:00 am
Juk, humbow, dried fish,
veggies, breads, soy milk.

.9m

← rammed earth

1.2m

Drive to village 9am.
Tour Hakka house.
Meet @ noon.

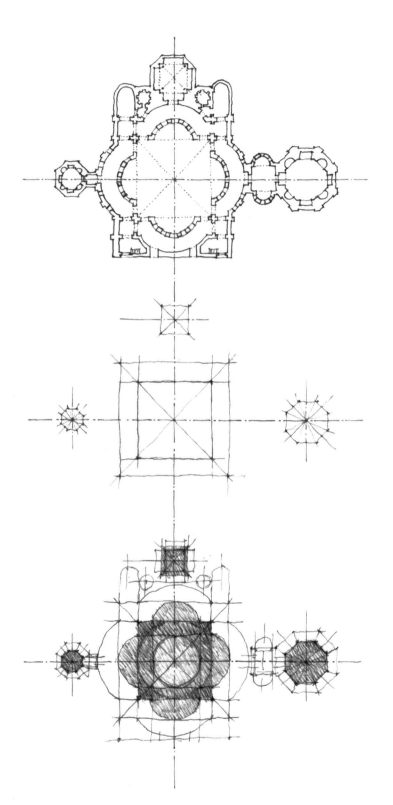

All drawings are, to some degree, abstractions of a perceived reality or an imagined conception. In design drawing, we operate at varying levels of abstraction. At one end of the spectrum lies the presentation drawing, which attempts to simulate as clearly as possible the future reality of a design proposal. At the other end is the diagram, which has the ability to explain something without necessarily representing it in a pictorial way.

- The hallmark of a diagram is its ability to simplify a complex notion into essential elements and relationships by a process of elimination and reduction.
- The abstract nature of diagramming enables us to analyze and understand the essential nature of design elements, to consider their possible relationships, and to quickly generate a series of viable alternatives to a given design problem.

Digital Diagramming

A distinct advantage of digital technology is its ability to accept and process information in a precise and accurate manner. We should not allow this capacity for precision to induce premature closure when exploring ideas with graphics software in the ambiguous, early stages of the design process.

We may use any of the drawing systems to stimulate our
visual thinking and to initiate, clarify, and assess ideas.

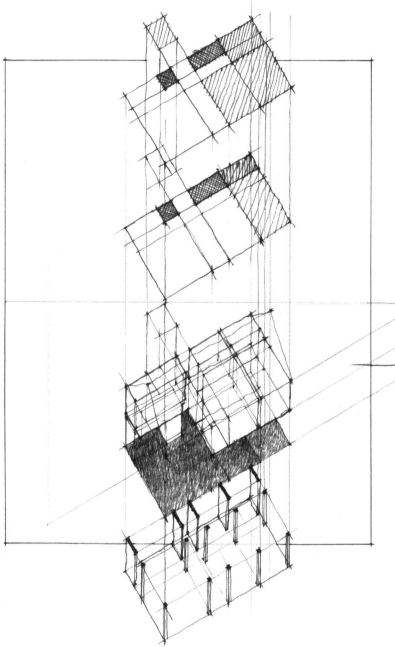

• When a diagram isolates a single issue or set of
  relationships for study, a two-dimensional format
  is usually sufficient.

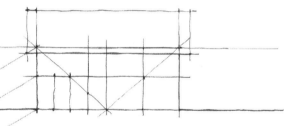

• However, when we begin to explore the complex
  spatial and relational attributes of a design, a
  three-dimensional drawing system may become
  necessary.

• Particularly effective vehicles for studying the
  volumetric massing and spatial dimensions of a
  design are cutaway, expanded, and phantom views.

Diagrams are visual abstractions that can depict the essence of concepts and things.

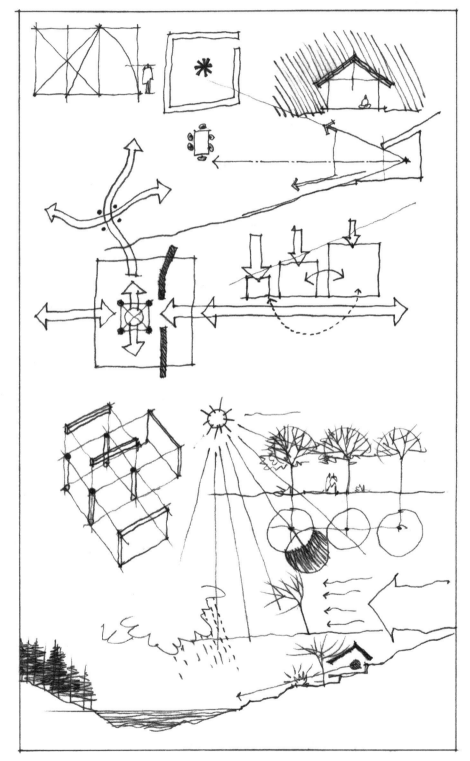

Concepts

- Scale
- Proportion
- Boundaries
- Shelter
- Outlook
- Axes
- Emphasis
- Hierarchy
- Entry and path
- Nodes
- Similarity
- Connections
- Movement
- Process
- Forces
- Zones

Things

- Structure
- Enclosure
- Landscape elements
- Sun
- Wind
- Rain
- Topography
- Light
- Heat

In addition to describing the essence of design elements, diagrams effectively examine and explain the relationships among these elements. To maintain a manageable level of abstraction in a diagram, we utilize the grouping principles of size, proximity, and similarity.

- Relative size describes quantifiable aspects of each element as well as establishes a hierarchical ranking among a number of elements.
- Relative proximity indicates the intensity of relationship among entities.
- Similarity of shape, size, or tonal value establishes visual sets that help reduce the number of elements and maintain a manageable level of abstraction.

To further clarify and emphasize specific types of linkages or the nature of interactions among the entities, we can employ a variety of lines and arrows. And by varying the width, length, continuity, and tonal value of these linking elements, we can also describe varying degrees, levels, and intensities of connection.

Lines

We use the organizing power of lines in diagramming to define the boundaries of fields, denote the interdependencies of elements, and structure formal and spatial relationships. In clarifying the organizational and relational aspects of a diagram, lines make both abstract and pictorial concepts visible and understandable.

Arrows

Arrows are a special type of connecting line. The wedge-shaped ends can signify one- or two-way movement from one element to another, indicate the direction of a force or action, or denote the phase of a process. For clarity, we use different types of arrows to distinguish between the types of relationships as well as varying degrees of intensity or importance.

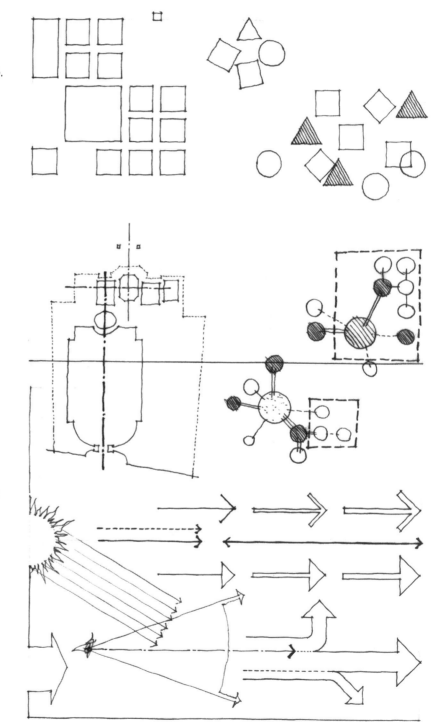

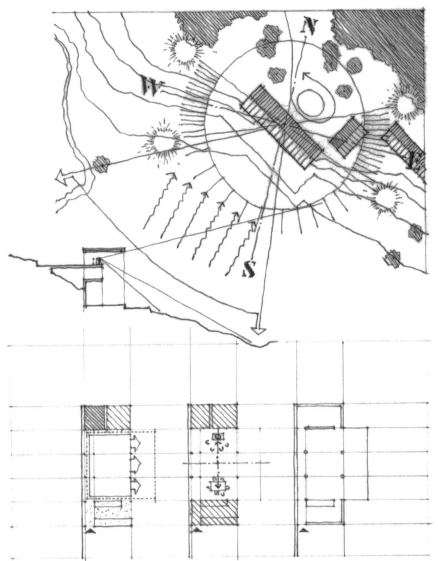

Diagrams can effectively address a diversity of design issues.

Site diagrams explore how the siting and orientation of a design respond to environmental and contextual forces.

- Contextual constraints and opportunities
- Environmental forces of sun, wind, and precipitation
- Topography, landscape, and water features
- Approach, access, and paths through a site

Programmatic diagrams investigate how a design organization addresses programmatic requirements.

- Spatial dimensions required for activities
- Functional proximities and adjacencies
- Relationship between served and service spaces
- Zoning of public and private functions

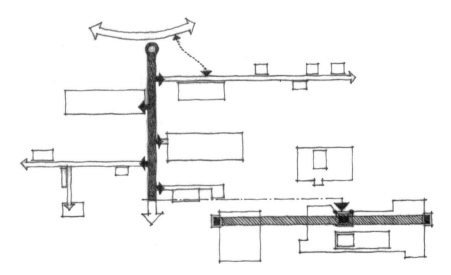

Circulation diagrams study how patterns of movement influence and are influenced by program elements.

- Modes of pedestrian, vehicular, and service travel
- Approach, entry, nodes, and paths of movement
- Horizontal and vertical paths

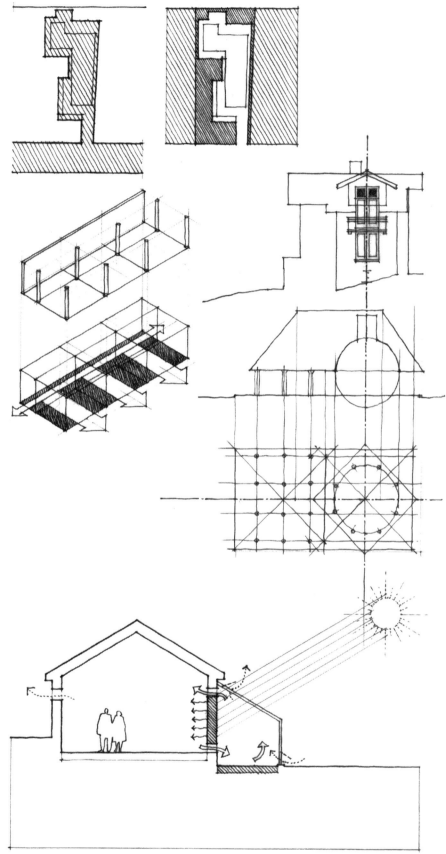

Formal diagrams examine the correspondence between structural pattern, spatial volumes, and elements of enclosure.

- Figure-ground and solid-void relationships
- Ordering principles, such as symmetry and rhythm
- Structural elements and pattern
- Elements and configuration of enclosure
- Spatial qualities, such as shelter and outlook
- Hierarchical organization of spaces
- Formal massing and geometry
- Proportion and scale

System diagrams study the layout and integration of structural, lighting, and environmental control systems.

The term "parti" refers to the concept or primary organizing idea for an architectural design. Drawing a concept or parti in diagrammatic form enables a designer to quickly and efficiently investigate the overall nature and organization of a scheme. Instead of concentrating on how a design might appear, the concept diagram focuses on the key structural and relational features of an idea.

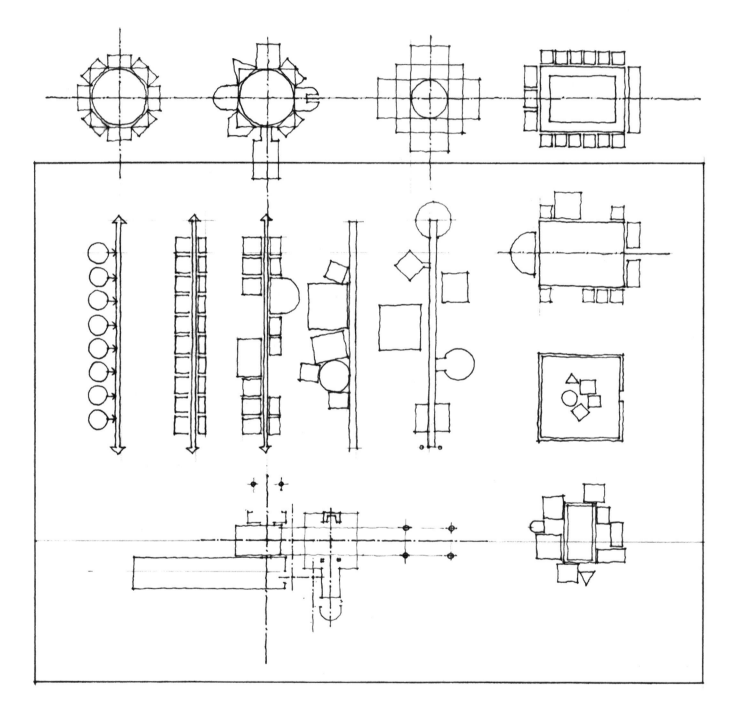

A suitable concept should of course be appropriate and relevant to the nature of the design problem. In addition, both a design concept and its graphic portrayal in a diagram should have the following characteristics. A parti diagram should be:

- Inclusive: capable of addressing the multiple issues of a design problem.
- Visually descriptive: powerful enough to guide the development of a design.
- Adaptable: flexible enough to accept change.
- Sustainable: able to endure manipulations and transformations during the design process without a loss of identity.

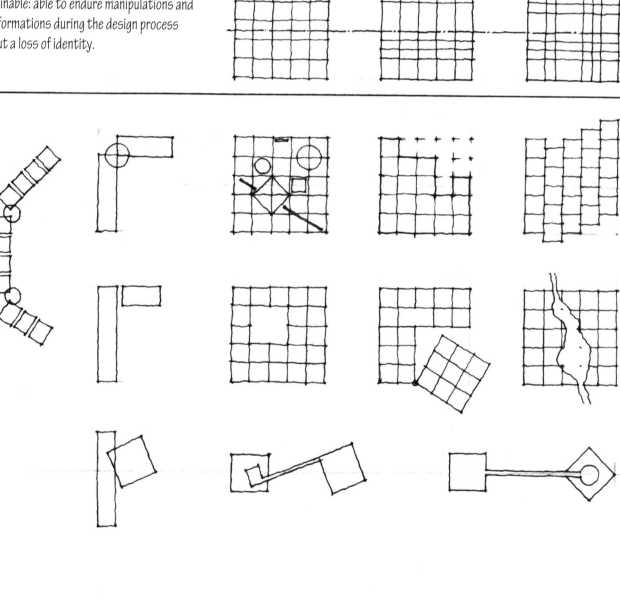

In generating, developing, and utilizing diagrams, certain principles can help stimulate our thinking.

• Keep concept diagrams concise. Drawing small condenses the information to a manageable level.
• Delete extraneous information as needed to focus on a particular issue and enhance the overall clarity of the diagram.
• Add relevant information when necessary to take advantage of newly discovered relationships.

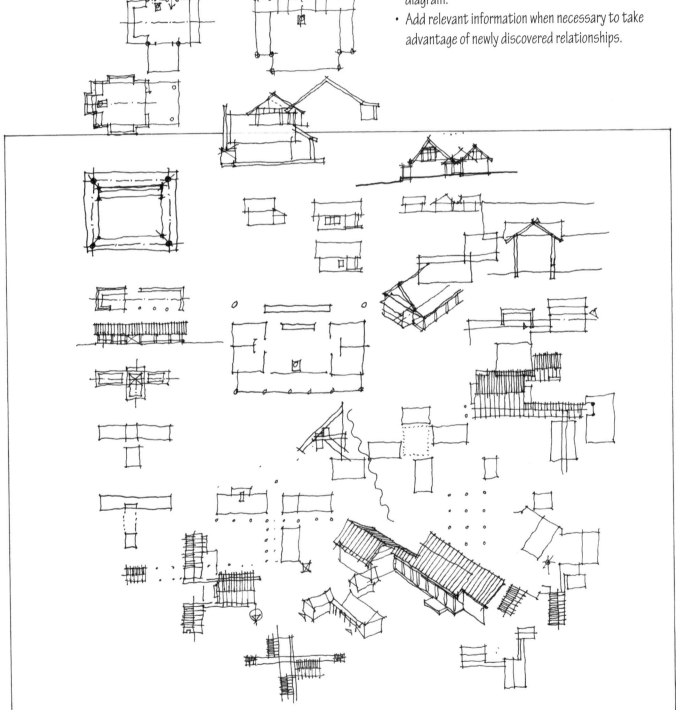

- Utilize the modifying factors of size, proximity, and similarity to reorganize and prioritize the elements as you search for order.
- Overlay or juxtapose a series of diagrams to see how certain variables affect the nature of a design, or how the various parts and systems of a design fit together to form a whole.
- Reverse, rotate, overlap, or distort an element or linkage in order to provide new ways of viewing the diagram and to discover new relationships.

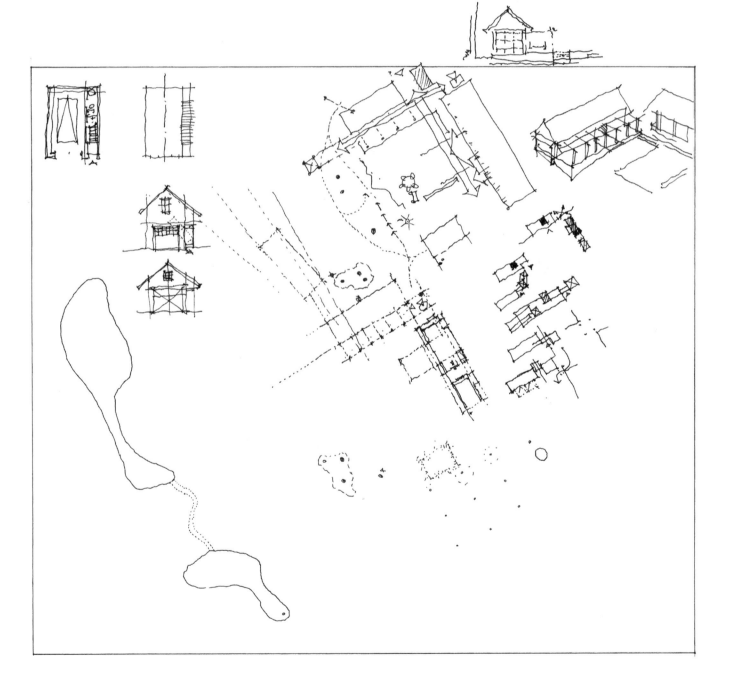

In conclusion, remember that drawing skills allow you to be eloquent, but you must first master the fundamentals. Whether drawing by hand or using digital tools, it takes discipline to construct a drawing properly and to match the message with the medium. It is hoped that this introduction to the basic elements of architectural graphics will provide you with a foundation upon which to build and develop the necessary physical and mental skills to communicate graphically with clarity and honesty.

"Art does not reproduce the visible; it renders visible."
—Paul Klee

A

B

C